Readers and Society in Nineteenth-Century France

Also by Martyn Lyons

A PALAVRA IMPRESSA: Histórias da leitura no século XIX (*with Cyana Leahy*)

AUSTRALIAN READERS REMEMBER: An Oral History of Reading (*with Lucy Taksa*)

FRANCE UNDER THE DIRECTORY

LE TRIOMPHE DU LIVRE: Une Histoire Sociologique de la lecture dans la France du 19e siècle

NAPOLEON BONAPARTE AND THE LEGACY OF THE FRENCH REVOLUTION

REVOLUTION IN TOULOUSE: An Essay on Provincial Terrorism

THE SPHINX IN THE TUILERIES AND OTHER ESSAYS IN MODERN FRENCH HISTORY (*co-editor with Robert Aldrich*)

THE TOTEM AND THE TRICOLOUR: A Short History of New Caledonia since 1774

Readers and Society in Nineteenth-Century France

Workers, Women, Peasants

Martyn Lyons
Professor in History and European Studies
School of History
University of New South Wales
Sydney
Australia

© Martyn Lyons 2001

All rights reserved. No reproduction, copy or transmission of this publication may be made without written permission.

No paragraph of this publication may be reproduced, copied or transmitted save with written permission or in accordance with the provisions of the Copyright, Designs and Patents Act 1988, or under the terms of any licence permitting limited copying issued by the Copyright Licensing Agency, 90 Tottenham Court Road, London W1T 4LP.

Any person who does any unauthorised act in relation to this publication may be liable to criminal prosecution and civil claims for damages.

The author has asserted his right to be identified as the author of this work in accordance with the Copyright, Designs and Patents Act 1988.

First published 2001 by
PALGRAVE
Houndmills, Basingstoke, Hampshire RG21 6XS and
175 Fifth Avenue, New York, N. Y. 10010
Companies and representatives throughout the world

PALGRAVE is the new global academic imprint of
St. Martin's Press LLC Scholarly and Reference Division and
Palgrave Publishers Ltd (formerly Macmillan Press Ltd).

ISBN 0–333–92126–7

This book is printed on paper suitable for recycling and made from fully managed and sustained forest sources.

A catalogue record for this book is available from the British Library.

Library of Congress Cataloging-in-Publication Data
Lyons, Martyn.
　　Readers and society in nineteenth-century France : workers, women, peasants / Martyn Lyons.
　　　p. cm.
　　Includes bibliographical references and index.
　　ISBN 0–333–92126–7
　　1. Books and reading—Political aspects—France—History–
–19th century. 2. Books and reading—Social aspects—France–
–History—19th century. 3. Working class—Books and reading–
–France—History—19th century. 4. Women—Books and reading–
–France—History—19th century. 5. France—Intellectual life–
–19th century. I. Title.
Z1003.5.F7 L96 2001
305.895'10730904—dc21
　　　　　　　　　　　　　　　　　　　　　　　　　　　　2001021624

10　9　8　7　6　5　4　3　2　1
10　09　08　07　06　05　04　03　02　01

Printed in Great Britain by Antony Rowe Ltd, Chippenham, Wiltshire

Contents

Introduction: the Biography of an Idea		vii
Chapter 1	**The New Readers of Nineteenth-Century France**	1
	The expansion of the reading public	3
	The fear of reading	11
Chapter 2	**Reading Workers: Libraries for the People**	17
	Bons livres, mauvais livres: the Catholic fear of reading	22
	Workers' education and self-help, 1830–51	24
	The Franklin Society and popular libraries	28
	Bibliothèques d'entreprises and the Ligue de l'Enseignement	35
	Conclusion	40
Chapter 3	**Reading Workers: Improvisation and Resistance**	43
	Conventional readers and working-class acculturation	44
	The Pursuit of Knowledge under Difficulties	48
	The uses and abuses of fiction	57
	Workers' libraries	65
	Workers as writers	70
	Working-class intellectuals as cultural intermediaries	76
Chapter 4	**Reading Women: from Emma Bovary to the New Woman**	81
	Women as novel readers	82
	The dangers of '*bovarysme*'	86
	The Catholic reading model	92
	The feminist reading model	95
Chapter 5	**Reading Women: Defining a Space of Her Own**	100
	The Catholic reader	103
	A female style of reading?	108
	Illicit and interstitial reading	116
	A space of her own: the problems of a *fille savante*	122

Chapter 6	**Reading Peasants: the Pragmatic Uses of the Written Word**	**129**
	Peasants on the margins of book culture	132
	Rural readers confront the world of print and writing	138
	Attempts to control peasant reading and the questionnaire of 1866	144
	From the 1880s to 1918: Peasant readers make independent use of the medium	149
	Conclusion	154
Chapter 7	**Reading Classes and Dangerous Classes**	**156**
APPENDIX A	Popular Uses of the Book in Early Twentieth-Century France	162
APPENDIX B	Thirty Works for Peasant Readers	164
Notes		166
Bibliography		191
Index		202

Introduction:
the Biography of an Idea

I date my interest in book history from one of Theodore Zeldin's lectures, given to the undergraduate class in which I was a student. There I learned one day that Baudelaire's *Fleurs du Mal* had been first published in a miniscule print-run of 1300 copies, and that Gide's *Nourritures Terrestres*, on it first appearance, had sold a mere 500. As I paused in the middle of breathless note-taking, it dawned on me for the first time that the shape of literary history might have looked very different to readers in the past, in comparison to the way it looks today. At the time, I was beginning to read some of what I supposed to be the masterpieces of French literature in the nineteenth century. Zeldin's admittedly unreliable statistics, however, flung randomly at his stunned audience, made me suspect that what readers in the nineteenth century valued in the literary production of their own day hardly coincided with the set books prescribed for study by the Oxford syllabus. Why was it that Gide, Stendhal and others too were apparently literary nobodies in their lifetimes? What then *were* the imaginative works which held nineteenth-century readers spellbound but which posterity had now utterly discarded? The study of books and literature had suddenly acquired a new historical dimension for me.

By the early 1970s I had developed an interest in and admiration for the Annales school of history. I knew that interesting work on *l'histoire du livre* was appearing in France, one of the early landmarks in the area being Furet and Dupront's two-volume *Livre et Société dans la France du XVIIIe siècle*. This, however, created a potential conflict with the intellectual tradition in which I had been trained. I felt that with a few notable exceptions, Oxford historians seemed irrationally hostile to the new school of French history. Many equated the *Annales* solely with statistical method; a few detested French theorizing of any sort. Once, towards the completion of my doctoral thesis, one Oxford historian scornfully remarked: 'I expect your bookshelf is full of things like Labrousse' (he was referring to the classic study of grain prices in eighteenth-century France). I was amazed that I'd given that impression, because economic history was far from being my favourite bedtime reading. In fact I naively regarded most of it as only marginally more riveting than the railway timetable. I was trained in the British empirical tradition, and I have always regarded a strong empirical basis and sound archival experience as absolutely essential for historical work. I had great respect for those who demonstrated these qualities but I saw no reason why this approach should exclude new methods and new problems.

My own book-history project was to culminate many years later in the publication of *Le Triomphe du Livre: Histoire sociologique de la lecture dans la France du XIXe siècle* (Paris, Promodis, 1987). In that work, I used some production statistics as a rough guide to the bestsellers of early nineteenth-century France. This had been an intimidating task, depending largely on the printers' declarations, recorded clearly but without indexes in large, dusty tomes, bound in green cloth, in the Archives Nationales. They were hard to use and hard to carry and they covered my clothes in a daily film of paper-rust. Apart from the laundry bill, there was another problem – the problem of how many of them one person could digest, for as book production grew, so the green tomes became more and more voluminous with every passing year they covered. I stopped at 1850, feeling virtuous, and confident that only the most foolish scholar would ever venture to try this self-imposed ordeal again. In addition, *Le Triomphe du Livre* presented my researches into the history of libraries and the expansion of retail bookshops into the suburbs and provinces.

I had found some answers to the questions posed by Zeldin's undergraduate class, but in the process new questions had arisen. In *Le Triomphe du Livre*, I had studied the development of the publishing industry, and discussed some of the ways books reached their audience, through itinerant peddlars (*colporteurs*), shops and lending libraries. But what happened *after* they had been acquired or borrowed by their readers? I wanted to go further than my maps and statistics had permitted, to ask some questions about readers and the reception of books. In the final chapter of *Le Triomphe du Livre*, which I saw as both a postscript and a way forward, I tentatively searched for means of analysing reading practices.

My first contacts, in 1984, with book historians at the Ecole des Hautes Etudes en Sciences Sociales provided me with some important revelations. Firstly, I was encouraged to discover that I was by no means alone in my turn away from the study of production towards the history of readers. I had been working in rather an isolated fashion from my distant base in Sydney, and this welcome news ended that isolation for good. Secondly, I realized that, contrary to accepted opinion, the sources for a history of reading did indeed exist if one looked for them. This book uses two kinds of these sources: the advice literature on reading, ordering what to read and not to read, which I refer to as the normative sources; and autobiographies, most of them written but some oral, which record individual reading experiences. Much of this book is about the fear of reading and the attempt to dispel it by controlling and organizing the reading of the 'dangerous classes'. It is also about the potentially subversive nature of every individual act of reading. Ever since those meetings in 1984, I have owed a continuing debt to Roger Chartier; and our relationship was cemented by a common enthusiasm for the running style of rugby which was then practised to good effect both in France and Australia. I have never ceased to be grateful for his insights, although my work remains less abstract than his, and more centred on individual readers and their everyday human experiences.

In Sydney I designed an oral history project on the history of reading which brought me face-to-face with flesh-and-blood readers. Together with Lucy Taksa, I recorded interviews with 61 elderly Australians in the Sydney region about the reading experiences they remembered since their childhood. The result was *Australian Readers Remember: an oral history of reading*, published in Melbourne by Oxford University Press in 1992. This work, which I regard as a very stimulating experiment, led me to put an even higher value than before on autobiographical sources. Oral autobiographies are, I would maintain, quite different in their narrative strategies and mode of creation than any other kind of source. I draw no easy parallels between oral autobiography and the written autobiographies of the nineteenth century. Both, however, provide a quasi-fictional text which the memory has shaped and re-ordered. They give priceless assistance to the historian about the responses of individual readers both in the past and in contemporary society. I refer to oral testimony wherever it is appropriate in this book.

In 1989 I was invited to contribute a chapter on the nineteenth century to the Franco-Italian edition of the *Storia della Lettura nel mondo occidentale*, which appeared first with Laterza in 1995, edited by Chartier and Guiglielmo Cavallo, and was later published by Seuil in Paris. Chartier proposed the title 'Les Nouveaux Lecteurs', and I accepted a scheme to discuss women, children and workers as readers. The present book has grown out of that chapter, although there are some very important differences between the two. The original chapter formed part of a work which aimed at an international coverage, whereas the present study has an exclusively French focus. Furthermore, I have not retained my original categories: in this work, I discuss workers, women and peasants. I felt that treatment of the peasants, who figured largely in the discourses on reading in the nineteenth century, was indispensable to the study. The material on the peasantry included here draws on my article "What Did the Peasants Read? Written and Printed Culture in Rural France, 1815–1914", *European History Quarterly*, vol.27, no.2, 1997, pp.163–97. I am grateful to the editor, Martin Blinkhorn, for permission to use this material here.

Several individual readers have seen drafts of my work. Since they come from very different disciplinary backgrounds, they have offered very different advice, and I am grateful for it all. They include Susan Grogan, Jean Hébrard, Sheryl Kroen, Ana Rossi and Cyana Leahy-Dios. I am grateful for the encouragement, advice or critical insights offered sometimes unwittingly by Barrie Rose in Tasmania, Jonathan Rose at Drew University, Colin Lucas in Oxford, Chips Sowerwine and Peter McPhee in Melbourne, Alan Forrest in York, Harry Ziegler in Lincoln, and Jeannette Gilfedder and Pat Buckridge in Brisbane. I am also grateful to Jacques Girault for his unstinted hospitality over many years. He has constantly directed me to new sources in connection with the labour movement, and kept me up to date with the resources of the Centre de Recherches d'Histoire des Mouvements Sociaux et du Syndicalisme in the rue Malher in Paris. In particular, I must thank Jacques for urging me to consider the libraries of the Bourses du Travail, discussed in Chapter 3.

I have had the pleasure of presenting some of this work to seminar audiences. I would particularly like to thank Jean-Yves Mollier for inviting me to his seminar at the Université of Versailles-St-Quentin-en-Yvelines. Any student of reading in nineteenth-century France must acknowledge, as I do, his fundamental works on the history of French publishing. My work on the reading experiences of nineteenth-century autobiographers has been presented to panels of the International Society for the Study of European Ideas at its meetings over the last decade, and to the congress of the International Committee for Historical Sciences at Oslo in 2000. In 1999, I thoroughly enjoyed and learned from a discussion in three languages with the very lively cultural history group at the Universidade Federal Fluminense in Niterói, Brazil. From time to time, the University of New South Wales has assisted me to travel to research in Paris. In 1999, I was able to enjoy an uninterrupted stretch of writing in an ideal working environment as Visiting Research Fellow at Corpus Christi College, Cambridge. I would like to thank the College and its Master at the time, Professor Tony Wrigley, for their hospitality.

These sorties would have been impossible without a secure home base. I am therefore leaving the most important and most obvious acknowledgements until last. The George Rudé Seminar in French History provides essential moral support for all who work on French history in Australia and New Zealand. The Australian colleagues who have made it thrive deserve every accolade. I am grateful, too, to other members of the team of specialists working on the History of the Book in Australia for their encouragement. I finally thank Jacqueline, Blaise, Holly and Claudine, for all their love and support.

Martyn Lyons

1
The New Readers of Nineteenth-Century France

On the eve of the French Revolution under half (47 per cent) of the male population of France, and about 27 per cent of French women, could read. By the end of the nineteenth century, however, functional literacy had become almost universal for both French men and women.[1] The statistics of literacy, based on the ability to sign one's name on a formal document, are only one way of measuring the enormous expansion of the reading public experienced by French society between the July Monarchy and the First World War. This expansion, as we shall see, was underpinned especially in its later stages by changes in the provision of primary schooling. It was supported by technological changes which revolutionized the production of print culture, especially the production of cheap fiction and the newspaper press. A mass culture of print was emerging, in which new categories of readers became consumers of print for the first time, and in which publishing strategies evolved to exploit new clienteles.

This book is about those new categories of readers, and about the problems they posed for nineteenth-century bourgeois society. It focuses in particular on three groups of 'new readers', namely workers, women and peasants. To call women 'new readers' may seem like stretching a point, since women had always been part of the reading public. But there is a sense in which all three of these important social groups were new and disturbing arrivals on the scene. Although both women and working-class readers had existed before the nineteenth century, they had never loomed as large until then, or posed such acute social and political problems. They can be legitimately considered as newcomers to the reading public because publishers (especially in the case of women readers) saw them for the first time as a significant and distinct market which offered new sources of profit, and required new strategies to exploit.

In addition to this, the appearance of lower-class readers posed new problems for élites. A democratic society depended on a literate electorate; but the spread of undesirable literature was blamed for the Revolution of 1848, the rise of religious indifference and the advance of socialism. The spread of literacy in the countryside was even held responsible for the rural exodus of the nineteenth century.[2] After 1870, France's defeat by Prussia provoked many different diagnoses of the national catastrophe; they included attributing defeat to a decline in the quality of reading, and the 'desacralization' of the book. More people could read than ever before, acknowledged Arnould Frémy, but the book itself was being swamped by an ocean of triviality produced by the newspaper press. The press encouraged rapid and superficial judgments, presenting 'an immense bazaar of facts, interests and ideas in which the most serious contemporary issues rub elbows daily with the most futile details of everyday life.'[3] Today's educators often complain that people read too little; the nineteenth century complaint was that people read too much, too indiscriminately, and too subversively. Although this study, then, is partly about readers themselves, it also investigates the fears and anxieties caused by the spread of popular literacy, and the means taken to direct lower-class reading into 'safe' channels.

The sources for this study are thus produced partly by individual readers themselves, and partly by those who interpreted women readers, worker readers and peasant readers as a threat to traditional notions of patriarchy and social stability. Sources include the autobiographies of readers, in which authors described and made sense of their reading experience and the way it had helped to define their personal identities. Not surprisingly, personal autobiographies are relatively plentiful for some groups, such as educated women, but extremely rare in others, such as peasants. A handful of workers' autobiographies, sometimes painstakingly compiled on the basis of an improvised literary culture, describe how the nineteenth-century autodidact acceded to the new reading public. Publishers, too, provide important evidence, in their advertising, marketing strategies and in the books themselves, which indicates their view of the reading public and of target audiences. The public debate about new readers surfaces throughout the nineteenth century in press and pamphlet discussion about the problem of working-class and peasant reading. It can also be followed in the public arguments on library provision in the 1860s, and in discussions of female reading models in both the Catholic and feminist press towards the end of the century.

The expansion of the reading public

Before 1830, the print-run of an average novel hardly exceeded print-runs which were common in the time of Gutenberg. Consider the production of two well-known titles which appeared at each end of the chronological spectrum 1830–1914. Stendhal's *Le Rouge et le Noir* was published in 1830 with a small print-run of only 750 copies. Although there was a second edition, this too had a print-run of only 750. Stendhal dedicated his work to 'The Happy Few': it is hard to say if his readers were happy but they were certainly few, at least until the process of his literary canonization developed over half a century later.[4] Within seventy years, by the early twentieth century, print-runs of popular fiction had been completely transformed. Pierre Loti's *Pêcheur d'Islande*, for example, published in 1889, achieved a huge circulation in Calmann-Lévy's cheap illustrated series priced at only 95 centimes per volume. By the end of 1906, *Pêcheur d'Islande* had an aggregate *tirage* of 110,000, and it had achieved a total run of half a million copies by 1919.[5] Stendhal published at the very beginning of the process of the industrialization of the book which later led to the mass production of authors such as Alexandre Dumas, Jules Verne and Loti. The mass production of popular fiction helped to integrate new readers into a national reading public which became increasingly homogeneous.[6] In the eighteenth century, the only books read throughout France were catechisms and devotional works; but by the end of the nineteenth century, readers in every part of the country were familiar with the same titles, such as *Les Trois Mousquetaires*, *La Porteuse de Pain* or *Les Misérables*.

The nationwide literacy statistics based on the signature test, which opened this chapter, offer only a crude yardstick of the growth of this reading public. They disguise important variations in the geography of literacy and the rhythm of its growth. While providing a preliminary answer to the question 'Who could read?', they are often insensitive to the class and gender composition of the literate population, as well as providing no guide to different reading competencies. Nevertheless, they are a fundamental starting-point.[7]

Historians often refer to the study of basic literacy conducted by the school inspector Louis Maggiolo in 1879–80.[8] Maggiolo's work set out to prove that the Church had done little to improve French literacy before the Revolution of 1789. He recruited local schoolteachers as voluntary researchers to record signatures on marriage contracts in selected periods going back to the late-seventeenth century. Sixteen thousand of them responded to the call. In fact, the results proved rather

4   *Readers and Society in Nineteenth-Century France*

inconclusive for Maggiolo's cause, for the rise in literacy had certainly predated the French Revolution. Maggiolo, however, had produced a very useful pioneering guide to the history of French literacy, for which historians have since been very grateful.[9]

As a result of Maggiolo's survey, France was conceived as two contrasting regions: the prosperous, educated and literate north and east, separated from the far less literate south and west by the so-called 'Maggiolo line', bisecting the country roughly from St Malo to Geneva. This simple division can be misleading, even in its own geographical terms. It tends to ignore the urban, literate Midi, the southern crescent running east from Bordeaux and Toulouse to the Mediterranean littoral, and curving north from Provence up the valley of the Rhône. On the whole, however, the lowest but fastest-growing literacy rates were to be found in regions south and west of Maggiolo's imaginary line of division.[10] For many parts of the Midi, the nineteenth century was a period of '*rattrapage*', of catching up with the north. The west, in comparison, found it more difficult to 'catch up'; in fact it could be argued that even by 1914 it had failed to do so. Some Bretons, however, would prefer to interpret this failure in terms of successful resistance against the colonizing impulses of the francophone state.

Maggiolo's survey was inevitably incomplete. Some local assistants had been more diligent than others. On the whole, towns were underrepresented in his data base compared to rural areas. The eastern departments of Alsace and Lorraine were part of Germany, so Maggiolo could not include them. Nor could he include the Seine department, since the records of the *état-civil* had been burned in the Paris Hôtel de Ville fire in 1871. In spite of Maggiolo's deficiencies, however, some conclusions can be extrapolated from his findings. The evidence of his extraordinary project suggested that the so-called Maggiolo line was vanishing from sight, just as soon as it had been revealed. The expansion of basic literacy everywhere was obliterating historic differences in the literacy rates of France's many and diverse regional cultures. The rural exodus of the nineteenth century, which brought thousands of country dwellers into growing cities, was also blurring the difference between urban and rural literacy rates. France was becoming a more homogeneous society in which readers everywhere were part of an integrated national book market, consuming the same bestsellers, and reading the same magazines.

Towns in the nineteenth century were usually more literate than the countryside, and large towns more literate than smaller ones. Older, administrative centres, which had a dense network of legal and educational institutions, were more literate than new industrial towns. In new manufacturing areas such as Roubaix-Tourcoing, where there was a high density of unskilled workers and recent arrivals from the countryside in search of work, the literacy rate could be temporarily depressed by early industrialization.[11] Paris itself already had an exceptionally high rate of literacy before the 1789 Revolution. In revolutionary Paris, 90 per cent of men and 80 per cent of women could sign their own wills. Signatures on wills, admittedly, are hardly representative. By definition, they do not include the poor, who owned no property to bequeath. But even in the popular *faubourg* Saint-Marcel, two-thirds of the inhabitants could read and write by 1792.[12] Here in the capital there existed a popular reading public familiar with the printed word, which provided a ready market for the print explosion detonated by every revolutionary crisis. In Paris, as in the provinces, there was always a significant correlation between reading-and-writing literacy and socio-professional status. Professional groups such as lawyers and clerics were highly literate and were likely to own their own libraries. Lower down the scale, shopkeepers and craft workers were more literate than domestic servants or unskilled labourers. Well-integrated Parisians tended to have a greater reading ability than recently arrived migrants from the countryside.

Literacy statistics regularly show male literacy outrunning female literacy. The structural gap, however, between male and female literacy rates was being closed, and by the end of the nineteenth century it had disappeared altogether. Female literacy, in other words, was now rising faster than that of men: women, too, were 'catching up'. The traditional gender discrepancy had always been most marked at the lower end of the social scale. At the end of the eighteenth century, for example, the day-labourers and silk workers of Lyon were twice as literate as their wives. In artisan circles, however, when women kept the front of the shop while their men worked in the *atelier*, things were sometimes different. Contact with the public, the need to record customer orders and keep accounts all tended to make women as literate as men in the *boulangerie* or the cobbler's shop.

The true extent of female literacy is probably disguised by statistics based on the signature test, because they do not take account of the level of reading-only literacy. Many women were able to read at least the catechism, without being able to write or sign their own name. Reading-only literacy was most common in culturally static areas, such as Brittany and the Massif Central, where the Catholic Church promoted partial literacy among women, but discouraged them from writing. Women's reading could perhaps be circumscribed within the needs of a Christian life, but writing was potentially a far more independent and critical activity. Reading-only literacy was found in urban areas, too, but here it was more likely to be the result of interrupted schooling.[13]

Perhaps the most influential factor in raising levels of female literacy was the changing nature of women's employment. In the last quarter of the nineteenth century, new white-collar careers opened up for women, in addition to their traditional roles in agriculture, domestic service and textile manufacture. Women found jobs as shop assistants and clerical workers and, eventually, as schoolteachers as well. These careers offered social mobility and were powerful incentives for female literacy, and they thus contributed to the feminization of the reading public.

For most of the nineteenth century, the infrastructure of primary schooling was patchy, and only partially reflected the grand projects of pedagogues and legislators. The Guizot Law of 1833 had laid the basis for a national system of primary schools, by planning for the creation of one school in every commune. The Guizot Law happened to be enacted in the middle of a growth spurt in primary schooling which occurred between 1821 and 1837.[14] It failed, however, to bring about rapid change in the medium term.

Catholic schools continued to play a vital role in education, especially at the primary level. Catholic teaching orders increased their primary school enrolments substantially during the Second Empire and, by 1876, two million students were officially enrolled in Catholic schools.[15] Teaching orders survived many anticlerical campaigns because their efforts were needed and usually supported by the Catholic laity. The Frères des Ecoles Chrétiennes were particularly influential. Because they refused to levy fees on their students, however, they were dependent on support from wealthy municipalities.[16]

The legislation of Jules Ferry in the 1880s is usually hailed as making free, secular and universal primary education a reality. The computerized study of enrolments conducted by Grew and Harrigan argues that the pattern of primary education in France was in place long before this, and that the main period of growth in primary enrolments may have occurred in the 1820s and 1830s. In this perspective, the spread of primary education was a continuous process. In that case, the advent of free and universal schooling in the Third Republic would have been the culmination of a long-term trend rather than a historic rupture with tradition.[17]

This remains debatable. Perhaps it is too superficial to deduce the existence of the new readers of the nineteenth century from enrolment figures calculated in different ways by the schools themselves. Enrolment figures are not necessarily a reliable guide to school attendance. The existence of a local primary school depended on popular demand rather than legislative decree. Setting up a local school was only the first step in a long struggle: parents had to be convinced that it was worth while for their children to attend. This was sometimes impossible in rural areas, except in winter when demand for agricultural work was at its lowest. At harvest-time, in contrast, country schools were deserted. In the Dordogne in 1836, only 8 per cent of eligible children attended school. In the Vienne in 1863, the attendance rate was only 6 per cent. A survey carried out in 1863 revealed that almost a quarter of French children in the nine to 13 age group never attended school, and that a third of the rest only attended for six months in the year.[18] These figures, it should be remembered, only apply to boys' school attendance. From the age of seven or eight onwards, a child's income might be vital to the family's survival, and the needs of the family economy took priority over reading and writing, the benefits of which no doubt seemed vague and remote to the majority of agricultural workers. Even in the 1880s and beyond, the concept of 'free' education remained problematic. Even if parents were not obliged to pay teachers, they nevertheless had to forgo the income of their children who attended school.

Primary school provision for girls expanded quickly in the Second Empire, after the Falloux Law of 1850 had called for the establishment of a separate girls' school in every commune with more than 800 inhabitants. It has been estimated that, by 1866, the number of girls attending primary school in France was equivalent to 93 per cent of the number of boys.[19] This did not mean that girls' education had thereby achieved near parity of status. Until the 1870s, the majority of girls were still taught by nuns, and they had a distinctive curriculum, which emphasized sewing, child care and domestic economy. In other words, girls were prepared for marriage and motherhood rather than for further intellectual endeavour. This domestic ideology implied a separate school system for girls. Mixed schools did exist, but this was out of financial necessity. Segregated teaching was generally preferred, because there were different objectives for boys' and girls' education. The republican Jules Simon explained: 'A mixed school is not a school for both sexes; it is a school for boys that receives girls.'[20]

The importance of formal education is a fundamental liberal principle; it is assumed to be essential to equality of opportunity, and to the development of informed citizens within a coherent national community. Its influence on the achievement of full literacy, however, should not be exaggerated. Until at least the 1860s, reading and writing were still taught separately, the student moving on to learn to write only after acquiring a rudimentary reading ability. Throughout the first half of the century, teachers used the laborious individual method of instruction. In other words, the teacher tested and advised one student at a time, while the rest of the class waited in turn for his or her attention. The schools of the Christian Brothers were the first to introduce the simultaneous method, addressing the lesson to the whole class at once. This method of tuition was well suited to learning the catechism, in which a collective response was required to a series of specific questions.

School equipment was often rudimentary, books were a rarity and there was frequently no permanent classroom. At Lons-le Saulnier, Guizot's inspectors reported that the school doubled as an armoury and a dance hall.[21] In the Meuse department, one inspector was surprised to find that the teacher's wife had just given birth to a child in the classroom. The teachers relied for their income on collecting fees from parents. This was not an easy task. Parental resistance had a variety of motives. As far as the authorities were concerned, their refusal to send their children to school was simply a reflection of crass peasant ignorance. The reality was more complicated. Some peasant heads of household may have regarded schooling with suspicion, as a threat to their own patriarchal authority. More importantly, the needs of the family economy were paramount, and schooling had to be paid for. Literacy skills seemed genuinely peripheral to the life and work of many peasants. Poorly paid teachers worked as barbers, tobacconists, gravediggers or town clerks to make ends meet. Many certainly lacked a sense of vocation: the main attraction of the profession was that after 1818, schoolteachers were exempted from military conscription.

The lack of qualified personnel put an intolerable burden on urban schools. In Montpellier, in 1833, there were between 100 and 220 students per class. In this overcrowded situation, the system of mutual education was popular. The eldest and, it was assumed, the best student was appointed monitor, and entrusted with the instruction of his peers. Reading itself commonly took the form of learning to recognize individual letters, isolated syllables and eventually complete words, which the teacher made the class recite. The student was not asked to explain the meaning of what was read, and in fact he or she rarely saw a book. More often than not, a more meaningful apprenticeship in reading took place outside the classroom.[22]

The growth of literacy depended on demands and incentives. The existence of a primary school did not in itself achieve much. What mattered more was whether parents saw a good reason, and some material benefit, to justify allowing their children to put in more than just an intermittent attendance. There is no doubting the growing demand for education from the working classes themselves. They aspired to greater personal dignity, or they were motivated by a more mundane desire for social mobility. Sometimes they sought some kind of emancipation in the light of the hostility of many employers to popular education. These demands for workers' education have been traced through the period of the Second Empire by Georges Duveau.[23] An individual example is the mason Martin Nadaud, who remembered his father's dogged insistence that his son should have an education, in spite of objections from his illiterate family.[24] Popular demands for education were often resisted by social superiors who feared the spread of education. In the south-west in the 1830s, landowners in the Ariège and the Albigeois were hostile to country schools, fearing that they would lose their labour force, or else that education would make their labourers more independent.[25] In the 1860s, landowners in Cognac made an agreement only to accept peasants and employees who were illiterate.[26]

The odds were, in the nineteenth century, that a local school had only come into being in the first place as a result of local pressures. Formal education thus responded to the demand for literacy rather than creating it. François Furet invited us to see the school institution as simply a catalyst for universal literacy, given a local environment which had already attained a certain cultural and literary threshold.[27] By the time a national system of primary education formally existed in the 1880s, most of the century's advances in literacy had already been made. Before this time, workers and peasants achieved access to the reading public through a range of informal channels. They improvised their reading by borrowing and using help offered by priests, family members and occasionally a benevolent employer. They used itinerant or qualified teachers who undercut their more established competitors. There were many ways to learn to read, in the family and in the local neighbourhood, before the advent of universal schooling.

The working classes began to enjoy greater leisure time in the last quarter of the nineteenth century. The 12–hour working day, first mooted in 1848, became law in 1874. In 1892, legislation stipulated a 10-hour maximum, and the much-heralded eight-hour day was legally instituted in 1919. This reduction in working hours left more time for reading, often previously seen as an activity confined to Sunday, the only time for rest. Indeed, a few hours of leisure every week opened up opportunities for a range of social and cultural pursuits besides reading, such as those sponsored by musical societies, sporting clubs and *bals publics*.[28]

So far this chapter has outlined the context and some of the conditions surrounding the emergence of a new reading public. We must also briefly consider the economics of publishing. New publishing strategies catered for a growing market of readers with low budgets. In the 1830s, Charpentier revolutionized fiction production by compressing the text into a single, small-format volume, instead of 'ventilating' it excessively to create several volumes for a secure market of libraries and *cabinets de lecture*.[29] This made novels cheaper and more portable. By 1838, following Charpentier, the standard format had become the 'grand in-18o', known as the 'jésus' or, in homage to its creator, as the 'format Charpentier'. At the same time, cheap monthly episodes reached a wider audience than the traditional, multi-volume format for novels. In the 1840s, *romans à livraisons* or *romans à quatre sous* were issued with an engraved illustration in 16-page sections for only 20 centimes each. Even Karl Marx's *Le Capital* was first encountered in 1872 by French readers in the form of weekly instalments. The serialization of fiction in the press, in the form of the *roman-feuilleton*, was being effectively exploited by Eugène Sue and Alexandre Dumas to reach new readers who may never have purchased a book. In an essay of 1839, Sainte-Beuve lamented what he called the 'industrialization of literature', arguing that mass production and the mercenary obsession with profit could never produce great art.[30]

The addition of new layers to the French reading public has to be understood in connection with developments in the publishing industry. Or, in other words, we must take into account changing conditions in the supply of literature, as well as the changing demand for it. Cheaper paper, and the spread of faster, mechanized printing presses allowed publishers to reduce the price of popular fiction in a continuing downward spiral. In 1855, Michel Lévy launched his collection of contemporary novels uniformly priced at one franc, which meant that the price of fiction had fallen to a mere one-fifteenth of its level before 1838.[31] In the mid-1890s, Flammarion and Fayard inaugurated an even more aggressive campaign, pricing their new series at only 60 centimes per title. Profiting from their huge market, a handful of successful publishing entrepreneurs joined the forefront of French capitalism. In the competitive publishing world of the first decade of the twentieth century, only the energetic, the daring and those who had a diversified portfolio of investments would survive.[32]

The fear of reading

The existence of a mass of lower-class readers was a new and troubling social phenomenon. Together with the prospect of an increase in untutored female reading, it was a source of anxiety for clerics, educators, liberals and politicians. France, it was thought, was reading too much, in the sense that a mass of inexperienced consumers was reading indiscriminately and without guidance. They were considered innocent readers, potentially easy prey for unscrupulous publishers and ruthless propagandists. Workers and peasants could be lured by undesirable ideas such as socialism, legitimism or bonapartism – the name of the demon changed according to the faith of the polemicist. The problem was defined not only in terms of *what* the new readers read, but also in terms of *how* they read. They would read unwisely, it was feared, unable to distinguish reason from falsehood, truth from fantasy. They might be tempted (in the case of women) by erotic desire and impossible romantic expectations. They would read superficially instead of purposefully without meditating and digesting their texts. The dangers, both moral and political, posed by new readers consuming a mass of cheap popular literature, were disturbing. In the debates on these issues, the social neuroses of the bourgeois were revealed.

The anxious dreams of the nineteenth-century bourgeois were peopled by all those who threatened his sense of order, restraint and paternal control. This book is concerned with a trio of them – the worker, the woman and the peasant – all embodiments of otherness in dominant bourgeois perceptions. These were exactly the characters nominated by Octavio Paz, in one of his essays on the Mexican condition, which identified the spectres that haunted the consciousness of dominant urban European civilization.[33] The peasant, according to Paz, 'represents the most ancient and secret element of society. For everyone but himself he embodies the occult, the hidden, that which surrenders itself only with great difficulty'. Woman, too, is a mysterious and enigmatic figure, a reminder of the radical heterogeneity of the world. The worker is a stranger and an individual, until he eventually comes to resemble the machine that he operates, and he is seen purely as an anonymous instrument of industrial production. In mid-nineteenth-century France, however, the typical worker had not yet become a member of the modern wage-earning proletariat. The pace of industrialization in France was consistent, but slow in comparison to the sudden transformation of the British economy, and it was localized in certain regions such as the east, the north and the environs of Paris. When Zola turned in the 1880s to the northern coal-mining proletariat for the setting of *Germinal*, he did so precisely because of the novelty of this social phenomenon, in the context of the national economy as a whole. The industrial worker had not yet lost his strangeness, and it was far from clear that he would become a docile subject.

By the 1840s, Paris was no longer the city it had been in pre-revolutionary times. In 1846, its population reached a staggering one million, and the city began to experience some of the problems that now beset all modern urban agglomerations: the spread of crime, disease, prostitution, suicide and other symptoms of social malaise. The cholera epidemic of 1831–32, which ravaged crowded lower-class districts but also swept away the prime minister, Casimir-Périer, was like a red alert for the nervous bourgeois of the July Monarchy. Louis Chevalier, using principally literary sources, carefully documented the growing apprehensiveness of social élites, and their sense that the barbarians were at the gates.[34] Teaching the population to read and write certainly increased the number of potential readers, but, according to *Le Radical* in March 1877, it would also multiply the number of potential revolutionaries.[35] The workers rose in Lyon in 1834, and in Paris in 1848. The insurrections of the south-east in 1851 proved that even sections of the peasantry had been won over to the ideals of the social-democratic Republic. The Paris Commune was repressed in a paroxysm of violence in which the depth of social panic could be measured. These social tensions, rarely articulated but always present, formed the context for the debates on lower-class reading.

How could the new reading public be controlled? This question worried élites, especially the church and, after 1848, the republicans as well. During the Bourbon restoration, the Catholic Church set out to reconquer the faithless congregations of a degenerate France who, it was considered, had betrayed the church and the monarchy in the revolutionary years. A series of Catholic missions urged their followers to do penance for the sins of recent French history, and to turn away from the twisted dogmas of the Enlightenment. A vitriolic campaign against *mauvais livres* accompanied this missionary activity, and between 1817 and 1830, ritual book-burnings were common in many parts of France.[36] At first Voltaire and Rousseau were the prime targets, but before long many other philosophical authors were publicly burned, fiction writers were proscribed and literature itself seemed suspect in the eyes of the Catholic missionaries.

This frenzy of counter-reformation intolerance was not repeated. Indeed, it had not always been approved by the upper clergy, who felt uneasy about the bigoted and inflammatory sermons of a few 'cossacks of fanaticism', as the Bishop of Avignon described some over-zealous book-burners.[37] Nevertheless, periodical admonitions about the danger of *mauvais livres* continued throughout the century. Episcopal condemnations of dangerous literature became more intense whenever the Church was fighting the rise of secular republicanism.[38] This applied particularly in the early years of the Third Republic, and in the crisis years of the 1880s for the Church when Jules Ferry brought a state system of primary education into being. The Church remained embattled with the Republic over primary school textbooks up to 1914. Condemnations of specific texts, however, usually went hand in hand with a positive campaign to provide the public with approved and edifying *bons livres*.

Under the Third Republic, literary surveillance reached a peak in the period of L'Ordre Moral in 1876–77. Bishop Turinaz led the attack on corrupting literature in his pastoral letters, issuing indiscriminate condemnations of the novels which were guilty of spreading immorality or simply of encouraging dangerous illusions.[39] Turinaz cited the prophet Zechariah who allegedly warned of the dangers of the dissemination of literature: 'Ego video volumen volans...haec est maledictio quae egreditur super faciem omnis terrae'.[40] Turinaz feared the devastating effects of *mauvais livres* for women and family life, and he argued that by undermining religious faith *mauvaises lectures* threatened the entire social order.

The Church's continuing fear of reading is usefully illustrated in the work of the abbé Bethléem. In 1908, Bethléem founded his *Romans-revue*, a monthly journal of book reviews for Christian readers, which enjoyed a long life up to 1970. Bethléem was a *curé* from the Nord, who had already published a guide to dangerous fiction, entitled *Romans à lire et romans à proscrire*, in 1904. This compendium of dangerous and suspect literature attained a print-run of 120,000 copies, and its success prompted Bethléem to keep it up to date with a regular periodical.[41] By 1914, editions of his journal would often run to a solid hundred pages.

Bethléem aimed to inform and to warn a *bien-pensant*, influential élite of priests and educators. Through them, he hoped to protect a new reading public which he assumed to be vulnerable and ill-prepared for the sensational fiction which was now produced more cheaply than ever. It was moreover sold in new outlets such as street-stalls and railways bookstalls where it found a new readership. Bethléem knew that educated readers would be discriminating and aware. But new readers, who were young and innocent, needed protection because they allegedly had no defences against 'realism'. 'Let's not forget', Bethléem wrote in March 1911,

> that some readers, especially female readers, and those living in the countryside and in circles using parish libraries, have only a very limited cultural baggage [*bagage de lecture*] and will be easily shocked by a description which is on the realistic side, even though it may be discreet, or by rather free illustrations. This is a matter of habit and upbringing.[42]

What kind of literature did Bethléem prohibit? Clearly, he wanted to warn readers away from any authors who were already on the Index of prohibited books. But there were others, too, whose influence he considered utterly pernicious. Casanova's memoirs were condemned, as were all Balzac's love stories and his *Peau de Chagrin*, 'a bizarre and sometimes smutty [*graveleuse*] work.'[43] Feydeau was 'completely disgusting' (*pleine de turpitudes*), while Hugo was also to be avoided. *Notre-Dame de Paris* was full of slander against the Church, while *Les Misérables* was unhealthy and subversive, a 'veritable socialist epic in prose, rehabilitating the convict, the single mother, the Revolution.'[44] Predictably, George Sand was beyond the pale as the 'high priestess of modern scepticism, a demagogue and a communist', and above all a critic of bourgeois marriage.[45] Eugène Sue, the 'self-styled messiah of the proletarians', was completely unrecommendable, and Zola was considered nauseous, obscene and repugnant. *Le Rouge et le Noir* was banned as an attack on *le parti prêtre*, and Bethléem noted the rumour that the positivist philosopher Taine had read it more than sixty times.[46] For his readers, this was heavy ammunition in the war against Stendhal. He condemned the indecency of Maupassant, the evil influence of Anatole France, and the immorality of Paul de Kock and Pierre Loti. The Catholic fear of reading thus extended to the most popular as well as to some of the most canonical authors of the century. Bethléem gave a poor report to Emile Guillaumin's *Vie d'un Simple*, now considered a classic memoir of peasant life, because it attacked the Church and the rich. He found Jules Vallès impious and nihilistic, and put the popular English novelist Mrs Humphry Ward on his blacklist for her anti-Papist views.[47] Bethléem seems to have made several mistakes in his coverage of translations of British authors. He recommended Scott in expurgated form, but he did not condemn *Jane Eyre*, and pronounced Margaret Braddon's Victorian melodrama *Lady Audley's Secret* (1862) as suitable for adolescents. This was a strange verdict in the circumstances, since the attractive blonde heroine abandons her child, murders her first husband, and contemplates poisoning her second. But all censors are fallible. He also failed to condemn Thomas Hardy, whose works acquired an emblematic value for women readers in search of their own emancipation.[48] In this way Bethléem struggled to keep up a rearguard action against secularization and the democratization of reading.

The reading public, especially its female half, was assumed by polemicists such as Bethléem to be weak and easily led astray by persuasive authors and publishers greedy for profit. From his point of view, a critical and right-thinking reading public relied on well-informed and responsible intermediaries. Readers needed direction. The good reader was one who read works officially endorsed by the Church.

Republican propagandists for *l'école laïque* defined their own view of reading and secular education in stark opposition to the Catholic Church. In practice, however, both Catholic and republican ideological systems converged at various points. As Mona Ozouf has suggested, both Catholic and secular schools could be interpreted, depending on the critic's ideological standpoint, as liberating forces, or the agents of bourgeois domination, or sites of a Foucauldian *grand renfermement*, which turned schools into draconian and quasi-military instruments of social discipline.[49] In some respects, Catholic and secular republicans had remarkably similar views of the vulnerability of the reading public and its need for supervision. In the eyes of republican educators, readers had been corrupted by a variety of pernicious influences, including socialism and bonapartism. Republicans attacked the Catholic Church itself among those reactionary forces accused of exploiting popular ignorance before the advent of the Third Republic. For them, secular teaching, not Catholic directives, should guide France's new readers. Michel Bréal, who was a supporter of Jules Simon and inspector-general of higher education, wrote in *Quelques Mots sur l'Instruction en France*, published by Hachette in 1872, 'Learning to read is an illusory advantage or a dangerous gift if you don't make your students capable of understanding and loving serious reading. That is the way we must protect them from seduction'.[50]

The republican world of reading, just like the Catholic world of reading, was peopled by new readers who, it was argued, needed guidance and supervision. They were vulnerable and ignorant and they required expert advice to immunize them against depraved thoughts and wild political fantasies. In place of the Church as the key intermediary and filter of good books, the republicans proposed a team of secular intermediaries – the schoolteacher, the librarian and behind them, the government of the Third Republic itself. Both Catholics and republicans alike spoke the same rhetoric of social or moral danger, of literature as an instrument for the seduction of the popular mind, of the need for guidance, protection and serious reading. Both promoted a style of reading they described as serious not frivolous, slow and meditative rather than desultory or extensive. Neither of them contemplated or encouraged the autonomy of the individual reader. Instead, they imagined millions of helpless, innocent new readers, swamped by the mass fiction pouring from the presses and quite unable to respond to it appropriately without instruction on how to read wisely. New readers were imagined to be dangerously incompetent but infinitely malleable. Catholic and republican educators had mutually antagonistic objectives but they were embarked on a similar mission, namely 'il faut les mettre à l'abri des séductions'.[51]

The chapter titles which follow – Reading Workers, Reading Women, Reading Peasants – have a double meaning. On one hand, they can be interpreted simply as introducing workers, women and peasants who read, their reading practices and experiences. On the other hand, what follows is also about how bourgeois society went about 'reading' workers, women and peasants, in other words how it imagined them and constructed them as a social problem. In the first interpretation, therefore, the reading groups are active and autonomous subjects of the story. In the second, they remain passive objects to be directed and kept in tutelage. In what follows, this deliberate ambiguity frames the study of cultural domination and the persistent ability of readers to resist that domination and to find their own interpretations. The reader's response cannot be assumed or predicted from prescribed texts and instructions on how to read them. Readers have a habit of subverting the intentions of authors and the projects of even the best-willed philanthropists. They go poaching, in De Certeau's phrase, for their own meanings, creeping furtively through their books to bag their prey, neither advertising their aims nor leaving any trace of their presence in the text.[52] Their footprints, however, may lie elsewhere, and the historian of reading must track them down.

2
Reading Workers: Libraries for the People

In mid-nineteenth-century France, reformers of both Catholic and republican persuasions searched for ways to nullify the appeal of cheap popular literature which they considered superstitious or immoral. They wanted to integrate the working classes more fully into the national community, by discouraging them from turning either to revolutionary utopias or to clerical propaganda. Campaigners for popular lending libraries, for example, often invoked the successful example of England. During the 1860s they noted that in spite of the cotton famine provoked by the American Civil War, the textile workers of Lancashire had remained politically quiescent. They marvelled at the fact that, despite two years of extreme hardship in the cotton-manufacturing centres of Britain, no serious social unrest had ensued.[1] What was Britain's secret? Observers thought that France could learn from the institutions which underpinned the new-found social stability on the other side of the Channel. Among these mechanisms of successful social control, they included intellectual institutions such as libraries. Perhaps, they speculated, some French equivalent of the Mechanics' Institutes or popular lending libraries could ensure the future docility of French workers. This chapter considers the assumptions of reformers about working-class reading and its political dangers, before going on to examine some of the answers offered by those who saw working-class reading as an urgent social problem.

The competing discourses on popular reading reviewed here ranged from the repressive to the philanthropic. The climax of repression came early in the century, and it can be identified with the intense clerical campaign against *mauvais livres* during the Bourbon restoration. In the 1850s, as we shall see in a later chapter, the administration of Napoleon III's Second Empire contributed further to limiting the spread of chapbook (*colportage*) literature. The middle-class, philanthropic reformers, most of them republican, found their voice a little later, in the 1860s, when the movement for library reform started to bear fruit. There were different responses, therefore, to the perceived threat posed by the democratization of the reading public. Those responses were usually located within the continual struggle for influence between the Catholic Church and the supporters of a secular Republic.

The Revolution of 1848 was a warning to France's dominant classes about the progress already made by socialist ideas amongst the workers. But long before 1848 itself, expressions of middle-class alarm about lower-class reading were already being heard. The fact that books were still expensive, or that illiteracy was still common, did not necessarily dampen middle-class anxieties about social unrest. Books could be borrowed cheaply from Paris's many *cabinets de lecture*, while working-class intellectual life depended heavily on reading aloud, perhaps to a semi-literate audience. Collective oral reading was especially noticed amongst the tailors. Charles de Rémusat, the Orléanist lawyer who became Minister of the Interior in 1840, recorded in his memoirs: 'Tailors, influenced by the readings they listen to as they pursue their sedentary work, generally had advanced opinions.'[2] This was the mild, composed reaction of an observer from a secure bourgeois background. Frédéric Le Play, the pioneer of sociological research into working-class life and culture, was more alarmist. He wrote in the 1860s about the tailors' custom of hiring an invalid war veteran to read to them:

> The workshops, by means of the readings which take place there, familiarise the apprentice tailor with the most revolting obscenities, or excite political hatred and passionate envy towards the upper classes to the point of exaltation...Sometimes one of the workers with a reputation as a speaker tells vulgar jokes or scraps of history re-interpreted as he likes, often taken from the most bloodthirsty episodes of the French Revolution. To sum up, apprenticeship coincides with a real education in debauchery and in ideas which society can feel justified in fearing.[3]

Between Rémusat's calm and comfortable youth and the panic of Le Play fell the shadow of 1848 and its immediate aftermath. The insurrection of the 'June Days' alerted the ruling bourgeoisie to the horrors of social conflict and the need for brutal suppression of the Parisian insurgents. Furthermore, the successes of Louis-Napoleon brought home the dangers of universal suffrage, and exposed the failure of liberal republicanism to establish a strong popular support base. The gap between bourgeois liberalism and the concerns of most workers and peasants was starkly exposed in both the Paris rising (although it was unsuccessful) and the inauguration of the authoritarian Second Empire of Napoleon III. The writer and historian Michelet expressed the danger in a letter written to his friend, the popular poet Béranger, in June 1848. Interestingly enough, he too saw class relations threatened by what the lower classes were reading. Michelet wrote:

> The press isn't reaching the people. You can see right now, in fact, that it is on one side and the masses are on the other. It leaves a great number of men as bonapartists (in other words idolaters) and most women either idolaters or Catholics. The masses can't read and don't want to read, because it's tiring if you're not used to it. The Republic must act on the masses, must demand that they read, which is impossible today. The newspapers, circulating libraries, schools for adults etc., will have an effect, but in the long term.[4]

The 1848 Revolution, therefore, and its imperial sequel, alerted the liberal bourgeoisie to the danger posed by a hostile proletariat, easily swayed by the rival ideologies of royalism, bonapartism or clericalism.

Reformers were generous with their advice about what the masses *ought* to be reading. They believed that approved useful reading, sanctioned by the élites, could perhaps neutralize the attraction of the radical press. Advice texts, however, tended to treat working-class readers like children, seeing them as a *bon enfant*, who needed to be nurtured, lured or cajoled into desirable cultural activities. Their authors proposed an ideology of self-improvement capable of integrating the artisan élite into the dominant bourgeois culture of the nineteenth century. Such normative literature – advice on what and how the reader ought to read – should not be discussed in isolation from its audience. Working-class autobiographies, which will be discussed in more detail in Chapter 3, allow us to offer some judgements about the reception of advice literature, and help us to estimate individual responses to the promotion of recommended books. In many ways, the attractions of the classics of French literature were clearly persuasive. At the same time, however, autobiographers were autonomous readers, whose social consciousness developed in independent and untutored directions. Working-class reading, therefore, was potentially a site of political contestation.

The provision of edifying literature was seen as a way of blunting social antagonisms and of moralizing the popular classes. In 1836, the deputy Delessert had in vain demanded the establishment of a system of popular libraries.[5] Delessert was the President of the Paris savings bank (Caisse d'Epargne), and saw saving and reading as complementary ways of instilling a sense of morality into the working class of the July Monarchy. His proposal was, in any case, a modest one: he envisaged libraries in the hands of the Christian Brothers, open on Sundays. His speech on the education budget expressed a common theme in library reform propaganda: the need to complete the work of Guizot's Education law of 1833, by encouraging students to put their reading to good use after they left school. As Curmer warned in 1846, formal education was not enough, if once it was over school leavers immediately picked up the *Tableau d'Amour Conjugal*, or licentious and subversive songs.[6] Workers who continued the reading habit beyond their school years might fall into the many traps which unscrupulous publishers laid for the unwary reader. 'People are avid for reading', wrote Louandre in 1846, 'but they read at random, at a discount, the rhapsodies which brutalise or deprave them.'[7]

Most of the polemical literature of the mid-nineteenth century about popular reading stressed paternalistic concerns for working-class thrift and morality. Their arguments focused on the dangers of drink and the evils of *colportage* literature. Attacks on popular drinking habits were very common amongst library reformers. When schoolteachers replied to a questionnaire from Charles Robert in the Education Ministry in 1861, reducing the popularity of the local *cabaret* appeared to be a very high priority. In the Haute-Vienne, one teacher felt that 'libraries would combat *cabarets* and cafés, those two most fatal institutions of so-called working-class civilisation.'[8] In the Saône-et-Loire, the library was seen as an attraction to rival the local bar, and Robert's corresponding schoolteacher cited Scotland in support, when he wrote

> In Scotland and Switzerland, the peasants relax after work in the evening and on holidays by reading. Our peasants usually go and spend their money in the bar. What else can they do? The Church, the school, the village institutions which might exert a moral influence, are serious, almost severe buildings. Whereas each village has five or six bars where people enjoy themselves so much![9]

Possibly this anonymous respondent was deluding himself about the state of inebriation, or the lack of it, usually to be found north of the

Tweed, but it is significant that he made comparisons with two Calvinist countries. The value placed by Protestantism on self-help, self-education and frugality was often seen by French polemicists on popular reading as a desirable influence. François Delessert, the President of the Paris savings bank mentioned above, was himself of Swiss Protestant origin.

Attacks on alcoholic excess were politically motivated. The *cabarets* were not merely drinking places, but also meeting-points where workers or peasants might read newspapers, and discuss political news. Martin Nadaud, who migrated from the Creuse to work as a stonemason in Paris, recorded in his well-known autobiography that, in 1834, he was in demand as a newspaper reader. Every morning, he recalled, he was asked to read Etienne Cabet's *Le Populaire* aloud to fellow-workers in the local wine bar.[10] In the North, the *estaminet* might be the focal point of a mutual aid society;[11] in the South, the bar might have been a similar focus for Provençal radicalism, the *chambrée*.[12] The other so-called source of moral ruin was the literature of *colportage*, the cheap chapbooks sold in rural areas by itinerant peddlars. Since the audience for this literature was chiefly a rural readership, the attack on *colportage* literature is more appropriately discussed in Chapter 6 on peasant reading.

Throughout the century, then, the topic of popular reading inspired a vigorous debate on France's social and political problems. Too much misdirected reading, it was argued, could lead to immorality and revolution. 'Correct' reading, however, variously interpreted, if made accessible to the popular classes, might prevent conflict and encourage thrift and industry amongst French workers. The debate which began after the 1830 Revolution, and intensified after 1848, continued during the Third Republic. After 1870, for example, Arnould Frémy lamented the end of a golden age of reading. The years immediately following the Franco-Prussian War and the Paris Commune were a period when the country's decline was intensely analysed and when intellectual introspection became very fashionable. It was tempting to attribute the French defeat of 1870 to anything an author wanted to complain about. Frémy did not resist the temptation, blaming the defeat at Sedan on the degeneration of French reading habits.[13] Reading, he argued, had become indiscriminate and superficial. The newspaper press threw together serious and trivial items in a state of daily promiscuity.[14] For Frémy, this kind of mixture was unhealthy, and it led to a fragmented style of writing as of reading. As a phenomenon promoted by illustrated magazines, it was furthermore an accursed English invention.

In contrast to Britain, the debate on reading in France was politically more highly charged. Régimes had been overthrown by revolutions in 1830 and in 1848, when a middle-class republican government had survived violent popular insurrection in Paris. Then, in 1851, a bonapartist *coup d'état* crushed what remained of this early revolutionary enthusiasm as well as the hopes of parliamentary Republicanism. Liberal reformers thus fought on several fronts at once: firstly, against the diffusion of socialist tracts, which they feared had contributed to the 1848 Revolution. Secondly, as Michelet put it, the main problem was to wean the masses away from bonapartism. An equally important need, for middle-class republicans and liberal imperialists alike, was to counter the influence of clericalism. For in the diffusion of improving works through lending libraries, the Catholic Church had taken an early lead. In the following consideration of some more specific responses to the problem of working-class reading, the Catholic Church should therefore come first.

Bons livres, mauvais livres: the Catholic fear of reading

Within the Catholic Church, the fear of popular reading provoked two responses: on one hand, the desire to suppress the dissemination of undesirable literature, and on the other hand a massive effort to produce and promote *bons livres*. Both campaigns were pursued simultaneously.

During the period of the Bourbon restoration between 1815 and 1830, the Church set out to reclaim the lost congregations of a degenerate French society, and to take back into the fold all those who, in the revolutionary years, were thought to have betrayed the Church and the monarchy. This missionary effort was accompanied by a violent campaign against *mauvais livres* and the perverse dogmas of the eighteenth-century Enlightenment. Between 1817 and 1830, missionaries organized *autodafés* in various parts of the country, at which impious books were publicly burned in ritual fashion.[15] The Catholic missionaries aimed to cleanse French society of the moral corruption and growing unbelief generated by the French Revolution. They wanted to instil a desire for repentance on the part of their audience, urging them to confess, to accept a collective penance or *amende honorable* in expiation of the nation's sins. The leading authors of Enlightenment works were identified as sources of moral contagion. In towns all over France, readers were urged to 'sacrifice' their books on Lenten bonfires. Voltaire and Rousseau, the missionaries preached, had engaged in an intellectual conspiracy against true Christianity. They were considered agents of the devil, and in carefully orchestrated ceremonies, copies of their books were thrown on the flames. After Voltaire and Rousseau, other philosophical works were destroyed, and before long works of contemporary fiction, considered frivolous or obscene, were added to the pyre.

How far any of this religious intensity touched ordinary workers is open to question. Certainly the missions drew large crowds in provincial cities, made up of peasants from the surrounding countryside as well as town-dwellers. According to the prefect of the Var, 15 000 attended the erection of the mission cross in Toulon in 1817. An even larger crowd of 40 000 was reported at Avignon in 1819.[16] There is plenty of evidence, however, that the urban lower classes were not enthusiastic about missionary activity and the campaign against *mauvais livres*. By the late 1820s, missions frequently reported that their sermons had to counteract the coolness (*froideur*) of the local population. In Brest in 1819, a public demonstration forced the expulsion of the missionaries from the city. In Rouen in May 1826, a missionary was assaulted and anticlerical protests continued for a month.[17] Missionaries frequently had to cope with stink-bombs thrown in church, or dead cats hurled into the congregation by disruptive youths.

In the 1820s, several cheap editions of the complete works of Voltaire and Rousseau were published, which aggravated the 'war of the books'. The Catholic missionaries, however, had begun their campaign to demonize the Enlightenment philosophers long before these publishing innovations got under way. Altogether, 37 editions of Voltaire's complete or collected works were published during the Bourbon restoration. In the same period, 31 new editions of Rousseau were announced by the *Bibliographie de France*.[18] Nevertheless, most of these multi-volume works were beyond the budget of ordinary artisans, and aimed principally at a bourgeois readership. The fear of Catholic missionaries that cheap, small-format editions would put the classics of the *philosophes* in the households of modest artisans and peasants was a wild exaggeration. Not until 1838 did Charpentier's new publishing formula, based on a compact text in a single volume in small format (the in-18o *jésus*) start to reduce prices significantly.

The Catholic response was not all bigotry and destruction. It had a constructive side, too. In 1820, the Bishop of Bordeaux established the *Oeuvre de bons livres*, which aimed to take *mauvais livres* out of circulation by buying them and exchanging them for Christian apologetics, lives of the saints and works of religious history. The work was inspired by ecclesiastics with a missionary purpose, who had rejected the French Revolution in refusing the oath to the Civil Constitution in 1791.

Prominent among them was Julien Barault, *vicaire* of the parish of St Paul in Bordeaux. At first, the newly formed Catholic library existed only in his private apartment. Soon he established a well-organized distribution network, which has led some historians to see him as a pioneer of the circulating library in France.[19] The librarians encouraged group family reading, but they strictly controlled each family's choice of title, and exercised their own informal censorship controls. Sometimes, a few offending lines might be blotted out, or a few pages removed, in order to preserve in circulation a text which only partially fulfilled the library's Christian criteria. In 1824, the project secured papal approval, which encouraged other bodies to affiliate, and also attracted subscribers, because they qualified for papal indulgences.

In 1827, the Société Catholique des Bons Livres was established in Paris to produce suitable literature for a new network of parish libraries. The Société Catholique des Bons Livres became a publisher in its own right, producing its own favourites such as Lhomond and Fénélon in small in-18o format. In 1833, the Archbishop of Toulouse launched a similar Bibliothèque des Bons Livres.[20] In 1843, his organization had a central stock of 25 000 volumes, with 4000 borrowers and 2000 loans per week in Toulouse itself. Christian libraries here and in other distribution centres lent edifying literature free of charge to workers and young readers.

We can see in hindsight that the Catholic libraries were fighting a losing battle against the long-term decline of traditional religious teaching. Their efforts, however, to rechristianize the working population were launched early in the century, in the favourable climate of the Restoration period. The Catholic Church was thus well placed to influence the new readers of nineteenth-century France.

Workers' education and self-help, 1830–51

The Second Republic introduced universal male suffrage and inaugurated a brief period of intense popular political involvement. Political clubs experienced a revival. The new Education Ministry under Hippolyte Carnot sponsored free public readings, on two evenings per week, where writers, lawyers and academics read for an hour or so, usually in uncomfortable unheated halls. Nevertheless, as many as 300 workers came to hear readings at the Conservatoire de Musique. The government chose the texts, usually from the classics of the seventeenth and eighteenth centuries. While such experiments lasted, workers and artisans succeeded in broadening their reading experience by adding

Lamennais, De Vigny, Hugo and Lamartine to the agenda.[21] For the most part, the programme of readings was uncontroversial, and their popularity waned in 1849. In April 1850, cuts to the education budget brought these public readings to an end.

The intense intellectual activity of 1848 thus ended in a period of increasing government control of the press and of popular literature, imposed by the Second Empire in the 1850s. Let us first, however, look backwards, towards the 1840s and the origins of the movement for an independent workers' culture from which the educational activities of 1848 derived. In particular, this was the period of two workers' newspapers, La Ruche populaire, launched in December 1839, and its rival L'Atelier, published from 1840 to 1850. Both are included here because they represented independent workers' initiatives which many conservatives found worrying. In addition, they offered advice on literature, and implicitly put forward certain models for working-class readers.

La Ruche populaire and L'Atelier were monthly periodicals, at least at first, until the Revolution of February 1848 stimulated L'Atelier into a more rapid rhythm of weekly or fortnightly publication. L'Atelier characteristically appeared in eight quarto pages, carrying an austere two-column text. It sold for three francs per year or 25 centimes for a single issue.[22] La Ruche populaire was more expensive. It charged six francs for its annual subscription, but it offered 32 pages in octavo size.[23] Perhaps the most important fact about both is that they were produced and written by workers for workers. The group involved with L'Atelier, for instance, included Corbon, a *sculpteur*, and Leneveux who was a typographer. Among regular contributors were Gilland, a locksmith, and Genoux, a *margeur* (margin-setter). They were skilled craft workers, many of them appropriately enough in the printing trade. Out of 75 contributors named by the journal, 26 were printers.[24] They represented an artisan élite, interested in self-education and workers' co-operation.

For some commentators the very existence of a workers' press was new and disturbing. For the author of one article in the respectable establishment journal La Revue des Deux Mondes, it seemed ridiculous for workers to discuss literature and publish their own poetry. It was absurd that workers should suddenly have literary pretentions, for 'the demon of pride has bumped against the artisan's door', he wrote, 'the worker dreams of literary fame; he is aiming for something he cannot reach.'[25] L'Atelier he thought was a worthy project, but it should not discuss politics. Thinking about ideas should be left to the intellectual classes. The real problem was the anxiety caused by *any* workers' organization that was independent of bourgeois tutelage. In practice, L'Atelier was not sympathetic to trade unionism. As the voice of skilled artisans, it preferred to work through associations of independent producers.[26]

The workers' press of the 1840s certainly aspired to such independence. It aimed not for revolutionary socialism, far from it, but hoped to express the unmediated voice of the worker, commenting on and challenging the official discourse of the bourgeoisie.[27] *La Ruche populaire* was the more ideologically eclectic of the two, offering a platform to Fourierists, Saint-Simonians, Owenistes and other socialists. *L'Atelier* by contrast was imbued with the Christian Socialism of Buchez, and was consistently in favour of a Christian education. It recommended evening classes run by the Christian Brothers, and condemned Voltaire as a vindictive hypocrite and a consistent enemy of the people for whom he had nothing but scorn.[28] The workers' press as a whole accepted a dialogue with progressive figures within the bourgeoisie, such as Eugène Sue in the case of *La Ruche populaire* or George Sand in the case of *L'Atelier*. In their notions of emancipation, working-class association and fraternity, they kept their distance from the communist aspirations of Etienne Cabet.

The philosophy of reading elaborated by the workers' press was a demanding one, but it served as a model for artisans interested in self-education. *L'Atelier* complained that workers were being corrupted by popular fiction. Novels and serialized fiction (*romans-feuilletons*) were denounced as a waste of time, as 'a poison which warps our intelligence, which in turn stimulates and enfeebles our soul.'[29] The attack on the *roman-feuilleton* echoed the misgivings of conservatives and Catholics about the runaway success of Eugène Sue's *Les Mystères de Paris*, serialized in the *Journal des débats* in 1842. *L'Atelier* denounced Sue for sensationalizing the hardship and misery which were a daily reality for ordinary workers. The paper disliked the scenes of 'debauchery' in the novel, and anticipated more modern reactions to Sue by finding that he had no fundamental answer to the social problems his fiction described. It castigated *La Ruche populaire* for giving Sue a favourable review.

The striking religious orthodoxy of *L'Atelier*'s views on Voltaire and Eugène Sue was reinforced by the journal's other reading advice to workers. It repeatedly recommended the magazine *Le Magasin pittoresque*, for the instructive information it offered, for example on the horrors of child labour in British factories.[30] In 1846, the journal was also a supporter of Michelet's book *Le Peuple*, in spite of his sentimental approach to the social question.[31] In November 1843, *L'Atelier* went further and outlined a course in workers' self-education.[32] The first requirement was a study of the French language, otherwise workers would not learn to express themselves effectively. Secondly, the journal recommended the study of history, with a particular purpose, namely to learn one's heritage, presumably both as a nation and as a class, and to envisage one's future destiny. Third on the list came the masterpieces of French literature, unfortunately undefined by *L'Atelier*, although its respect for the canon seems clear. Fourthly, the worker should read some law and politics in order to appreciate better his rights and duties, and lastly, his library might include something useful to improve his professional and technical competence. Education would best be achieved, according to *L'Atelier*, on a mutual basis, through groups organized in the workplace (which sounds very much like the informal classes Martin Nadaud recalled organizing in Parisian workers' lodgings in the late 1830s). If the Frères de la Doctrine Chrétienne were involved as well, that would be all to the good.

This very general reading advice contained nothing subversive or objectionable except, as we have noted, that it was predicated on the workers' own independent efforts. Michelet would have approved the emphasis on history, while teaching the law was on the face of it innocuous. The literary canon went unchallenged. The advice to cultivate technical expertise was absolutely in line with the emphasis on 'useful knowledge' promoted by the Mechanics' Institutes in Britain and their admirers in France. *L'Atelier*'s programme of study was doubly significant for what it left out as well as for what it actually recommended. There were two glaring omissions. Firstly, there was no explicit mention of political economy. The emphasis on studying legislation had as its primary aim simply the development of an awareness of citizens' rights and obligations. It implied no critical stance towards the institutions of the bourgeois state, no analysis of the workings of capitalism. Workers were apparently not encouraged to pursue any kind of sustained critique of the liberal economy even, it seems, from a Christian perspective. The second omission is that of any recreational literature. As we have seen, *L'Atelier* identified the *roman-feuilleton* as pulp fiction which perverted working-class morality and consciousness. Its strictures extended, it seemed, to all kinds of fiction. Even poetry, including the worker-poets who were being published by *La Ruche populaire*, did not find a place on *L'Atelier*'s recommended programme of study. Workers' reading, in this view, had a functional purpose, enabling them to communicate more effectively, to work more skilfully, and to understand their history. The self-educated worker, *L'Atelier* warned, may have to endure isolation and his intellectual efforts may provoke the ridicule of fellow-workers – the classic situation of many autodidacts. But he should persevere, sacrificing his leisure time and resisting the temptations of drink. Workers' reading, as recommended by *L'Atelier*, was a serious and demanding business.

The last issue of *L'Atelier* appeared on 31 July 1850. It was the victim of a press law which demanded a large financial deposit from every periodical. Although it may have had as many as a thousand *abonnés* at its peak in February 1848,[33] its moderate views lost their popularity in militant circles thereafter. The decade of the 1840s, culminating in the Revolution of 1848, had opened a brief window of opportunity, when certain groups of mainly skilled workers aspired to develop their cultural autonomy. Under the bourgeois Republic, followed by the early years of Napoleon III, that window now closed.

The Franklin Society and popular libraries

As we have seen, Catholic organizations had been disseminating Christian literature to the masses since the 1820s. Several decades later, liberals, too, felt an urgent need to influence the direction of popular reading. If religious associations could propagate good works in their own interest, asked the republican Jules Simon in 1863, why could not lay associations do the same?[34] Simon argued for the establishment of popular lending libraries, which could guide the reading of adults beyond their school years.

Existing public or municipal libraries lent books only rarely. They opened for limited hours which were not designed to attract lower-class readers. In Lille, for example, the library had been open until 9 p.m. during the Second Republic, but in 1852 this arrangement ceased, and the evening session was not restored until 1865. Even then, lending was prohibited. One disgruntled Lillois described the local library as a kind of shrine where workers in their blouses and clogs were frowned on.[35] Without more flexibility, French libraries had little hope of capturing the attention of the century's new readers. Librarians, who as yet received no professional training, tended to see their main duty as preserving the treasures of the library, rather than making the books available to the general public. Apart from a few local scholars, many traditional libraries were visited only rarely, and in any case they did not maintain a large stock of general literature. By 1851, therefore, when British legislation first enabled local councils to levy one penny in the rates to subsidize local libraries, French public library provision was in an antiquated condition and lagged far behind British and American public libraries. Jean Hassenforder's comparison of the state of lending libraries in two cities of comparable size – Leeds and Lyon – at the beginning of the twentieth century, showed that the gap had still not been closed. The comparison was entirely in favour of Leeds. While Leeds had a central library with 14 branches open all day, Lyon had only six popular libraries, open in the evenings only.[36] The need for reform was patent. Even when it came, however, libraries still tended to regard readers, and especially working-class readers, with suspicion. Many librarians thought workers would steal the books, and were extremely reluctant to lend at all. In 1886, the Bibliothèque Forney in Paris opened its reading room with two policemen on patrol to keep an eye on the readers.[37]

Library reformers and popular educators pushed for libraries which would lend at least a section of their stock, and which would open in the evening, to allow workers to use the library at the end of their working day. They ultimately aimed to establish a republican curriculum in opposition to both clerical influence and the bonapartist dictatorship. They were clear what they were against: impiety, obscenity, socialism and religious bigotry, as peddled by the *colporteurs* and certain popular novelists. None of this, in the view of Jules Simon, provided the manual worker with fare to entertain him and give sustenance to his spirit, refreshing him, ennobling him and lightening his burden.[38] What sort of literature would achieve this ideal?

Most French reformers, like their English counterparts, agreed that popular libraries should offer works of sound morality and useful technical knowledge. A few others thought that works on French history would also serve to cultivate the popular classes. For a true and ennobling moral sense, they recommended the ancients and the French classics of the seventeenth century. When the Franklin Society, dedicated to the spread of popular lending libraries, drew up its model catalogue for a new *bibliothèque populaire*, it included Fénélon, Pascal and Bossuet, Plutarch's *Lives*, as well as Corneille, Racine, Molière and Lafontaine.[39] It did not neglect foreign classics, for the Franklin Society catalogue also included Dante, Milton, Shakespeare and Schiller. The Society viewed its task in these terms: each member was asked to imagine that

> a delegation of foremen, workers, factory employees, peasants and artisans came to ask him to designate the main works suitable for the shelves of a library of 400 or 500 volumes, which would entertain or instruct their readers while remaining aloof from politics and from religious controversy.[40]

Jules Simon apparently took great pleasure in prescribing book lists for the education of the people. He felt that popular readers needed a dose of Seneca to drive out almanacs, works of piety, ridiculous fairy tales and Eugène Sue. The man of the people was 'un grand enfant', who was not to be let off lightly, although the Franklin Society hoped to see annotated editions of the classics, which would presumably help him with his homework.

The Franklin Society, which received government authorization in 1862, issued a regular journal from 1868, which is the historian's main source for its activities in encouraging the establishment of lending libraries and advising on the most desirable book stock. The Society's governing board (*conseil d'administration*) was made up at its foundation of intellectuals, politicians and highly placed government officials. Thirteen of its 66 members, or 20 per cent, described themselves as professors, men of letters or members of a distinguished academy, such as the Académie française or the Académie des Sciences Morales et Politiques.[41] Nine founding members were senators, deputies like Jules Simon or former deputies, and 14 were either jurists or *fonctionnaires*, like Charles Robert, general secretary to the Education Ministry. There were five schoolteachers or school inspectors, three bankers and three industrialists. They included a strong contingent from the east of France, including Jean Macé, then a teacher at Beblenheim, and leading Mulhouse manufacturers Dollfuss and Thierry-Mieg. As we shall see below, this group was extremely active in promoting libraries for workers, and in backing the Ligue de l'Enseignement. Thus except for the presence of five aristocrats, including Baron Alphonse de Rothschild, and a solitary working-class representative (the Parisian lithographer Girard), the encouragement and direction of working-class reading was firmly in the hands of the *haute bourgeoisie*.

The Society took its name from the most influential role model of the self-improving artisan, who kept recurring throughout the literature of advice to workers – that of Benjamin Franklin, scientist, statesman and autobiographer. Franklin's autobiography was a key reference text amongst the advice literature for self-educators. It provided the most complete model available in recent times to illustrate how a man of humble social origins could achieve success in many fields of endeavour. Franklin's own writings were adopted to construct an image of him as a perfect reader. Franklin was the architect of his own fortunes. The son of a soap and candle-maker, he belonged to a modest family. Like so many autodidacts, he interrupted his early education, and yet the young Benjamin showed a great devotion to books. As a printer's apprentice, he enjoyed the benevolent assistance of a patron who allowed him to borrow from his private library. Franklin, in the image publicized by his autobiography, lived frugally, did not drink, and carefully saved money to buy books from secondhand dealers. He was a man of regular habits, always punctual (unlike many of his fellow-workers), who organized his life so as to give himself maximum leisure time for reading and study. Franklin also took the initiative in establishing a circulating library. His life story was fashioned to impress upon readers the virtues of self-denial and the avoidance of strong drink, both animated by the passion for intellectual discovery.

The advice literature on working-class reading directed workers towards certain literary genres which were considered edifying, and away from others. Non-fiction was preferable by far, especially scientific manuals aimed at improving the technical expertise of artisans. The advice texts were trying to shape working-class literary culture in a way that would limit distraction and escapism, in order to develop practical talents and improve the quality of production. Once again, English models were admired by French reformers. Plon, for example, produced a French edition of Samuel Smiles' *Self-Help* in 1869. In the *Bulletin de la Société Franklin*, General Faré gave it a fulsome review, and concluded that *Self-Help* alone 'was worth an entire library'.[42] Benjamin Franklin was a prestigious icon of self-improvement in France, just as he was in the English-speaking world. His name signified 'instruction, travail, économie, moralité', although it was recognized that Franklin's rigorous technique of self-examination was probably too demanding for French workers.[43] Both French and British philanthropists tended to reproduce the same rhetoric.

Library reformers did not simply seek to direct working-class reading into certain educational channels; normative literature such as *Self-Help* also offered instruction on *how* to read. This literature discussed the reading methods best suited to self-education, outlining ways of extracting the maximum profit from texts. The profitable use of time was essential. Readers who borrowed books and rarely bought them sometimes only had a limited time available before they were due to return them. But maximizing the use of time was more than a technique for dealing with short-term book loans – it was part of the autodidact's *habitus* of austerity and self-denial. Self-taught workers shared a puritan philosophy of life in which all waste was sinful. Ben Franklin's maxims were again enlisted here, for they too advised: 'Lose no time; be always employed in something useful, cut off all unnecessary actions.' Consequently, self-educating readers were urged to make use of every odd hour or half-an-hour in the day. The time thus saved could be put away profitably, as it were, in a savings bank. The educators thus proposed a new economy of time, in which it became a valued currency which bore interest for the careful investor.

The best way to use the scraps of time available for reading was to train the memory to work harder. It was quite possible for self-educated workers to memorize long passages, and even entire volumes. This was a valuable skill for those who could never hope to possess a large private library where texts were always available for consultation. The reader was guided towards an intensive style of reading, in which memorization, personal note-taking and constant re-reading were aids to learning. Fragmented reading styles appropriate to light magazines were deplored.

The popular lending libraries, which began to appear in the late 1860s, selected their stock carefully. They hoped to provide technical advice and sources of reference. They were to offer works on practical drawing, surveying and agronomy. The Franklin Society recommended specific titles on agriculture, horticulture, family hygiene and pharmacy. Popular libraries, then, would not only be an aid to moral education. They would also constitute a repository of everyday practical knowledge at the disposal of the local community.

Since some reformers felt that nineteenth-century novels had a corrupting influence, it was logical that recreational literature should play a minor role in their ideal popular library. The Franklin Society, however, was practical about popular tastes for fiction. In its 1864 catalogue of 516 titles recommended to any organization setting up a library, 'instructive works' accounted for 69 per cent of the titles, religious works for 3 per cent, and fiction for 28 per cent.[44] This is of course a rough guide. Some titles straddled the boundary between fiction and 'instructive works' and were difficult to classify. The novels of Jules Verne are a good example: they were often classified by the Franklin Society not as fiction, but as instructive works of travel and geography. In practice, the popular libraries spawned by the Franklin Society carried between 35 and 45 per cent of their stock in novels or other literature.[45] This was still far below the percentage on novels which readers actually borrowed.

The Franklin Society, however, remained cautious about working-class consumption of novels. Even good novels, it was felt, could divert the serious reader from the healthy and useful books he really needed. They encouraged fantasy, and enfeebled the spirit. As one member of the Franklin Society wrote:

Real life does not easily lend itself to these romantic impulses. Hence disillusionment, disgust and moral wretchedness beyond measure. When you have seen close up the havoc that honest novels wreak in simple working lives, you are frightened by the responsibility you assume when you encourage this kind of reading.[46]

Although some of Dickens was acceptable, together with standard classics such as *Paul et Virginie* and *Robinson Crusoe*, very few modern novels were approved by the Société Franklin, except for the patriotic fiction of Erckmann-Chatrian.[47] The Society's 1864 catalogue refused to accept any Balzac novel except *Eugénie Grandet*.

The Commission des Bibliothèques Populaires, which met after 1882 under the auspices of the Education Ministry to recommend suitable books for lending libraries, took an extremely restrictive view. It rejected the speeches of the socialist leader Louis Blanc as 'polemical'.[48] In 1885, Macchiavelli's *The Prince* was rejected, and the Commission also found Eugène LeRoy's novel of peasant protest in the Périgord, *Jacquou le Croquant*, too dangerous. So, too, were Fouché's *Memoirs*, and Hugo's *Notre-Dame de Paris* (at least at first). The Commission was very reluctant to accept Jules Verne, Pierre Loti or Anatole France as edifying authors.[49] Authorities were careful not to encourage sexual immorality and female infidelity. They rejected *Anna Karenina* as proper library material in 1885, but the Commission welcomed Tolstoy's more didactic story *Resurrection* in 1911. It rejected George Sand's letters to Alfred de Musset in 1897. Almost all Thomas Hardy's stories were considered unsuitable for French working-class and peasant readers, beginning with *Tess of the D'Urbervilles* in 1901. The literary advisers regarded Ibsen as far too explicit, until they let in *The Enemy of the People* in 1903.

The safe authors were those who wrote in a conservative national tradition. These were the classical writers of the seventeenth century and contemporary novelists such as Erckmann-Chatrian. Walter Scott and Fenimore Cooper were also approved. When one Parisian employer analysed the characteristics of the well-disciplined worker in 1870, he described him as a reader of recent French history, by authors such as Lamartine.[50] This he considered the best antidote to the impossible socialist dreams of Cabet or Louis Blanc. He would no doubt have welcomed the inclusion of the historian Lavisse on the list of books approved by the Commission des Bibliothèques Populaires by the 1890s. By this time, Brunetière, Déroulède, Alexandre Dumas and Conan Doyle had also found their way onto the approved list. Only after 1905 did the commissioners relax their bans on authors such as Gorky, Verne and

Thomas Hardy. Even a library edition of Sue's *Le Juif Errant* was accepted in 1905; perhaps the rallying of republican forces in favour of the separation of church and state made Sue's anti-Jesuit prejudices respectable at last. Some authors, however, never obtained their seal of approval: these included Emile Zola and Oscar Wilde.

Popular lending libraries, whether established by the efforts of private philanthropy or under municipal sponsorship, spread rapidly in the 1870s, and by 1902 there were as many as 3000 *bibliothèques populaires* in existence.[51] Yet they only partially fulfilled the expectations of the bourgeois philanthropists who sought to foster and direct working-class reading practices. The correspondence of the Franklin Society during the late 1860s and the 1870s resounds with the despairing cries of librarians, frustrated by incorrigible readers who insisted on choosing dubious novels in preference to the moral works they were offered. Government controls imposed another obstacle to the smooth development of popular lending libraries. Private bodies needed prefectoral permission before setting up a new library and sometimes the prefects demanded the right to inspect the catalogue annually. The French state exercised such a meticulous supervision of voluntary philanthropic associations that in 1876 the government even sent affiliates of the Franklin Society a memorandum prescribing the exact dimensions of the index cards to be used for their author catalogues.[52] The main problem, however, was the demanding nature of the reading which the reformers prescribed. As Chalamet of the Franklin Society conceded in 1883, the study of literary classics had possibly been exaggerated. 'One should not forget', he paternalistically advised, 'that most of our population... are intellectually no more than grown-up children; and you don't feed children solely on coarse bread and heavy food.'[53]

The library reformers had aimed to provide sound literature for working-class readers. Most of the borrowers, however, in the lending libraries at the end of the nineteenth century, were not of working-class origin. Every library naturally drew on social groups in its particular *quartier* or *arrondissement*. From the records of Parisian municipal libraries and from the correspondence of the Franklin Society, we can see that many soldiers used the library at the Invalides, and a large number of office workers borrowed from the library in Batignolles. Leaving aside local characteristics, however, analyses of borrowers have suggested that the clientele of lending libraries fell roughly into four main groups.[54] Firstly, there was a substantial number of *rentiers* and *propriétaires*, or in other words bourgeois with no profession, who made up more than 20 per cent of library borrowers in Paris. Many readers in this category were women. A second group, which usually composed between a quarter and a third of urban borrowers, was made up of clerks and office workers from local businesses (*employés*). A third group of students and schoolchildren was very important both in Paris and in provincial cities. A fourth category, finally, was made up of workers, who might constitute between 10 per cent and one-third of the library's readership.

Precise social classifications are always hazardous, and when a librarian describes a customer as an 'ouvrier' it is never completely clear whether he is a craftsman or a factory worker. For this reason, the above breakdown of library users only attempts to provide a broad outline of their social status. Nevertheless it seems clear that the poorest classes were in a minority amongst library users. The lending libraries were not carrying out their assigned task of promoting moral values among and integrating the workers, since they only represented a small proportion of the readers. Readers from other social categories outnumbered them, and sometimes they were in a majority of 85 per cent. The typical library user at the end of the nineteenth and beginning of the twentieth centuries was not a worker, but a *rentière*, a white-collar worker or a student from the local *lycée*. It would be more accurate perhaps to characterize such library users as *petit-bourgeois*, and to see lending libraries as a means of incorporating not the working class, but rather the lower middle classes into the dominant literary culture of nineteenth-century France.

Bibliothèques d'entreprises and the Ligue de l'Enseignement

The Franklin Society was not the only voluntary philanthropic organization through which the liberal bourgeoisie attempted to direct and incorporate workers' reading. It was simply the one which has left the best records of its activities. Similar objectives inspired those employers who set up workplace libraries in their own factories. Similar objectives also lay behind Jean Macé's Ligue de l'Enseignement. These projects overlapped; as we have seen, Macé was a founder member of the Franklin Society, and so were some of the Alsace manufacturers who were interested in creating factory libraries.

Macé, born of working-class parents in 1815, had studied on a scholarship at the Collège Stanislas in Paris, and had supported the Republic in 1848. His connection with eastern France began in 1851, when he took refuge from the bonapartist coup in the small town of Beblenheim, north of Colmar. There he developed his interest in working-class education, and from this base he drew existing organizations such as the Société d'Instruction Elémentaire and the Association Philotechnique into a new national campaign. His earliest adherents were a tram conductor, a stonecutter and a policeman, and he also recruited Bastelica, inspirer of the Marseille branch of the Workers' International. On the whole, however, this was a movement of local élites rather than of workers themselves. The movement's educational imperatives were framed by the concerns of the republican bourgeoisie, intent on overcoming the effects of Catholic propaganda. For their historian Katherine Auspitz, disciplining the poor was an implicit rather than an explicit objective. The progressive bourgeoisie promoted a work ethic and wanted to achieve an obedient labour force. At the same time, Auspitz describes the Ligue de l'Enseignement as a progressive republican network which represented a kind of counter-cultural alternative to bonapartism in the 1860s.[55] In a similar vein, Philip Nord described such networks as the infrastructure of a republican political culture, which prepared the Third Republic and assisted the triumphant transition to republican democracy after the 1870s.[56]

Macé's Ligue, established in 1866, has been described as a 'weapon of war against clericalism', although Macé himself seems to have regarded his work as a religious crusade, part of his Christian duty to provide intellectual sustenance to the blighted industrial region of eastern France.[57] The Ligue always remained a local effort, based on Macé's work in establishing libraries in the Haut-Rhin. In his book *Morale en Action*, Macé described the organization of libraries and study circles in Beblenheim and nearby towns.[58] He charged readers five centimes for every volume lent, believing that the local population would be suspicious of anything provided free of charge. One feature of the organization was the very high rate of participation by local Rhineland manufacturers, especially those of Protestant origin, who perhaps saw libraries as way of improving rather than distracting their labour force. A committee of 24 members organized the creation of popular libraries in the Haut-Rhin, and of these 11 were manufacturers or officials of the Société de Mulhouse. Dollfuss the cloth-manufacturer was a collaborator, and so were members of the Thierry-Mieg and Koechlin families. They represented a Protestant oligarchy of benevolent entrepreneurs, acting with the support of freemasonry and the backing of the Rabbinate of the Haut-Rhin.[59] The library at Guebwiller, between Colmar and Mulhouse, was also launched by a Protestant schoolmaster, aided by local industrialists.[60] It stocked the *Magasin pittoresque*, the great French literary classics, Shakespeare and Walter Scott.

When Audiganne published his descriptions of the working-class milieu in every region of France, he picked out Alsace, and especially Mulhouse, as a model environment.[61] Audiganne's account was full of references to the shocking events of the 1848 revolutions but, at the same time, he measured the progress that he considered had been made since then in promoting inter-class harmony. Welfare institutions, charitable organizations and mutual help societies all helped to achieve this, in his view, whether put in place by workers themselves or by an enlightened *patronat*. He thoroughly approved of workers' libraries in factories and, like many other commentators, he praised British precedents such as the Mechanics' Institutes.[62]

Education reformers were very conscious that industrialization had created a workforce which was much more vulnerable to undesirable influences than was the traditional craft worker in his small workshop. Jules Simon, a supporter of the Franklin Society and the Ligue de l'Enseignement, saw that modern industrial conditions easily led to moral decline, drunkenness and ignorance. The power of women to exert a beneficial influence was also reduced when they left home to work in factories. Simon, who became Education Minister in 1871, and was briefly prime minister of the Republic before being dismissed by President MacMahon in 1877, epitomized some of the anxious attitudes of the liberal bourgeoisie.[63] He had studied working-class areas in Lyon, Lille, Mulhouse and Rouen. He took social inequality as a given and accepted the principles of liberal economics. He opposed the National Workshops in 1848, and voted against including the right to work in the constitution of the Second Republic. His main aim was to encourage the workers to live a moral life, and to dissuade them from resorting to strikes, without violating *laisser-faire* principles. This was always the framework within which bourgeois philanthropy, including library and educational reform, operated. As a result, there was a residue of social tension in the movement for workers' reading, directed as it was by wealthy bourgeois and employers. The socialist newspaper the *Nouvelliste de Rouen* pinpointed this issue in an article in 1870. The paper wondered what lectures on Benjamin Franklin and Christopher Columbus might have to do with actual working-class concerns, especially, the paper added, when they were organized by 'les gros bonnets'.[64] The bourgeois reformers were never prepared to surrender control of the institutions they had created to direct working-class reading.

When the Parisian employer Denis Poulot wrote his provocative survey of workers' attitudes in 1870, workers' reading played a significant role in his argument.[65] Poulot's book was an attack on the laziness and drunkenness of the workforce, and its resistance to the discipline of the modern workplace. His descriptions were possibly used by Emile Zola in *L'Assommoir*, his novel based on Parisian working-class life, and centring on the theme of alcoholism. Poulot classified workers into eight categories, labelling most of them either *ouvriers*, of whom in general he approved, or those he called 'les sublimes', about whom he had little to say that was good. He provided a pen-portrait of the typical worker in each category. 'Le vrai sublime', a drinker of strong spirits, is only very rarely a reader, according to Poulot. He may occasionally show an interest in the crime and scandal pages of the newspaper (*les faits divers*), or he might listen to his fellow-workers reading.[66] The orators who might be reading to him were the political dreamers in the workforce, and they were certainly identified by their reading. In Poulot's unflattering character sketch, they read Cabet's *L'Icarie*, Louis Blanc's *La Révolution*, Hugo's *Les Châtiments* and his character assassination of Napoleon III, *Napoléon le Petit*. Political orators seek inspiration in their reading, according to Poulot, not true instruction. They have read a lot, and are full of social and political theories.[67]

Poulot's book reveals a boss's view of his workers' disobedience and irregularity, as well as workplace slang and culture. In a sense his complaints are indirect evidence of the worker's resistance to the demands of capitalism, even though Poulot is writing to denounce their insubordination. He puts forward his sketch of the ideal worker, who is also defined by his reading, and his serious attitude towards it. The ideal employee, Poulot's *ouvrier vrai*, is a regular worker, who works at least 300 days in the year, is never absent on Mondays, and is prepared to put in some overtime if necessary on Sunday. Not only is he willing and pliable in this way, but he fulfils two other essential requirements of those who sought to direct working-class reading: he takes care of his money and is never in debt, and he never gets drunk.[68] He reads above all for self-instruction. Poulot's ideal worker knows of Cabet's communist writings, but rejects them as impossibly utopian. He enjoys a *Histoire de la Révolution*, presumably Michelet's version. On the 1848 Revolution, he reads not Louis Blanc's socialist version, but the liberal, bourgeois histories of Lamartine, such as his *Les Girondins*. In fact, Poulot would have his workers reading history whenever possible.

Poulot's second category of worker is also an example of near-impeccable discipline, even if he might drink occasionally, and does not quite match in his employers' eyes the absolute perfection of *l'ouvrier vrai*. He rejects frivolous novelettes in favour of the edifying and instructive *La*

Gazette des tribunaux or *La Science pour tous*. Poulot's portrait allows him the luxury of a second-hand copy of Sue's *Le Juif errant*.[69] Denis Poulot thus offers us a scenario based on personal observation, which contains a severe critique of worker behaviour, and at the same time outlines the employer's ideal, in which serious reading accompanies the desirable virtues of discipline, regularity and sobriety. His view of workers' reading embodies a consistent genre hierarchy, in which history is by far the favourite genre. Then come, in descending order of importance, reading for useful knowledge, and fiction. The *'sublimes'* hardly read at all, except for news of sensational murders. The troublemakers nurture their political fantasies on socialist political writings and Victor Hugo. Like the other bourgeois philanthropists discussed here, Poulot attributed enormous importance to what workers were reading or not reading, and he had very definite views on what kind of literature ought to be absorbing their leisure time.

One of the most dedicated industrialists of Alsace was J.-J.Bourcart, who in 1864 established the study circle at Guebwiller, and built new premises for it.[70] Imitating the British model of Mechanics' Institutes, Bourcart reasoned that intelligent workers would produce better work than ignorant workers, and appreciated the need to develop their education. He realized at the same time that evenings spent in study also discouraged wasteful expense and idleness. He foresaw that after a long 12-hour working day, his workers might resist the regimentation of their leisure time by their employers. He consequently gave his workers considerable freedom to organize their own discussion groups, allowing them to elect their own representatives and choose their own teachers. Nevertheless, workers' autonomy had its limits, and Bourcart reserved for himself the power to dismiss troublemakers. Out of Guebwiller's 6000-strong labour force, 500 workers were affiliated to study groups, following for the most part courses in French, drawing, arithmetic, physics and chemistry.

A report compiled by Jean Koechlin-Dollfuss in 1864 mentioned eight local establishments in the Haut-Rhin with schools, of which four had libraries, while Koechlin *et cie* had a library but no school.[71] These five libraries had a total of 3000 volumes in both French and German, comprising travel, history and moral tales, but nothing religious or political which might be controversial. No charge was made for use of these libraries. Many more *bibliothèques d'entreprise* were set up after the 1860s, especially in companies involved in the book trade itself, such as Hachette, and in the public service, such as the library for customs employees founded in Le Havre in 1873, and another for tobacco workers also in Le Havre established in 1876.[72] These ventures were usually linked to apprenticeship training and in-house evening courses.

In eastern France, the Ligue de l'Enseignement thrived under the protection of local prefects. Elsewhere in France it made only slow progress. In Rouen, textile manufacturers such as Bessièvre were supportive. At Maromme, north-west of Rouen, Besselièvre made 200 volumes available to his employees.[73] There was some degree of success in the Yonne department, a traditionally anticlerical part of central France. In 1868 a popular library for workers was established in the *chef-lieu* Sens, which opened until midnight twice per week. It stocked Macé's own works, as well as Voltaire's histories, Michelet's *Jeanne d'Arc*, and works by Franklin. Napoleon III's own writings on pauperism were available, which made this a highly orthodox selection.[74] The Mayor of Sens himself was even induced to participate in public readings. Police spies attended and reported that he read for two hours from Thiers' history of the Consulate and Empire to an audience of cobblers, farmers and *vignerons*.[75]

The ultimate aim of Macé's project was to secure a compulsory system of secular state education. His fortunes declined in 1877, with the ascendancy of the *Ordre Moral*, whose prefects were no longer in sympathy with his organization. Branches of the Ligue were closed down. At La Rochelle, the Ligue's despairing ex-president, facing the extinction of his organization, asked the prefect 'Will you then declare that reading poses a public danger?'[76] For so many of France's regimes in the nineteenth century, this was precisely the perception. Macé's goal, however, was eventually achieved with the passage of the Ferry education laws in the 1880s. After this success the Ligue, and perhaps bourgeois radicalism itself, lost its main impetus. Macé, the cause of secular education won, became a senator in his old age. The Ligue's archives were later destroyed by the Vichy regime.

Conclusion

> The most common aspect of the writings which are being disseminated at present, and which are published in the most popular format, is to divide society into two classes, the rich and the poor, representing the former as tyrants and the latter as victims; to arouse the envy and hatred of one against the other, and thus to nurture in our society, which has so much need of unity and fraternity, all the elements of a civil war.[77]

Reading Workers 41

In these alarmist terms, the Republic's Minister for the Interior expressed the fear of reading amongst the new, lower-class readers of the nineteenth century. He wrote, admittedly, in 1849, when social tensions ran high, and the conflicts of the 1848 Revolution had not yet been resolved. Nevertheless, the debate on lower-class reading engaged those from all positions on the political spectrum at different times throughout the century.

Along with other contemporary problems such as working-class drinking, improvidence and lack of religion, working-class reading was part of the complex of issues known as 'la question sociale'. For the Catholic Church, a correct and expurgated reading list could bring back to the fold the millions lost in the turmoil of the 1789 Revolution and the subsequent reign of the usurper. A return to the sermons and morality of the seventeenth-century literary classics could restore the faith and fortify wavering souls in the true doctrine of the Church. Republicans, too, had their reading agenda for a working population which seemed far too ready to accept Catholic, bonapartist or royalist ideas. It included history, useful knowledge, and the classics of antiquity. Through organizations like the Franklin Society and the Ligue de l'Enseignement, they promoted this agenda through a much-needed library reform. In contrast to Britain, their action came late, not achieving momentum until the decade of the 1860s. This was fully a generation after the Mechanics' Institutes and the Society for the Diffusion of Useful Knowledge which French commentators sometimes held up as models to be emulated. When the effort was made, it owed a great debt to non-Catholic employers and philanthropists who were aiming to construct the institutions of a secular, republican state. All these groups sought a counterweight to cheap sensational fiction and illustrated magazines. They encouraged working-class self-education and struggled to influence the literary culture of working-class readers.

Some workers' circles, like the contributors to *L'Atelier* in the 1840s, made similar pronouncements about desirable workers' reading. On occasions, however, the reading they proposed was too demanding. Working-class readers did not necessarily share the classical education which had formed the western European middle class. They were not always familiar, in Bourdieu's phrase, with the cultural capital which the nineteenth-century middle class had inherited, although many of them proved eager to claim a share of that cultural legacy. Working-class autodidacts, on the other hand, could find some common ground with their social superiors in the ideology of self-improvement, with its emphasis on self-denial and instructional reading. Working-class readers remained autonomous in their choices. They took advice, absorbing it and at the same time resisting its attempts to control their cultural life. Self-educated workers maintained a strong sense of class consciousness. For them, in spite of advice literature and encouragements to read, equal access to knowledge was a goal not a given. As we shall see in the following chapter, they were prepared to organize their cultural life without middle-class supervision.

3
Reading Workers: Improvisation and Resistance

Although the views about workers' reading put forward by the Church, republicans, librarians and manufacturers are important for any study of working-class reading culture, we cannot build a history of workers' reading on these sources alone. The opinions represented in these competing discourses about reading are just that – opinions, about what workers *ought* to be reading – and they only tell one side of the story: they say little about what workers actually read. The advice offered by concerned élites is much more valuable if it can be complemented by some information about how the audience of working-class readers reacted to it. As Jonathan Rose urged in a provocative article, we must 'interrogate the audience'.[1] This chapter tries to do exactly that, and to offer some clues about readers' responses. The clues come from the evidence of independent working-class libraries, and from the accounts given by individual workers about their own reading experience. These sources enable us to envisage workers not just as a passive body of readers ready to be shaped and disciplined, but as active readers who attempted to construct a distinctive reading culture of their own.

The core of this discussion lies in the autobiographies of workers themselves. I have consulted 22 autobiographies in all, 18 of them by men and four by women. Fourteen of them deal with the period before 1851, eight concern the period between 1848 and 1871, and another nine refer to the period of the Third Republic (naturally there is some overlap here). Working-class autobiographers rarely failed to give a description of their reading, and some of them outlined the detailed reading programme which had guided them. In relating their reading, they traced their triumphant struggles to acquire a literary culture. They established authentic foundations for their own literary aspirations. Their books were the instruments which fashioned a new working-class intelligentsia. The eager search for book knowledge was vital to the intellectual emancipation on which political action was based; it also provided the knowledge and discipline required for moral, rational self-improvement.

The emphasis on reading was echoed by many members of this working-class intelligentsia, and it raises important questions for a historian of books: what did the working-class autobiographers read? Given the expense of buying books, how did they acquire their reading matter? When did they read, if their days were filled by long hours of exhausting manual labour? Above all, *how* did they read – collectively or alone, silently or orally, eagerly, obsessively or casually, like the 'nonchalant' readers encountered by Richard Hoggart?[2] They exploited a variety of resources to acquire reading matter, and struggled to read in the face of grinding poverty and other material difficulties. And yet what they regarded as 'useful knowledge' did not always match the definitions of utility promoted by philanthropists, educators and politicians. Workers made their own choices, dictated by their own interpretations of their needs.

Working-class autobiographers had quite distinctive methods of literary appropriation. Although many of them attended formal school, their attendance was usually brief and irregular. The need to earn a living as soon as possible, or to travel in search of work, precluded sustained periods of schooling. The autobiographers were 'autodidacts', men who had taught themselves most of what they knew. Their literary culture was improvised, developed haphazardly outside the structure of educational institutions. In its respect for the literary canon, however, the reading of the autodidacts seems extremely deferential to the literary monuments of bourgeois culture. This ambiguous reverence for official culture lies at the heart of working-class *autodidaxie*. Yet it never prevented working-class readers from proclaiming their class identity or making clear where their fundamental class loyalties lay. They lay, in the vast majority of cases considered here, with the working-class roots from which they had sprung. From this angle, we can justifiably call their reading culture a culture of resistance.

Conventional readers and working-class acculturation

Self-taught workers were a special group: they were usually skilled workers, distinguished by their greater ambition and articulateness. We should not take them as representative of the mass of workers as a whole. To put them in context and in perspective, we should consider

Improvisation and Resistance 45

the typical situation of working-class readers before asking how a few of them managed to transcend it.

One insight into the world of more ordinary working-class readers is provided by the sociological investigations conducted by Frédéric LePlay into working-class households. LePlay and his associates were only partly concerned with workers' reading; what interested them most of all were the family network and the family budget, which was carefully detailed in their reports. LePlay wanted to test his theories about family size and structure, and their relationship to social stability and moral values. These notions, he believed, were applicable not only in France, but in the rest of Europe as well, and even beyond. In fact, his inquiry increasingly assumed pretentious globalizing tendencies. He called his individual studies 'monographs', and the essential item under his microscope was the family. He was not concerned at all with unmarried workers. Although reading was not his main target, his accounts of working-class leisure activities did supply precious inventories of reading material available. LePlay's comments, therefore, were conditioned by his particular priorities and his anxiety about the decline of working-class moral values. He deplored the disintegration of family ties, and religious indifference amongst workers, while their resentment against the bourgeoisie shocked him.[3] Nevertheless, he and his collaborators visited and reported on real working-class households and this is the value of their contributions.

LePlay's original reports date from the period 1849–52, that is to say the aftermath of the Revolution of February 1848 and the June Days – a moment, it need hardly be said, of high bourgeois anxiety. A further series of reports was compiled from information collected later, between the mid-1860s and the late 1880s.[4] Frédéric Barbier's analysis suggests that 65 per cent of working-class households investigated by LePlay owned books.[5] In 19 per cent of cases, these consisted only of works of piety, while in 41 per cent of cases, the only books the household possessed were school texts (*manuels scolaires*). Novels appeared, according to Barbier's count, in 35 per cent of the working households cited by LePlay. This is only an indication of the books which were owned and which were present in the home, not of the works actually read by the family. They do, however, begin to suggest a conventional dependence on religious reading, as well as the impact of schooling on working-class culture.

The Parisian ragpicker (*chiffonnier*) investigated during the Second Republic had a personal library of about 30 volumes, the majority of them conventional religious works.[6] In the large room he rented with his small family near the Panthéon he had a Bible and two New

Testaments, two psalters, an *Imitation de Jésus-Christ*, some prayer books, Fleury's *Histoire sainte*, some edifying works for children, and a copy of Silvio Pellico's *Mes Prisons*, often used as a Catholic didactic work. In fact, many of the ragpicker's books were of Protestant inspiration, for example *La Patrie du Vieillard*, translated from English, and children's stories by Madame Guizot. In spite of this denominational mixture, his family's reading was thoroughly orthodox and met with the approval of his social superiors. Some of the books had been donated by a friendly Jesuit, and a philanthropic bourgeois family had paid for the ragpicker's daughter to attend a Protestant school. He read the Bible *en famille* and appeared a model of the socially integrated worker. This example might have made LePlay ecstatic, if only he had been capable of such extreme emotions. The ragpicker was a worker whose culture was framed and nurtured by clergy and *notables* – if such examples could be multiplied, the nightmares of the bourgeoisie might be dispelled.

LePlay's family monographs abound with such examples of orthodoxy, like the fisherman of Martigues who kept *livres de messe* in his parents' room, pious works in his aunt's room, and both recreational and pious reading in his young daughter's room.[7] Others borrowed books from the Catholic Bibliothèque des Bons Livres, encountered in chapter 2.[8] Not surprisingly, large families found it more difficult than small ones to acquire cultural capital. The exemplary ragpicker already mentioned had only one child, but the *charron* (wagon repairer) from Montataire in the Oise, investigated in 1884, had six children and owned only 'about fifteen volumes in poor condition'.[9] Book ownership, as Barbier points out, remained at a feeble level in households with seven members and upwards.

Barbier's statistics of LePlay's subjects do not tell the story of the changes occurring between LePlay's first efforts in 1849 and his subsequent compilations thirty years or more later in the century. As 'new' members of the reading public, workers were undergoing a rapid and significant process of acculturation. They were beginning to borrow books from libraries, like the *charron* from Montataire, who borrowed from his factory library.[10] They were becoming familiar with the daily press, like the porcelain-worker (*faiencier*) from the Nièvre who in 1864 bought *Le Petit Journal* regularly.[11] Above all, their own children were introducing them to a new world of reading, as the growing presence of school texts and school prize books frequently indicated. LePlay and his team thus discovered working family libraries in which the traditional dog-eared collections of a few almanacs and pious works were being superseded by new kinds of literature, namely books demanded by their children's education, and novels and histories denoting a thirst for a more general cultural awareness.[12] The desire for more general and recreational reading is demonstrated in the evidence of library borrowing patterns. All lending libraries affiliated to the Société Franklin provided information on the main categories of titles in demand. The Society's model catalogue of 1864, discussed in chapter 2, had allocated 28 per cent of its ideal stock to novels, while two-thirds of the stock was to consist of instructional works.[13] This profile, however, did not correspond to the preferences of borrowers. A few examples will serve to illustrate the general pattern. At Marieux in the Somme (1867–69), a small *bourg* of about 500 inhabitants, 69 per cent of loans were novels.[14] At Thann in Alsace (1868–69), the librarian reported to the Société Franklin that almost two thirds of loans were of fiction or poetry.[15] At Brive (1872), to take one more example, novels, theatre, poetry and children's literature accounted for 75 per cent of all loans.[16] The Société Franklin found the popular demand for novels rather than educational literature frustrating. Readers were not responding as programmed.

The evidence of loans from Parisian libraries, summarized in Table 3.1, suggests that readers rejected the moralizing aims of philanthropic reformers, and instead saw the libraries as a means of satisfying their demand for entertaining literature.

The figures for 1882 are based on a breakdown of 363 322 loans, and do not include titles consulted within the library itself.[17] We can consider the first three categories as 'instructive' literature, that is, history, geography and sciences. The table suggests that the level of borrowing in these categories would have disappointed the library reformers. Taken

Table 3.1 Borrowings from Paris municipal libraries, 1882–1894

Category	Total for 1882 (per cent)	Total for 1894 (per cent)
History & biography	8.0	7.70
Geography & travel	10.0	12.12
Science, arts & education	11.0	8.45
Poetry, theatre, foreign languages, literary criticism	13.5	15.48
Novels	55.0	51.54
Music	2.5	4.75

together, they only represented between 28 and 29 per cent of all loans, which was hardly enough to justify the allocation of two thirds of library shelving to this kind of book.

Within these categories, the most successful genres were invariably history and biography, accounting for between 5 and 10 per cent of titles borrowed in most Parisian libraries, together with geography and travel, which normally accounted for between 4 and 10 per cent. Borrowers often overlooked more difficult or technical works on politics or science. Amongst historians, Thiers was a popular author, especially for his *Histoire du Consulat et de l'Empire*. Travel literature was popular, but some of it was not so much instructive as entertaining, if not plainly fictional, as in Jules Verne's *Voyages extraordinaires*.

By the end of the century, ordinary readers had an insatiable appetite for imaginative literature, especially novels which, to the chagrin of well-meaning librarians, accounted for over half of all loans from Parisian public libraries. Librarians consoled themselves at first with the thought that sensational fiction would at least accustom people to reading and to using libraries, and that, consequently, readers would gradually move on to higher things. It was hoped that 'those who come looking for a brief moment of distraction will little by little be brought to appreciate instructive and fortifying reading'.[18] This was the 'landings' theory of lending libraries: getting the customer to enter on the ground floor was just the first step, leading in gradual stages to the higher storeys of more elevated reading. If the reader could be induced to climb the staircase to the first landing, anything might be possible. But there was little evidence that readers were 'maturing' in the desired fashion. The demand for recreational reading showed no sign of diminishing. Librarians remained perplexed by the refusal of their readers to read what was thought good for them.

The mass of working-class readers, therefore, were gradually becoming integrated into the new reading public, either through their children's school reading, or through their own interest in the best-selling fiction of Alexandre Dumas or Jules Verne. A minority of working-class readers, however, was determined to go further, and set out to apply its energy to the search for intellectual emancipation. We must now turn to this group of self-taught workers.

The Pursuit of Knowledge Under Difficulties

The 'Pursuit of Knowledge Under Difficulties' was the title of Edward Craik's successful work of advice literature for self-improving British workers, first published in 1830 under the auspices of the Society for the Diffusion of Useful Knowledge.[19] The slogan applies equally to the attempts made by French artisans to develop an improvised reading culture of their own, in the face of material handicaps and sheer hostility.

The nineteenth-century self-taught worker had some spiritual ancestors. One was the farm boy Valentin Jamerey-Duval, who lived and worked in Lorraine in the early-eighteenth century. Jamerey-Duval was illiterate until he came across an illustrated edition of *Aesop's Fables*. He induced his fellow-shepherds to explain the pictures which had impressed him, and to teach him to read the book. From then on, by his own account, Jamerey-Duval was unstoppable, devouring chapbooks, pious literature and indeed any literature he could borrow locally. He repaid the efforts of his early companions and tutors by reading and reciting stories for them. His apprenticeship underlines the importance of illustrations in the literary culture of the illiterate.[20] It also relied, as it did for many of Jamerey-Duval's nineteenth-century counterparts, on the co-operation of his fellow-workers.

As well as learning to read, he also travelled. Sometimes, the worker's travels expressed a cultural as well as a geographical break with his or her origins. Jamerey-Duval journeyed in search of new knowledge and understanding, relishing new experiences and interrogating people he met to learn what he could from them. His search for new places signified a cultural displacement, as he tried to establish entirely new cultural co-ordinates.[21] He eventually found employment as librarian for the Duke of Lorraine. Reading and travelling had both extended his cultural horizons.

Jacques-Louis Ménétra, the eighteenth-century Parisian glassworker, is a better-known example as a result of the publication of his racy autobiography in 1982.[22] Like the majority of artisans in the capital, Ménétra was not only literate but a skilled writer and narrator. If we consider his reading, however, his literary culture seems limited. He rarely mentions books at all, except for the Bible, *Le Petit Albert* (a contemporary book of popular magic), and three titles by Rousseau, whom Ménétra may have met in person. Although Ménétra does not appear to have been a great reader, he often went to the theatre: his literary culture was experienced through a mixture of the oral, the visual and the printed word. Both oral transmission and working-class co-operative effort were to remain important in nineteenth-century workers' access to literature.

The literary culture of the autodidact was improvised and self-directed. By definition it owed little, if anything, to formal education.

Self-taught workers had a love-hate relationship with formal education. They resented the fact that it remained the preserve of the rich and privileged. At the same time, they retained a strong belief in its value, and several autobiographers devoted considerable space to a discussion of their own education. In practice, autodidacts usually had some experience of schooling, but their encounters with school were brief and erratic. As we have seen, educational opportunities for working-class children were sparse and unreliable for most of the nineteenth century. Their reading competence, and that of the autodidacts, was to a large extent a form of literacy without education.

Many were deprived even of the opportunity to learn to read. Perhaps the most harrowing tale of thwarted educational possibilities comes from the long-time illiterate, Norbert Truquin, the son of a northern metal-worker. Born in the Somme in 1833, the young Truquin was put to work for a woolcarder in Amiens at the age of seven. For three years, his employer forced him to sleep in a coal-hole under the stairs, and to get up at 3 a.m. to light the fire, and only then did he card wool, from 4 a.m. to 10 p.m. daily. He was, he tells us, regularly beaten.[23] Truquin's release came in 1843 when his employer died, but this left Truquin unemployed, living by begging and collecting vegetable leftovers from other people's garbage. He was taken in by a group of prostitutes, until a police raid again left him homeless. Truquin had a series of jobs, as he took to the roads, working as a brickmaker, a *colporteur* and a *fileur de laine* (weaver), all before the age of 13. He could neither read nor write, but he had heard of the socialist writer Cabet by 1846, and he came to think of himself as a free-thinker.[24] In one factory, he heard a fellow-worker reading aloud from Cabet's *Voyage en Icarie*, but this worker was dismissed.[25] This incident testifies both to the importance of oral transmission in working-class reading, and to the fragility of any attempt to develop an independent reading culture in this period. Truquin was in Paris in 1848, describing the Revolution from the perspective of a street *gamin*. He rediscovered his father, and persuaded him to emigrate to Algeria. Truquin had acquired strongly anticlerical opinions, but he still had had no opportunity to learn to read.

Truquin stayed in Algeria for seven years, working as a servant to army officers. In 1855, he returned to France, and to the misery of work in the Lyon silk sweatshops. He discussed history and politics with fellow-workers, and he heard the *Courrier de Lyon* read aloud, although he regarded it as a paper which continually slandered the working class.[26] Without any formal education or reading competence, Truquin had learned from direct experience about the exploitative nature of capitalism. In 1870, he was arrested for participation in the Lyon Commune. Once again, oral reading amongst his fellow-workers continued Truquin's education. He persuaded other prisoners to read to him from Fernand Cortez's history of the conquest of Mexico.[27] Truquin had clearly developed a great interest in history, although historians, in his opinion, only wrote to praise the upper classes. The great philosophers were no better, Truquin decided after visiting the ancient sites of North Africa, for the great minds of antiquity cared nothing about the emancipation of the slaves who maintained their illustrious civilizations.[28]

Truquin's interest in the Spanish conquest of Mexico also illustrates his curiosity about Latin America, which now captured his attention. Having suffered in the poor conditions of Lyon's ailing silk industry, he was attracted by the promise of new, agrarian-based social experiments. Still illiterate at the age of 37, he left in 1872 to help establish a socialist colony in Argentina. He returned briefly to France before his definitive emigration with his wife to Paraguay. His experience of Paraguay confirmed his anti-Jesuit opinions, but in all probability it was here that he eventually became literate. He finished his autobiography, *Mémoires et aventures d'un prolétaire*, in 1887, and it was published in the following year by Bouriand, a socialist publisher in Paris.

Norbert Truquin had spent much of his life trying to fight hunger and homelessness. No wonder that his autobiography, like many other workers' autobiographies, recorded such basic information as the price of bread and how much he earned. Such materialist concerns are a distinctive feature of working-class writing in the nineteenth century. In spite of his hardships and peregrinations, he had acquired a class-based culture, which was inspired by socialism and anticlericalism, and was well-versed in history. He asked questions, discussed issues with fellow-workers, and responded critically to the literature that he listened to. His 'knowledge' developed out of his life experiences – physical hardships, two revolutions and prison. Truquin had no roots and no craft-based training, and he suffered from his own illiteracy. He was deprived of an education, and his employers continued to prevent workers' access to culture. Nevertheless, he had by his mid-fifties acquired enough expertise to write his own autobiography, which concluded with a ringing call to social revolution.[29] Even in the most hostile of environments, a workers' literary culture could be formed.

However brief the experience of formal schooling, it nevertheless authorized some emphatically negative judgements from workers. The Frères des Ecoles Chrétiennes were not exempt. Their schools, which were free of charge but reliant on municipal subsidies, tended to cater for the artisan élite to which many autodidacts belonged. They were not always popular, however, with poorer students. Antoine Sylvère, whose father was a share-cropper (*métayer*) and his mother illiterate, delivered a scathing indictment of the school he attended near Ambert (Puy-de-Dôme) in 1894.[30] He recalled the unremitting use of the cane by the Soeurs Blanches, and decided that the textbook used by the Christian Brothers (*Les Devoirs du Chrétien*) was so detestable that it was a direct cause of the spread of anticlericalism. Learning with the Frères was particularly difficult for those like Sylvère (known as Toinou) who spoke only *patois*, and were compelled to learn in French. But this was not the only reason for Toinou's resentment. The Frères denounced 'the disgusting [*immonde*] Zola', ' the execrable Voltaire', 'the notorious [*trop fameux*] Renan', and their tirades against freemasonry put children in terror of the 'flamaçons'.[31] The Frères des Ecoles Chrétiennes, according to Toinou, provided the local bourgeoisie with silent, submissive workers, whom they beat and humiliated into a terrified obedience. But he was not one of them.

Perhaps it was natural that men deprived of educational opportunities should denigrate schooling. Working-class autobiographers were men who had obtained an education through their own efforts, and they were proud to have fashioned their own culture. It was natural that they should value the lessons of life and experience over classroom learning. For several of them, schools were purveyors of useless erudition and false knowledge. As Martin Nadaud put it, his writing offered his working comrades 'a book written in good faith which will not lead them astray into false and deceptive tricks of subtlety'.[32]

The autodidacts pursued their desire for study and self-improvement with a determination that was sometimes obsessive. Indeed, it had to be, if they were to overcome the immense material handicaps that stood in their way. Sacrifice and ingenuity made up for the lack of money, light, space and time to read. Gabriel Gauny, as a poor Parisian *gamin* in the *faubourg* St Marceau during the second decade of the century, even collected discarded wrapping-paper used to pack seeds, sugar or coffee. It was usually made of old books and newspaper, and provided him with an unlikely source of reading-matter.[33] Gauny's difficult life as a child of the *faubourgs* did not prevent him from starting an apprenticeship as a carpenter, joining the Saint-Simonians, and developing a philosophical theory based on the palingenesis of souls. But this lay in the future. The publishing initiatives of the 1830s had reduced the price of novels without yet making them affordable to working-class readers. Another problem was the lack of light for reading. Windows were rare, and candles were expensive. In the 1830s and 1840s, oil-lamps were available, and after the 1850s, paraffin lamps were introduced. In many working-class households, however, the lamp might only be lit when all the family was present for the evening meal. Parental opposition to reading was sometimes an effective deterrent, too. Martin Nadaud's memoirs are a reminder of this, for Martin's father had to overcome vigorous opposition from the boy's mother and grandfather in order to send him to school.[34] This phobia had literary echoes in Stendhal's *Le Rouge et le Noir*, in which *père* Sorel harshly abuses young Julien as a 'filthy bookreading dog' (*chien de lisard*).[35] The hostility of employers to workers' self-education could be equally lethal, if not more so, if we follow the recollections of another worker-autobiographer, Jean-Baptiste Dumay. Dumay's father had died in a mining accident before he was born in 1841, and his 18-year-old mother married his illiterate stepfather. Dumay started work as an apprentice fitter in the Le Creusot factory at the age of 13. His life of militancy was to be bound up with Le Creusot, and its all-powerful masters, the Schneider family. In 1868, aged 27, Dumay founded a workers' reading and study group, which he named the *Bibliothèque Démocratique*. He claimed it had 300 members, but as well as offering a library, it was also the nucleus of a strike organization and a republican opposition group.[36] In 1870, Dumay was sacked, but at the time of the Commune Gambetta appointed him briefly Mayor of Le Creusot. Dumay's reward for supporting the Commune in 1871 was a sentence to hard labour for life, but he succeeded in escaping to Switzerland. In 1879, he returned to France, became a travelling photographer, and worked to establish a metalworkers' trade union. Once again he was at Le Creusot, where he opened a bookshop. Schneider refused to tolerate this, and factory workers who bought newspapers at Dumay's bookshop were sacked.[37] Dumay made no secret of his opposition to the church, and joined the Le Creusot workers' Mutual Aid Society. One of his final local victories was to mastermind a performance of the Marseillaise in Schneider's hearing outside the factory.[38] The bookshop closed in 1881. Dumay was later elected deputy for Belleville, the culmination of a life of militancy which had been inseparable from encouraging fellow-workers to read. It had also been impossible for him to resist constantly provoking his erstwhile employer, who stood firmly in the way of the dissemination of undesirable literature in or near his factory.

Working-class autodidacts embarked on the pursuit of knowledge with vast enthusiasm and little discrimination. They confessed to a ravenous appetite for literature of all sorts, which they admitted in retrospect was poorly directed. Only later did some of them organize their study into a pattern with fixed objectives. This indiscriminate and eclectic reading seems to have been a necessary initiation stage. The autodidact began by accumulating knowledge quite arbitrarily. He or she lacked the experience or education to classify his or her cultural acquisitions, or place them in a hierarchy of importance. In Pierre Bourdieu's terms, they lacked both economic capital and cultural capital; or, in other words, they had neither the resources to buy books, nor the educational qualifications to guide their reading preferences. Without the literary landmarks offered by formal schooling, the autodidacts were cultural usurpers, adopting independent and 'heretical' modes of cultural acquisition.[39] They looked back with mixed feelings on this stage of exploration and rapid, unsystematic consumption. The goal of self-improvement dictated a different kind of reading. Reading should have a clear purpose, and there was little room for casual browsing. The autodidacts criticized themselves for reading without clear direction, and for not concentrating on 'useful' literature.

Autobiographers thus described an early stage of ignorance. At a certain point, however, the reader would be struck by the revelation that his or her reading had been desultory, indiscriminate and poorly directed. He or she determined to pursue a more purposeful reading plan in future. This turning-point has been effectively described by Nöe Richter as 'the conversion of the bad reader', when the autodidact resolved to renounce his 'bad' reading habits.[40] At this point, the self-improving artisan or worker made his or her own reading time, and set his or her own programme. A planned programme of reading had the obvious advantage of defining clear objectives, and a certain sense of satisfaction was no doubt achieved as each stage of the reading programme was passed. A stern self-discipline was required. Gabriel Gauny, who we encountered as a young boy reading discarded wrappings on the streets of Paris, came to regard personal abstinence as a prerequisite for a spiritual life. His personal 'économie cénobitique', as he called it, recommended extreme frugality in the consumption of food, drink and clothing. Diogenes and St John the Baptist were his models, epitomizing the renunciation of worldly goods, and the stigmatization of immorality.[41] Moral, spiritual and material improvement demanded neatness, sobriety and moderation in all things. Self-denial was part of the *habitus* of the self-taught working-class reader. Nevertheless, self-imposed reading courses were sometimes so ambitious that they exacted a heavy price in terms of the reader's mental and physical energy.

Teenage reading crises were not unusual. In 1860, Xavier-Edouard Lejeune drove himself to a breakdown by the age of 15. He came from an upwardly mobile artisan family, and had already started work two years earlier as a Parisian shop assistant. Part of his spare time was spent reading the newspaper to his uncle, an illiterate *quarante-huitard* (veteran of the 1848 Revolution).[42] Inspired by his adolescent reading of Châteaubriand and Alexandre Dumas, he became a subscriber to a *cabinet de lecture*. He read every night, until his mother, probably anxious about his health, reduced his candle ration.[43] Then Lejeune resorted to the second-hand *bouquinistes* along the Seine, devouring the classics of the seventeenth century, and of the Enlightenment, as well as Goethe and Shakespeare. He experienced the eclectic phase of indiscriminate reading common to many autodidacts. As he put it later, his self-improving reading caused a mental maelstrom: 'Just like the turbulent waves of a torrent crashing over the rocks, these new things erupted in my young mind, and created a chaos there that nothing could restore to order.'[44] Following these efforts, he started reading adventure novels in instalments. At the age of about 15, he had a severe crisis. The result, however, was positive: from this breakdown, his literary aspirations were born, and he began to write his autobiography. 'In spite of every obstacle', he confidently concluded, 'I found myself before long in possession of most human knowledge.' This desire to encompass every field, often coupled with a sense of their own ignorance and inferiority, was typical of the intense attitude to reading shared by many self-taught workers.

Working-class readers improvised and borrowed from friends, neighbours, priests or schoolteachers. They patronized second-hand booksellers such as the *bouquinistes* who kept stalls along the *quais* of the Seine. If employers or social superiors occasionally offered a helping hand, autodidacts usually grasped it, even if they remained suspicious of middle-class patrons. A collective effort could compensate for the lack of individual resources. As a soldier in Metz in 1846, Sebastien Commissaire joined with other members of his barracks to 'sub-let' two-day-old copies of progressive newspapers from a local bookseller.[45] At the same time, they exploited their own informal networks to obtain books. Family ties and professional or religious connections were sources of intellectual aid rooted in the working-class milieu itself. Working-class networks protected the autodidact's autonomy as a reader, and may have filtered his or her responses to the texts read. They ensured that he or she did not always respond predictably to the literary culture diffused by middle-class mediators.

Working-class networks could provide literature and education to workers otherwise deprived of them. Informal borrowing systems developed in the workplace and workers gave up their time to tutor one another. As a result, literacy could be developed and used in the context of a militant working-class tradition. Consider the oral testimony of an anonymous worker from the north of France, born the son of a nail-worker in 1892. His official schooling was interrupted at the age of seven, but a group of militants continued to take his education in hand. He recalled:

> When you reached the age of seven, school was over, totally! Young people don't realise what the situation was like, 50, 60, 80 years ago. They ask you 'So how did you learn to read? How could it be done...?'... Well, there were the old guesdist militants... They were good teachers who put on an evening school to teach us to read and write. They gave lessons. They taught us problems, maths. They did half an hour of theory on what had happened, on the revolutions, action and after all, at that particular time, it was very rich from the point of view of social issues. My father was born in 1852, and he brought us up in the memory... he told us about the Commune. He was a member of the socialist party and naturally, he told us about Louise Michel. You see, we were brought up with the attitudes of people who had rebelled against injustice.[46]

This militant, known here simply as A., later became secretary of the St Nazaire branch of the French Communist Party. His story shows how even learning to read could become part of the informal process by which working-class culture was transmitted from one generation to another, and by which historical memories and myths were perpetuated.

Given this independence, it is not surprising that the efforts of social superiors were not always welcome, or received with the gratitude or deference expected. Claude Genoux provides a good example, at the other end of the century, of conflicting attitudes to offers of assistance from individual bourgeois and aristocrats.[47] Genoux was the 12th child born to his Savoyard family, who learned to read, write and count in an orphanage in the *faubourg* St Antoine in Paris. In 1821 Genoux escaped from the Hospice des Orphelins, and found employment as a domestic servant with an *avocat* in Blois. His employer took time to teach him French, Latin, Greek, history, geography, physics and mathematics. In 1822, however, Genoux again ran away, rejecting an opportunity for self-improvement.

Genoux travelled to Italy, and went to sea. In 1825–26, a Turin sea-captain taught him mathematics, astronomy and navigation; but he also beat him, and Genoux ran away yet again, to become a shoeshiner in a Chambéry hotel. Many wealthy tourists passed through this alpine resort. Genoux met Werdet the publisher, and befriended a Russian prince, but once again he failed to capitalize on these contacts. Genoux's culture had been mediated through orphan school, then by individual bourgeois and aristocrats. Claude Genoux found generous patrons at every stage of his life, but he had always been their servant, and he hated the subservience of livery.

The examples of Truquin, Gauny, Dumay and Genoux quoted here all succeeded in the 'pursuit of knowledge under difficulties', as the very existence of their autobiographies testifies. Poverty deprived them of all but a smattering of formal education, and condemned them to improvise. They stole time to read, and they carved out moments of privacy from the continuous stream of demands from families or employment. By borrowing from various sources, exploiting working-class networks or the generosity of relatives and assorted patrons, they manufactured their own culture.

As we have seen, their improvised methods of cultural appropriation carried certain unresolved ambiguities. Autodidacts could despise the worthless subtleties of scholarship, but at the same time, they mourned the lack of a sustained formal education. Their reading, furthermore, depended in part on middle-class benefactors – the friendly Jesuit; the rare sympathetic employer, perhaps the librarian who lent books while turning his nose up at the borrower; liberal and learned men of all kinds who took an interest in the progress of education. In spite of this need for middle-class patronage, 'self-culture' was still seen as a means to the independence and emancipation of labour. It is a paradox of *autodidaxie* that out of this very dependence on bourgeois help was to come self-reliance and the desire for emancipation. Only the successful autodidacts present us with these contradictions. The fate of those who tried the road to self-improvement, but failed, at one or other of the obstacles described here, can only be imagined.

The uses and abuses of fiction

In constructing a working-class reading culture, working-class intellectuals had little patience with popular novels. In their preferences for non-fiction, they joined company with middle-class library reformers in urging workers to rise above the tide of pulp fiction which, by the end of the century, was engulfing lending libraries. Two worker-intellectuals, Henri Tolain and Agricol Perdiguier, take us further into the *habitus* of this emerging working-class intelligentsia. The models they proposed will lead us towards a discussion of the reading choices of the self-taught workers themselves.

Tolain was a Parisian bronze-worker with Proudhonist sympathies who played a major role in founding the International in France.[48] At first sight, his literary views showed a great respect for the 'high' literary culture which movements like the Franklin Society encouraged workers to share. In 1865, Tolain, writing in the short-lived weekly *Tribune Ouvrière*, regretted the banality and sensationalism of the popular novel. Pulp fiction, in his view, was a corrosive influence and an insidious poison, infiltrating the working household and sapping its sense of morality. Newspaper fiction, he wrote, was sprouting

> like a poisonous mushroom. Secretly or in broad daylight, it proudly struts its wares or furtively slides under the poor man's roof. Even if papa by chance bans it as unhealthy fare, Lisa will hide it in her bodice. The tyrant can do nothing, and his ban adds the bitter taste of the forbidden fruit to the palpitating attraction of the drama.[49]

Perhaps significantly, Tolain here blamed the female reader for promoting the harmful effects of serialized fiction, and his reference to the fall of Eve reinforces his gender prejudices.

Tolain condemned novelists who had no morality and no concept of justice. He criticized the rotten distortions inherent in the sensational novel. He did not shrink from condemning Goethe's *Werther* as a selfish, weepy lover, and Balzac's Madame Marneffe as a female monster. He echoed the strictures of *L'Atelier* in the 1840s against the novels of Eugène Sue. If we examine his ideas more closely, however, it is clear that he does not reject fiction outright. Tolain simply had his own agenda for the ideal novel. What he demanded from the genre was a clearer personal conviction on the author's part, and an awareness of social and political issues. What he valued in novels, and found wanting amongst popular contemporary writers, was precisely that sense of social justice and social reality which would make fiction meaningful and uplifting to working-class readers. Tolain cites Hugo's *Notre-Dame de Paris* as a novel with such ideals, and in spite of Madame Marneffe he grudgingly praised Balzac as a master of social observation. Everything else, however, was dross, nothing but overwrought sentiment and banality. The novel itself was not condemned, but Tolain expected novelists to be philosophers with principles and a message to impart.

When Agricol Perdiguier compiled a list of basic books for a worker's library, many of his selections echoed the advice list of the Franklin Society. He recommended technical manuals on building or agriculture, and studies of the metric system which would form the nucleus of a skilled worker's professional reference library. As well as this, his list included Homer and Virgil, the Bible, Fénélon, Corneille, Molière, Racine and Lafontaine, besides some Voltaire, Montesquieu, Rousseau and Schiller.[50] Perdiguier, however, did not passively accept all the edifying booklists offered by paternalistic middle-class reformers. He went further than the Franklin Society, insisting on including some history of the French Revolution, and popular favourites like Eugène Sue's *Mystères de Paris* and Hugo's *Notre-Dame de Paris*. As Georges Duveau pointed out, his choice was eclectic, ranging from learned works such as Montesquieu's *Esprit des lois* to fantasy novels such as Madame de Graffigny's *Lettre d'une Péruvienne*.[51] His list of recommendations included George Sand's *Le Compagnon de la Tour de France*, a work whose hero Huguenin is thought to be based on Perdiguier himself. In addition, his ideal library did not omit works by the worker-poets themselves.[52]

In fact, Perdiguier's ideal library bore a striking resemblance to his actual personal library, as it was outlined by Jérôme-Pierre Gilland, editor of *L'Atelier*, who visited Perdiguier in Paris in 1840, and reported the occasion in *La Feuille du village* in 1851.[53] Gilland noted Perdiguier's interest in French history, and his complete works of Rousseau and Voltaire, in small-format, easily portable collections. He possessed plenty of Greek authors, and the plays of Corneille, Racine and Molière. He had an encyclopaedia, bought in instalments, and the *Magasin pittoresque*. Gilland stressed that such a library could be accumulated if the reader looked for cheap editions and publications which could be purchased by affordable instalments.

Gilland's account had its hero-worshipping aspect. Perdiguier was a well-known figure, popularized by George Sand, and elected to the Legislative Assembly in 1849. Admittedly, this acceptance in bourgeois circles did not help him to get his memoirs published in the 1850s, when newspaper editors found him of little interest.[54] Nevertheless, Perdiguier saw himself as a pioneer and he was an important model for other workers. Publishing the contents of his library, and his personal advice on what a worker's library should contain, thus had authoritative status. The appearance of such reading lists as his always carry certain unspoken assumptions. The importance of the author delivering the advice is taken for granted. Such lists usually assume the authority of the past, and consider contemporary literature as nearly worthless. Perdiguier was only a partial exception to the rule that all notable books were by definition written long ago: he advised reading a few contemporary authors, especially George Sand and Victor Hugo, Béranger and Lamartine. But his greatest admiration was reserved for the literature of antiquity and its seventeenth-century descendants. Reading lists like the one offered by Perdiguier also assume that a clear, undisputed verdict is possible about what the best books to read actually are. They imply that there is a finite number of works which will satisfy the reader's needs, and that he or she will regularly return to this small number of select high-status texts. Like Tolain, Perdiguier was a reader with a high respect for canonical texts, but perhaps not all members of the working-class intelligentsia would have been happy with Perdiguier's insistence on the value of the humanities, including Greek and Latin authors.

Perdiguier loved the classics of French literature. Born near Avignon in 1805, the seventh child of a joiner, Perdiguier had attended his village school, where all his early schoolbooks were in Latin. This was hardly a problem, Perdiguier claimed in his autobiography, because he would not have understood them even if they had been in French. All he knew as a young boy was his native Provençal.[55] His personal acculturation thus proceeded through learning French, and reading Aesop's *Fables* and the Bible, which he found at home. In his autobiography, written in exile in Belgium and Switzerland after the *coup d'état* of Louis-Napoléon, he told stories of life as an apprentice carpenter, and as an artisan on his obligatory travels through France. His memoirs testify to the love of the theatre and of classic authors. He described carpenters in the 1820s reading aloud to themselves Ducis's eighteenth-century adaptations of Shakespeare and Racine's *Phèdre*, and his own delight in the purchase of a set of Voltaire's tragedies.[56] As Jonathan Rose has argued in a British context, such preferences for 'high culture' do not necessarily reflect a conservative political stance on the part of working-class readers. The impact of any text on an individual is hard to predict. Canonical literature, according to Rose, is as likely to radicalize the worker as it is to mollify him.[57] Perdiguier, as already noted, was an adversary of Napoleon III.

Tolain and Perdiguier, therefore were critical readers who each had a clear agenda for their ideal working-class reader. While Tolain wanted to combat the evils of pulp fiction, Perdiguier wanted to pass on his love of humanities, the theatre and the benefits of a classical education. But what did the other autodidacts read in their dedicated pursuit of self-education and intellectual emancipation?[58] To some extent, the autodidacts accepted advice to concentrate on utilitarian reading, together with a knowledge of uplifting canonical works. Many of them felt that purely recreational fiction was a waste of their time. Their responses to self-improving literature, however, were not uniform. Although they often read the same books, it is not always possible to predict what they thought of them. The history of their responses is a reminder that the impact of any text on an individual reader is never predetermined. The historian of the reception of books inevitably encounters a wide range of reader responses. Between a text and its appropriation there exists a metaphorical space, according to Chartier, an *espace lisible*, where the reader formulates his or her independent interpretation.[59] Workers conducted their own dialogue with the texts they acquired, and were quite prepared to question the assumptions of liberal political economy. They searched for answers to problems arising from their own experience of life and work, and that search could lead them towards socialism and rationalism. Of course, these were not always the destinations that their moral guardians had in mind.

Individual readers constructed their own meanings from their texts, but there were nevertheless some common features in the autodidacts' reading practices. They shared similar preferences and similar evaluations of different literary genres. To some extent, in the codes of practice they adopted, they unconsciously formed what Stanley Fish termed an 'interpretive community' of readers.[60] They developed common reading strategies, based on convergent assumptions about what constituted good literature. The classical literature of the seventeenth century was one common meeting-point, while Rousseau was the dominant radical presence in the library of many autodidacts. The writing of Châteaubriand was another strong influence. Volney had an international influence on working-class anticlericalism, and so did Voltaire. The autodidacts read and responded individually but in spite of obvious divergences, they shared common interests and devoured the same imaginary library.

A few certainly used their reading in politics and economics to develop socialist ideas. French socialism, however, had many different sources. One was the writing of Etienne Cabet. Nadaud read the workers' journal *L'Atelier*, and he also recalled being asked to read Cabet's paper *Le Populaire* aloud in Parisian wine-shops in 1834.[61] Cabet's ideas had a following in Lyon, where, as has been noted, the illiterate Norbert

Truquin first learned about them. Working-class readers encountered other strands of socialist theory. Claude Genoux, the chimney-sweep turned printer, also came into contact with the workers' paper *L'Atelier*, and he was familiar with the Christian socialism of Buchez.[62] Joseph Benoît, a Lyon silk worker, belonged to yet another strand of French socialism. His radicalization developed in conditions of hunger, unemployment and insurrection in the Lyon silk shops during the 1830s. He also owed a debt to his reading of Buonarroti's history of Babeuf's Conspiracy of the Equals in 1796, first published in 1828. Benoît read the *babouviste* newspaper *Fraternité*, to which he later contributed in his own right. He was a committed communist who saw Cabet as a rival influence on the workers of Lyon.[63]

Rousseau was an ever-present influence for Benoît and many other working-class readers. Perhaps Benoît was particularly receptive to Rousseau because his father had sent him to school in Geneva. Rousseau was not merely a recognized author, but a source of radical inspiration. Voltaire and Volney were two more authors read by the community of self-taught working-class readers. French working-class readers in the nineteenth century encountered Voltaire as an author who had already attained a certain canonical status. Highly valued by bourgeois readers, Voltaire's works were recognized by the early-nineteenth century as part of France's literary heritage. Thus the apprentice fitter Constant Lepage's first acquaintance with Voltaire was with a 70-volume edition of his works, which he found in the library of his *déclassé* bourgeois father in Le Havre.[64] Voltaire also reinforced the anticlericalism of many militants, fuelled at the same time by a reading of Volney, Holbach, Meslier or indeed of religious history itself, which could inadvertently demonstrate to readers the follies and iniquities of the Crusades, the wars of religion and the Inquisition. They devoured history, scientific works and tried to master foreign languages. Louis-Arsène Meunier, the starving muslin-weaver from the Perche, became an itinerant schoolteacher in the 1820s, but felt ridiculed by his social superiors for his ignorance of Latin. So he taught himself Latin, with some assistance from a local lawyer. The phenomenal Meunier claimed that he read eight hours per day for six years, committing large sections of Rollin's *Ancient History* to memory. He had borrowed the work from a friend, and read it through twice within three weeks before returning the loan.[65]

Fiction and recreational reading, however, were not the sort of literature we might normally expect serious autodidacts to be enthusiastic about. Victorine Brocher, the militant *communarde* who was sentenced to death as a *pétroleuse* recalled rather grimly that in her family 'we read progressive newspapers.'[66] Those who experienced a 'conversion' to more serious and purposeful reading looked back on fiction-reading as a frivolous waste of time. In this vein, the Saint-Simonian Suzanne Voilquin recalled evenings when she read to her mother from novels borrowed from the local *cabinet de lecture*. Looking back in her autobiography, she felt that all she had derived from this experience was a kind of false consciousness. 'From those novels', she wrote, 'I drew false ideas about the realities of life.'[67] All the same, women readers tended to have a more tolerant attitude to fiction than their male counterparts. Suzanne Voilquin read George Sand and referred to her often.

In placing a low value on fiction, working-class readers echoed Tolain's criticisms of contemporary novelists. On the other hand, many working-class autobiographers, like Tolain and Perdiguier, took a personal and selective approach to fiction. Both men and women read some of the classic novelists of their century. Châteaubriand and Hugo were especially remembered by the autobiographers.

Châteaubriand was an important influence on two autobiographers in particular. His *Génie du Christianisme* made an impression on Constant Lepage, when he read it in 1847 aged 22. Lepage was surprised, because he had approached Châteaubriand with suspicion, regarding him as a legitimist and a devout Catholic. Châteaubriand overcame this mistrust, and worked a kind of religious conversion on Lepage who found him a refreshing contrast to Voltairean scepticism. He went on to read *Réné*, *Atala* and *Les Martyrs*.[68] About ten years later, the young Xavier-Edouard Lejeune, about to start work in Paris at the age of 13 as a draper's assistant, was also inspired by Châteaubriand. He dated the origins of his intellectual curiosity from the day at his school in Montmartre when he received the *Génie du Christianisme* as a school prize. He was then only 11 years old, but Châteaubriand had turned him into a writer. He wrote:

> with what ardour, with what passion I read and read again this immortal masterpiece of poetry and style! I can say that my mind, closed and narrow until that time, was suddenly opened to the sublimity of nature and to intellectual horizons that I had never known.[69]

Châteaubriand seemed capable of causing a sudden spiritual awakening.

Victor Hugo, too, had a part in the self-taught worker's ideal library, because he could be read as a social radical. Victorine Brocher clearly took time off from her progressive papers because she reported that she was inspired by *Les Misérables*, which she read in a *cabinet de lecture* in the mid-1860s, and re-read annually thereafter.[70] She described it as a great work of social philosophy, well worth the one franc per day she paid to borrow it. Working-class readers knew what they wanted from imaginative literature. Lamartine's *Méditations*, for instance, were admired, but readers also noted Lamartine's political affiliations. In the workers' paper *La Ruche populaire*, a dressmaker, Cécile Dufour, paid tribute to Lamartine's fame, assuring that his works were lovingly passed from hand to hand by working-class readers.[71] Dufour was nevertheless shocked by passages in Lamartine's novel *Jocelyn*, which suggested that Louis XVI had been an innocent victim of bloodthirsty popular violence. Stung by this criticism from a popular reader, Lamartine tried to defend his political record, and attempted to mollify Dufour by offering her a free copy of *Jocelyn*.

Working-class readers respected the classics of bourgeois literary culture, but they judged them according to their own values of realism and understanding of their struggles. They read Corneille, Racine, the masterpieces of the classical seventeenth century. They studied dead and foreign languages. Claude Genoux's reading, for example, included Dante and Petrarch, Cervantes, Kant and De Staël, or at least so he claimed (but he no doubt had plenty of time for reading while employed as a ship's cook on a whaler to Peru and Kamchatka). Genoux, the former chimney-sweep, devoured Walter Scott, *Don Quixote*, Rousseau's *Confessions* and Volney, or so the literary allusions in his autobiography would suggest.[72] He read Florian and D'Urfé, but found Lamartine's *Méditations* superior to anything. None of this was of any practical use in his profession.

The worker's literary culture was therefore wide-ranging. It was by no means restricted to socialist economics or works on explicitly proletarian themes. Self-education had opened up a world of literary classics which the autodidacts enthusiastically entered. They turned to the official monuments of French and European literature. The self-improving artisan was acquiring a bourgeois or learned culture which was potentially alien to him. Xavier-Edouard Lejeune, inspired by Châteaubriand, devoted his reading to 'the works of the great men of every epoch and of every country: historians, philosophers, poets, founders of nations and religions.'[73] This was not the whole story. Self-taught workers were not passive readers, and the fact that they were attracted to high-culture literary masterpieces did not determine their individual responses to these texts. Working-class readers drew on works of 'high culture', but measured them according to their own needs and standards. Their readings of the literary canon remained personal and unpredictable. Many read works of liberal political economy in order to reject their principles in favour of socialism. They read novels, too, but made use of them to reinforce their notions of contemporary social injustices.

Workers' libraries

There were plenty of signs, in the second half of the nineteenth century, that *le grand enfant*, the popular reader, had a mind of his or her own. Without prompting, and through their own autonomous efforts, workers established their own libraries. Small groups of workers started to come together to build the infrastructure of a distinctively working-class reading culture. The only knowledge we have of their achievement often comes from their enemies, either local élites anxious about the purposes of any independent working-class organization, or administrators keen to bring all independent initiatives under government surveillance. Thus in 1838, police in Lyon became aware of a reading club (*société de lecture*) in the working-class district of Croix-Rousse. Its stock included works by Saint-Just, Marat and Robespierre, in pamphlet form distributed by the Parisian publisher Pagnerre. The club also produced a poster of the French Revolution's Declarations of the Rights of Man, to be put up in bars, workshops and public places.[74] The reading club clearly intended doing some republican proselytizing as well as furthering its members' education.

A further example of working-class independence surfaced in the industrial city of St Etienne in 1867. Two popular libraries had been established there in the previous year, to the consternation of the city notables, and especially its clerical élite. The local newspaper *Le Mémorial de la Loire* attacked the libraries, and *Le Progrès de Lyon* defended them. The polemic entered national politics when a group of Catholic notables sent an official complaint to the imperial senate, where the literary critic Sainte-Beuve made a stirring speech in support of freedom of thought.[75] Conservative opponents accused Sainte-Beuve of embracing atheism, and he was even challenged to a duel (he brushed this aside). Since the Ministry of Education was not prepared to police every library shelf in the country, the notables of St Etienne did not ultimately receive satisfaction.

The workers of St Etienne had made their own choice of books, refusing passively to accept the recommendations of local worthies. Clerical petitions against them objected to Voltaire's *Dictionnaire philosophique, Candide* and *Zadig,* and Rousseau's *Confessions* and *Emile.* They objected to George Sand and to Eugène Sue, who allegedly attacked marriage, excused suicide and justified adultery. They considered the workers' choice of Rabelais dangerous, along with Michelet (for *La Sorcière*), Renan (*La Vie de Jésus*) and Lamennais (*Paroles d'un croyant*). They feared that the inclusion in popular libraries of works by Enfantin, Louis Blanc, Fourier and Proudhon would promote dangerous social doctrines. This was an exceptional example, because Sainte-Beuve's solitary intervention gave it national publicity. The dispute is a useful reminder, however, that workers made their own autonomous choices of reading, even when this directly antagonized social conservatives.

In 1863, the *bibliothèque populaire* which had been set up in the third arrondissement of Paris came under fire from the Ministry of the Interior, because its organizers had tried to evade mayoral surveillance.[76] This was the first such library to appear in Paris, created in 1861 on the initiative of the lithographer Girard. It still exists at 54, rue Turenne, and can be visited. A second *bibliothèque populaire* soon followed in the 18th arrondissement. By 1879, eight such libraries were functioning in the capital, and this level of activity was sooner or later bound to interest the authorities. The Prefect of Paris intervened to 'normalize' the borrowers' register and to impose uniform opening hours of every evening between 8 and 10 p.m.[77] The offer of financial assistance depended on accepting these requirements, and in this way an independent workers' institution fell under the bureaucratic tutelage of the prefecture.

The research of Pascale Marie has cast further light on the rise and fall of the Société des Amis de l'Instruction, which founded several Parisian libraries, including the library in the third arrondissement already mentioned.[78] Workers themselves administered the society's libraries. They paid a subscription and were responsible for the purchase of new acquisitions. After 1868, however, the Minister of the Interior insisted on supervising and censoring the catalogues. One exceptional feature of the library in the third arrondissement is worth noting: it opened its doors to women. In 1882, the Amis de l'Instruction had 18 libraries, if we include the five that the society managed in the suburbs, and the positivist library in the rue Réaumur. There were 8000 subscribers in all, 25 per cent of them female; 40 per cent were workers or artisans.

At the start, the book stock reflected the organizers' preference for instructional works. There were technical manuals, and works on chemistry, electricity and mechanical drawing. As well as this, the Amis de l'Instruction stocked some examples of the positivist and scientific literature of the period, such as Darwin's *Origin of Species*. History formed a third substantial category, especially works on the history of the French Revolution and the nineteenth century. In 1862, history accounted for 2 per cent of titles in the catalogue of the library of the third arrondissement.[79] The Amis de l'Instruction showed few socialist leanings. Neither Fourier, Proudhon nor Cabet appeared in the 1862 catalogue, and the Society did not acquire any literature on the Paris Commune. Only in the catalogue for 1909 did works by Louis Blanc and Jean Jaurès appear. By this time the public's voracious demand for recreational literature was influencing the society's acquisitions policy, and it was thus losing its distinctive character. It had been a pioneer in the fragile struggle for worker's intellectual emancipation, free both of clerical influence or government supervision.

This struggle was continued in the 1890s by the Bourses du Travail, which provided trade unionists with their own libraries, and consciously tried to assist the education of militants. The work of the Bourses du Travail is often associated with Fernand Pelloutier, although he did not create the movement and was to die early of tuberculosis in 1901 at the age of 33. Pelloutier, however, spent his energies striving firstly to bring trade unions together in the Bourses du Travail, and secondly to federate the local branches into a national organization. The Bourse du Travail had four broad objectives, as outlined by Pelloutier himself.[80] Principally, it acted as a mutual aid organization, finding job placements, offering unemployment relief, assistance in case of accident, and a travel subsidy to enable workers to move to a new job. These services represented the mutualist legacy of *compagnonnage*, now incorporated into the work of federated labour *syndicats*. Secondly, and most importantly for our purposes, the Bourse du Travail was to be an institution for workers' education, with a lending library and study courses. Thirdly, it was a centre for political propaganda, and fourthly, its task was resistance, in other words it tried to accumulate strike funds. Most importantly, the Bourses du Travail were to be staffed by workers and administered by union delegates, and only union members could join it. These, at least, were the ideals, but dependence on the benevolence and funding generosity of public authorities always threatened to compromise them.

There were anarchist aspects to Pelloutier's ideas, and to the Bourses du Travail themselves, at least between the establishment of the Bourse in Paris in 1886, and the expulsion of the Confédération Générale du Travail from its ranks in 1905. Indeed, the very notion of workers uniting to organize their own autonomous institutions, including libraries, has anarchist potential. In the case of Pelloutier and the early Bourses du Travail, this tendency was underscored by the ideals of anarcho-syndicalism. Pelloutier believed, for example, in the revolutionary potential of a general strike of all workers, and he repudiated the compromises and vacillations of parliamentary socialism. Workers, for Pelloutier, must emancipate themselves by their own efforts, for parliamentary legislation could never be trusted to achieve this. None of these radical sentiments prevented Pelloutier and the Bourses du Travail from working for 'possibilist' reforms, a shorter working day, and better medical care for workers, or from simply helping them to find a job.

The libraries of the Bourses du Travail would be workers' universities, the place where workers would find material to help them understand their predicament and the social organization which oppressed them. Pelloutier envisaged libraries which would assist the training of a militant, from technical literature and the latest works on Darwinism and natural science, to imaginative literature by contemporary authors such as Anatole France and Emile Zola, not forgetting the literature of social theory and political economy from Adam Smith and Saint-Simon to Marx and Kropotkin.[81] The militant needed to develop a historical consciousness, too, through a study of the French Revolution, represented in the library of the Paris Bourse du Travail by Michelet, Aulard, Buonarroti and Jaurès. Histories of the Paris Commune were also on the shelves.[82] With the help of these books, the worker was to be taught 'the science of his own misery' (*la science de son malheur*). Working-class reading, in this view, had revolutionary potential.[83] Pelloutier's motto was 'Instruire pour révolter' (Educate to rebel).

In 1892, when the Fédération des Bourses du Travail came into existence, there were 14 Bourses in existence. By 1898, there were 51, grouping a total of nearly 1000 different *syndicats*. By 1900, Pelloutier claimed his federation embraced 48 per cent of all unionized workers in France.[84] The network grew even faster after his death and there were 143 Bourses du Travail in existence in 1911.[85] By this time, however, they had become far more conservative. In any case, they did not all have a library, and in fact the only substantial library attached to a Bourse du Travail was to be found in Paris, at headquarters in the rue du Château d'Eau. Most provincial Bourses were lucky if they had a regular acquisitions budget and a stock of more than two or three hundred books.[86] It was in the Paris Bourse library, with its stock of 5000 volumes, that the experiment took shape.

The library was open to all, but only union members had borrowing rights. It was open on weekdays and Saturdays from 9 a.m. until 11 p.m., but it closed at noon on holidays. The library was subsidized by the local municipality, and its acquisitions included official donations as well as direct purchases. Between 1898 and 1905, according to the librarian's acquisitions register, the library's new stock reflected some of Pelloutier's priorities. The main categories of new books were:[87]

Social sciences, statistics and economics – 36.7 per cent
General literature – 17.8 per cent
Technical works and manuals – 13 per cent
History and Geography – 10.65 per cent
Horticulture – 6.2 per cent
Natural sciences (inc anthropology) – 6 per cent
Philosophy, religion, education – 2 per cent

Clearly, the category of 'general literature' was an important one, and the Bourses du Travail did not exclude fiction. In fact, Pelloutier himself had argued that the libraries should show a healthy 'eclecticism' rather than rejecting bourgeois humanist culture outright.[88] This was just as well, because borrowers demanded fiction: in 1906, 81 per cent of loans were in the category of general literature.[89]

Just as with other attempts to define a specifically workers' reading culture, which have already been discussed, so too the library of the Paris Bourse du Travail treated fiction critically and selectively.[90] The sensational fiction of the *roman-feuilleton* was rejected, just as Henri Tolain had rejected it, and Eugène Sue amongst many other of its masters was not to be found on the library shelves. Working-class culture consistently preferred realist or naturalist novels, especially those with an authentic working-class setting. The library therefore gave priority to 'anti-bourgeois' fiction. Essentially, this meant Balzac and Zola, and in fact these two authors between them accounted for almost half of all novels bought by the library. The stock had 40 works by Balzac and 34 by Zola, supplemented by George Sand, *Madame Bovary* which might also be considered anti-bourgeois, the *dreyfusard* Anatole France and Octave Mirbeau. The library made some concessions to its clientele's taste for fiction in stocking some Victor Hugo and Jules Verne as well.

The Bourses du Travail had difficulty in maintaining their initial drive for militancy. Although the movement had tried to create an independent worker's cultural centre, it had never in fact been fully autonomous. The authorities insisted that the librarian was nominated by the prefect. Moreover, purchased acquisitions only formed a minority of the library's stock. The rest came from individual donations or as gifts from official bodies, the municipal council, government ministries, and the Chambre des Députés, who wanted the library to provide reference documentation of a general administrative nature.[91] No wonder the library's historian questioned the integrity of its radical mission, when trade union representatives were not wholly responsible for library acquisitions. These contradictions were resolved in 1905 at the expense of the unionists, who now lost control of the Bourses du Travail. They fell under prefectoral control, and relied increasingly on public authorities to maintain the Paris library. The reference stock was maintained, but the library's original militant function became redundant. The prefecture, for example, donated the ultra-nationalist works of Déroulède, and titles on colonialism, both of which were quite contrary to the anarcho-syndicalist ideology of the earlier Bourses du Travail.[92]

The Bourses du Travail had briefly tried to shape a distinctively workers' culture which was realist, egalitarian and rebellious, while showing some respect for bourgeois literature. Like other workers' libraries mentioned, the experiment had been challenged by the workers' own demands for fiction; but it was eventually stifled by state administrators and public authorities. In fact, the Bourses du Travail, despite their revolutionary rhetoric, had always been dependent on their benevolence.

Workers as writers

Workers were not just readers; they also wrote. If we are fully to measure their achievement in constructing an independent literary culture, we must also consider the phenomenon of workers as poets and above all, as autobiographers. The writing careers of those workers who did break into print may also help to explain their relationship with an apprehensive bourgeoisie, faced not only with the advent of a mass of 'new readers', but also with the arrival of a new category of writers.

Working-class authors searched for the means to legitimize their writing efforts and, almost inevitably, they imitated literary figures from the world of high culture. Yet the derivative nature of their literary projects encountered sneers rather than applause. The unschooled worker who doffed his cap to the prestigious authors of the past had pretensions which the cultivated élite might regard as a mockery of the literary canon. Bourdieu accurately characterized the paradoxical situation of the autodidact in search of acceptance:

The traditional kind of autodidact was fundamentally defined by a reverence towards high culture which was the result of his brutal and premature exclusion from it, and which led to an exalted and poorly directed devotion to it, inevitably perceived by the agents of official culture as a sort of caricatural homage.[93]

The autodidact did not easily cross the cultural chasm which separated him from those who claimed natural membership of the literary world. Several workers became published poets. Poetry was not the preserve of a distant, learned culture; it could be re-worked by working-class readers and it was produced and published by working-class writers. Their poetry, however, was often an extension of the oral culture which they inherited, and which survived in popular song. Moreover, worker-poets did not always write in French, preferring local languages which were closer to popular usage. The *coiffeur* Jasmin, for example, wrote in Occitan, looking ahead to the renaissance of regional languages which occurred in the mid-nineteenth century.[94] Poetry was closer than prose to popular oral tradition, it could express an emerging class-consciousness, and it found ready outlets in nineteenth-century newspapers.

Working-class autobiographies are another clear indication of a growing self-awareness and mastery of the printed word. Without formal tuition, without ghost-writers and without literary credentials, a group of remarkable individuals set out to write their own stories. They provide a personalized history of the working class in this period, a time when the oral transmission of that history had begun to decline, and before modern oral history and been invented.

The autobiographies consulted in this chapter were published either as books or in contemporary periodicals, usually in the author's lifetime, although a few have only recently been discovered, like the notebooks of Xavier-Edouard Lejeune, the retired draper's representative, who died in 1918 after keeping the contents of a lifetime's writings a secret even from his wife. They were unearthed by his grandchildren, one of whom happened to be Philippe Lejeune, a leading critic of autobiographical writing. Another attempt to delay publication was made by the French socialist Benoît Malon, who ordered that his memoirs should remain unpublished for at least ten years after his death (which occurred in 1893). His followers obeyed with interest – the memoirs did not appear until 1907.[95] Only a tiny proportion of working-class autobiographies were privately published. Victorine Brocher's memoirs, published at the author's expense in Lausanne in 1909 under the name 'Victorine B.', was a rare French example of private publication. In the 1840s, workers' writing was published in periodicals such as *La Ruche populaire* and *L'Atelier* (although even the worker-poets needed the sponsorship of intellectuals such as Lamartine and George Sand). In France, the publication of autobiographies only took off after 1848, and reached a peak in the period 1870–1914. Autobiography was regarded very much as an English genre, and working-class autobiographies did indeed proliferate more freely in nineteenth-century Britain. The 1866 edition of the Larousse Dictionary described autobiography as an English invention, still rare in France.[96] In 1888, the critic Brunetière complained about the invasion of '*littérature personnelle*' and its egotism, 'the morbid and monstrous development of the self'.[97]

The medium used by working-class writers must be examined in its own right. They wrote autobiographies for different purposes, to warn, to instruct, to record, and to preach – to name but a few. Some were inspired by nostalgia, some by vanity, others by anger. They wrote at different times of their life, some reflecting on their past in old age, others taking new stock of themselves as a result of a personal trauma, a few writing to reassess themselves and resolve what we might now call a mid-life crisis. Gilland took advantage of a prison sentence to write his *Biographie des hommes obscurs* in 1849, and Agricol Perdiguier looked back on his life as a victim of imperial persecution in 1854. Others wrote a brief sketch of their life to preface a publication of their poetry or songs. They wrote in different styles, adopting traditional literary conventions, but sometimes escaping those set formulas to express the more authentic voice of the 'unlettered' author. We must examine the purpose of the autobiographical enterprise, as well as the literary modes that dominated their autobiographies.

Three genres in particular stand out: the success story of the self-made man, the militant's memoirs and the literature of *compagnonnage*.[98] The autobiography of Jacques Laffitte, who was one of 12 children of a carpenter and became a leading figure under the July Monarchy, belongs to the first category. His autobiography was clearly a public document, celebrating the achievement of a self-made man who had played a leading political role after 1830, and had contributed to the arrival of Louis-Philippe on the French throne. Born in Bayonne in 1812, Laffitte became a clerk, and used his employer's library to read Bossuet and Fénélon, Molière, Corneille, Racine, Lafontaine, Voltaire and Rousseau. Like many ambitious young men, he made the *montée* to Paris, after first eliminating an important handicap to his social climbing – he eradicated his Bayonnais accent. A *parvenu* of the Empire, Laffitte became governor of the Bank of France under Louis XVIII. He boasted in his autobiography of his 'gilded mansion' on the fashionable Chaussée d'Antin. Laffitte reproduced his political speeches in full in his memoirs, and one chapter was vainly entitled 'Le Roi et Moi'. Most of his memoirs were confined to the activities of his political persona. They impress the reader with the author's overpowering sense of self-importance.[99] His vanity was characteristically male, expressing the pride of men whose sense of self-worth was intricately bound up with a public career and the exercise of political power. The autobiography of the self-made author was in this sense a highly gendered text.

Working-class women writers came into their own, however, as authors in a second popular genre, that of the militant's memoirs. Their interest lay not in material success, but in self-emancipation. The author's gradual radicalization and perceptions of the sources of oppression were the true subject of these autobiographies. In addition, their writing had a historical purpose – to tell the story of the century's revolutionary struggles from a true perspective, in other words from the point of view of the protagonists and victims. A good example is the autobiography of Victorine Brocher, published in this century like so many militants' memoirs by François Maspéro. Her story centres almost exclusively on her experiences of 1848, and of the Paris Commune. It is a passionate account of the February Revolution and of the massacres of the Commune, during which she was an ambulance worker. The author gives day-by-day accounts of these revolutions, culminating in the discovery that she had been sentenced to death as a *pétroleuse*. Her narrative reflects the problems of material life with which nineteenth-century workers commonly struggled: the price of bread, the problem of finding shelter, and the levels of wages are often detailed. Victorine Brocher wrote exactly what she paid for butter and potatoes, and she described the illnesses and diet of her children, which was a vital concern in the siege of Paris, when she unwittingly found herself eating mouse paté.[100] Even if the style of working-class autobiographies was frequently derivative, they expressed specifically proletarian concerns. Frequently, and Brocher was no exception to the rule, this kind of autobiography took on a profoundly anticlerical or atheist animus, which spared neither Catholic nor Protestant.

In the third common genre, the Tour de France provided the framework for autobiographies of *compagnonnage*. They professed to relate the 'inside story' of *compagnonnage*, its rituals, apprentice's songs, customs and jargon. They did not hesitate, either, to relate the drinking bouts, internecine quarrels and frequent industrial accidents which were part of the *compagnon*'s life. Skilled workers were more likely to write autobiographies than industrial, factory workers. A large group were skilled artisans in the clothing or building trades, like the mason Martin Nadaud, or in printing and bookselling (trades which produced many literate writers and future journalists). The clothing trade always offered opportunities for skilled female labour. The autobiographers, then, were a skilled élite, but we should not for all that assume a direct and natural correlation between skilled crafts, political militancy and intellectual ambitions. As Jacques Rancière has pointed out, political engagement and intellectual effort often developed outside a strong craft-based culture.[101] Indeed, they might emerge in opposition to the corporate identities of well-established trades. We should not then be surprised to find worker-autobiographers who were peripatetic, at least for a part of their life. They are often encountered on the margins of the stable world of a working-class professional culture which had not fully integrated them.

The nineteenth-century decline of the traditional world of *compagnonnage* was an essential feature of the consciousness of writers such as Agricol Perdiguier. *Compagnonnage*, that system of mutual help and protection which enabled workers in skilled trades to regulate the labour market to some extent, was very important to Perdiguier. For him, the *compagnon*'s Tour de France, finding work and companionship in a series of provincial cities, had been a crucial rite of passage to maturity and professional expertise. *Compagnonnage* brought a sense of identity, of rootedness in a professional community, but at the same time it was divisive. Members of different orders of *compagnons*, the various Devoirs, were rivals engaged in running gang warfare. They fought pitched brawls with each other which sometimes resulted in fatal casualties. It was hard to see how any class solidarity could develop out of such violent antagonisms and the jealous, exclusive spirit of *compagnonnage*. The corporate ethos of the *compagnon*, however idealized by George Sand, could not perhaps generate the culture of militancy required by working-class organizations at the end of the century. Amongst the working-class autobiographers, perhaps Dumay and Bouvier, who both had direct experience of factory work, came closest to expressing a modern class-consciousness in their concern with labour grievances.

Most working-class leaders cited here struggled to protect their interests in the teeth of advancing industrial capitalism. They wrote at a moment of crisis, when skilled craftsmen were forced to compete with each other for shrinking job opportunities. They were not necessarily part of a cohesive class consciousness, and their conception of working-class solidarity was partly conditioned by the experience of *compagnon-*

nage. They were well aware, however, that they were recording a disappearing way of life, either to preserve the memory of their artisan culture for posterity (in the case of the carpenter Joseph Voisin)[102] or in order to bury it altogether (in the case of the Girondin Jean-Baptiste Arnaud). Artisans were credulous and prejudiced, according to Arnaud, and his didactic autobiography urged them to put violent professional rivalries behind them. Progress depended, he argued, on working-class unity which would replace the divisiveness of the societies of *compagnonnage*.[103]

Working-class writers were usually conscious of writing history for public consumption, but at the same time, writing an autobiography fulfilled an inner need. Autobiography was a step in the process of defining one's identity, both as an individual and as a member of a group or class. The act of writing itself brought greater self-knowledge and self-assertion. Autobiography was an affirmation of the self, as a unique individual and as a member of the working class. Philippe Lejeune described autobiography as principally the 'history of a personality', and envisaged the autobiography as a pact which the writer makes with himself or herself.[104] The purpose of the pact, Lejeune argues, is to redeem a flawed destiny, and to rescue a personality which has doubted its own value. The Le Creusot worker Dumay, surveying a life-history of struggle and illusion, concluded with satisfaction that he had added his weight to a worthwhile cause ('I have the great personal satisfaction of being able to say that as far as my strength allowed I pushed forward the chariot of human progress').[105] The autobiography thus invests a life with meaning, and proclaims: it was not all in vain after all.

The problem for these 'new writers' was to find a suitable language and style in which to make their stories. Jacques-Etienne Bédé's editor, for example, lists the author's many grammatical mistakes, wrong use of tenses, incorrect agreements and bad spelling.[106] They were untutored and unsophisticated writers, but however uneducated they were in a formal sense, working-class authors brought a great deal of cultural baggage to the task of writing. They had inherited or acquired a sense of correct literary tone, and they adopted linguistic or stylistic modes encountered in their own reading. They plundered their existing capital of images, metaphors and narrative techniques for the style best suited to the expression of their own individual identity.

Self-taught writers were naturally self-conscious, and aware of the existence of a long literary tradition, which they had to adapt for their own ends. Bédé, who led a strike of Paris chair-makers in 1820, wrote his life as a late-eighteenth-century melodrama. In his autobiography, Bédé continually addresses God or destiny in a romantic style reminiscent of Ducray-Duminil – 'O sort épouvantable!' ('O cruel fate!'), etc. A carefully crafted *mise en scène* frames his father's death which opens the story. In a terrible thunderstorm, with thunder crashing, a heavy beam tragically fell on him in his mill. At the sight of this accident, his uncle swooned and 'almost lost his life' *(faillit perdre la vie)*.[107] The narrative reads like a novel throughout. Bédé entitled it, in the style of Ducray, 'Etienne et Maria ou le Triomphe de l'Amitié'. He provided the triumphant ending which the genre demanded: in 1820, with the devoted support of his friend Maria, he was released from a prison sentence with a royal pardon. The *dénouement*, however, has a final novelistic twist. Until the end, Bédé concealed the real identity of the beloved Maria who worked loyally for his release from jail. The reader learns that Maria is not in fact Bédé's wife, but the wife of a comrade Bicheux, to whom the work is dedicated, and whose real relationship with Bédé can only be surmised. Historians of labour have appreciated and exploited Bédé's work as a valuable source for early-nineteenth-century labour struggles, but they have not always appreciated the narrative strategies and novelistic style which order the text.[108]

Xavier-Edouard Lejeune provides another example of a self-taught writer using the literary models of the great romantics. It was, as we have seen, Châteaubriand's *Génie du Christianisme* which turned him into a writer in the first place. His poetry imitated Hugo, and he copied Balzac in entitling his memories of work in a department store 'Scènes de la vie de magasin'. The press was another important influence. Lejeune frequently cut out articles from the newspapers which he avidly read between 1860 and 1918. At his death, he left notebooks of newspaper cuttings, which he had collected and glued into the pages.[109] Like all self-taught writers, he struggled to learn his craft from the models he knew.

Working-class writers, therefore, were an articulate but inexperienced minority. A few, like Laffitte, wrote to demonstrate that they had achieved bourgeois respectability. Others wrote to educate others in a spirit of militant defiance. Their work was inevitably derivative, as they improvised a literary style and a narrative structure to announce their presence alongside the paragons of 'legitimate' culture.

Working-class intellectuals as cultural intermediaries

For the nineteenth-century autodidact, reading served an emancipatory purpose. At the same time, it was the crucial instrument in the development of a broadly humanistic version of 'self-culture'. French working-class readers and writers adopted similar reading and writing practices, in the teeth of poverty, material hardship and a lack of privacy endured by the working classes as a whole. There were some common patterns in their reading preferences and critical judgements. For these reasons, they can be said to belong to a distinctive interpretive community of readers. That community was a loose and informal one: loose, because it was fissured along national and along gender lines, and informal, because there was no single institutional framework to shape their self-made literary culture.

The reading practices of the autodidacts emerged from a common aesthetic of self-denial and earnestness. The social psychology or *habitus* of the self-taught worker, however, exhibited some characteristics of nineteenth-century bourgeois culture (thrift, sobriety, respectability). Working-class readers distanced themselves from the crowd of fellow-workers. Reading was a solitary activity, and individual working-class readers were often shunned by their fellow-workers, or treated as peculiar anti-social recluses. The worker who read, Agricol Perdiguier recalled, was an object of ridicule (*un objet de raillerie*).[110] A few might have welcomed this ostracism, as it gave them more time and solitude to devote to reading. But individual readers had an uneasy relationship with fellow-workers. Their reading opened up for them a world of middle-class culture and middle-class values, which accentuated the ambiguity of their position.

Working-class autobiographers could complain about workers' ignorance and drunkenness in language which would not have been out of place in the mouths of their social superiors. They therefore risked unpopularity. When Jean-Baptiste Dumay had objected to the religious instruction received by his children at school, he was singled out as a troublemaker. 'My house', he recalled, 'was more than ever treated as a house visited by the plague.'[111] Dumay probably meant that the authorities were responsible for treating him like this; but men like Dumay faced ostracism by other workers too, as well as by employers. Jean-Baptiste Arnaud described French *compagnons* as 'blind, credulous, worshippers of prejudice' (*crédules ouvriers, aveugles et idolâtres de leurs préjugés*).[112]

A distance opened up between the working reader and the ordinary worker, often filled with a poorly disguised antipathy. Even language barriers appeared between ambitious working-class intellectuals and their fellow-workers. Laffitte, in order to facilitate his Parisian *embourgeoisement*, had got rid of his Bayonnais accent. For Perdiguier, as for

Nadaud, learning French and discarding their local language (Provençal in Perdiguier's case) and pronunciation were part of their intellectual progress.

Nadaud was for a long time a worker with his feet in two different worlds. As a regular seasonal migrant from the Creuse to the French capital, he was part-Limousin, part-Parisian, speaking with a natural Limousin accent which he gradually lost as his life centred more permanently on Paris. As an autodidact, he despised the apathy of his fellow-masons, and yet was eager to do something for their education. He characterized the duality of his position as that of a revolutionary vanguard. 'In each occupation', he wrote, 'groups formed amongst the proudest and most intelligent workers, who spurred on the masses and made them ashamed of their indolence and apathy.'[113] Nadaud identified himself with 'the proudest and most intelligent', leading the rest out of ignorance and indifference. As a reader and an autodidact, he was detached from other workers, but at the same time he appointed himself their guide and leader.

Working-class intellectuals had a very keen sense that they were different. They knew they belonged to a small group more determined and more far-sighted than most other workers. They tended to adopt reading practices which reinforced their sense of distinction. In their loneliness, they were tempted to think of themselves as a select band of visionaries. Joseph Benoît described the small working-class vanguard of the 1830 Revolution:

> Amidst this crowd, these dense masses, there were generous hearts to whom the secrets of the future had been, if not unveiled, then revealed to their restless and tortured conscience... But these men were few in number and isolated in the middle of the confused mass as if in a desert.[114]

My purpose, however, is not to argue that the nineteenth-century autodidact was on the road towards *embourgeoisement*. I have tried to suggest that his or her predicament was far more complex than that rather simplistic term implies. The improvisation of a culture often followed middle-class models, but between what the autodidacts read and how they responded as readers there was scope for many possible outcomes. Some autodidacts certainly emerged from the working-class throng determined to distinguish themselves irrevocably from it, but few denied their class origins entirely. The situation was ambiguous. The working-class intellectual did not share what he or she perceived as the laziness and prejudices of the majority of workers. At the same time, he or she did not necessarily share middle-class versions of respectability either. Men like Benoît and Nadaud described themselves as part of a revolutionary vanguard, but autodidacts in general were cultural intermediaries, working-class activists with a broad knowledge and their own interpretation of a hallowed literary tradition.

Unlike middle-class sympathizers, who saw self-improvement in terms of individual discipline, working-class autodidacts often viewed self-help in collective terms. 'My life', wrote Agricol Perdiguier, 'is linked to the life of workers in general, in speaking of myself I speak of them. I regard as one [je fais communs] our work, our habits, our customs, our faults, our prejudices, our qualities.'[115] The extent to which Perdiguier actually succeeded in speaking for all workers is open to dispute, but although he counted himself amongst a vanguard who had acquired some education, he still expressed a sense of solidarity with other workers.[116] In similar vein Gilland, the adamant locksmith of the *faubourg* St Antoine, declared 'I love my position, I love my tools and even though I could have made a living from my pen, I would not have wanted to stop being a working locksmith'.[117]

Political radicalization was filtered through the values of an informal but distinct community of readers, with its own evaluation of the uses of fiction, poetry, history or science. Print culture was vital to this politicization, although it also depended on oral transmission. Private networks, verbal rumour and report, reading aloud in wineshops and elsewhere all played a role in the spread of left-wing militancy. The autodidacts then are best seen as cultural intermediaries, standing between the learned culture which became accessible to them, and their working-class roots, from which their education had partially detached them. In spite of the cultural shifts they made, these exceptional working-class readers rarely lost contact with their origins.

As long as reading and writing were unusual activities, they would entail a huge sacrifice and the risk of ostracism by fellow-workers. But the acquisition of a bourgeois literary culture did not necessarily deflect the working-class reader from the political struggle. On the contrary, it could have a revolutionary purpose. As Norbert Truquin urged in a plea with which a historian can only sympathize:

> It is urgent that all those who work and endure the vices of our social organisation should count only on themselves to overcome their difficulties [*se tirer de l'affaire*] and by means of solidarity build a better present and future for themselves. It is therefore imperative

that every one of them contributes his stone to the common edifice, by publishing his notes, notebooks, memoirs, in a word any document which might help destroy the iniquities of the old world and hasten the coming of the social revolution.[118]

Truquin's plea for the preservation of a working-class archive is especially interesting because it emerges from a reading culture with which we are no longer in touch. The cultural practices of the nineteenth-century autodidacts have been buried by a century of social change. Universal schooling made their improvised reading culture superfluous. The rise of new forms of leisure has made their intensive reading practices seem obsolete. A general process of acculturation has transformed all of us into consumers of culture and of commercialized entertainment rather than independent seekers after self-emancipation. The compulsive reading of nineteenth-century self-taught workers is a distant reminder of individual potential, when driven by a passionate desire for intellectual liberation.

4
Reading Women: from Emma Bovary to the New Woman

'The great preoccupation of French provincial women is novel-reading', wrote Stendhal in 1832, 'hence the immense consumption of novels that takes place in France.' He went on: 'In the provinces, there is scarcely a woman who does not read her five or six volumes per month; many read 15 or 20; and you would not find a small town without two or three *cabinets de lecture*.'[1] Stendhal's survey of the feminine book market carefully distinguished between two kinds of readers. On one hand, there were respectable Parisian readers, who typically demanded the octavo editions of Walter Scott published by Gosselin – novels, as Stendhal put it, for the *salons*; on the other hand, there was the small-format 'roman pour les femmes de chambre', full of absurd tear-jerking scenarios for readers of the provincial *petite bourgeoisie*. Although the provincial woman might sometimes attempt the respectable octavo novel (*roman de bonne compagnie*), she would not be able entirely to understand it. Stendhal's comments betray the prejudices of a Parisian intellectual towards the mediocrity of provincial culture. He wrote, however, as a practising author, who admired Scott for satisfying both these female publics at once.[2] His testimony is doubly significant. It underlines the importance of women readers for the nineteenth-century fiction market. At the same time, in the condescending tone in which Stendhal discusses 'novels for chambermaids', we can also glimpse one of the dominant and enduring images of the female reader. In the nineteenth century, and even today, she was and is constructed as a superficial consumer of light romantic or sensational fiction, which required little intellectual effort from the reader. This chapter is concerned with such representations of women readers, and by attempts to replace them. Later in the century, both Catholics and feminists promoted alternative reading models to their female constituencies.

Women as novel readers

During the Bourbon Restoration, various publishers produced series of works directed at the growing female readership. Not all of them included novels. For example, the *Bibliothèque choisie pour les dames*, launched by Lefuel and Delaunay in 1818, offered selections from Greek writers like Homer, Herodotus and Aristotle. This collection was sold by subscription; it originally promised 72 volumes, and the publishers at least succeeded in producing 36 of them by instalments up to 1821.[3] The *Bibliothèque des dames chrétiennes*, produced by Didot *aîné* between 1820 and 1825, was another long-running series offering sermons, spiritual guides, works by St Augustine and extracts from other theological authorities. This series was a vehicle for Lamennais, who wrote prefaces to and commented on many titles.[4] These early literary series for women had two features in common. Firstly, they were in small-format and easily portable editions. The *Bibliothèque choisie pour les dames* appeared in in-18o, while the *Bibliothèque des dames chrétiennes* was in the miniature in-32o format, ideal for private prayer and for taking to church. Secondly, they reproduced short pre-digested extracts, or *morceaux choisis*. The female subscriber was not expected to trudge through the entire *Iliad*, and the Christian woman could meditate on the words of the Church fathers in small easily-absorbed 'bites' or *opuscules*.

The female reader, however, was targeted above all as a consumer of novels and aristocratic memoirs. Didot *aîné's Collection des meilleurs ouvrages de la langue française, dédiée aux dames* produced many such private memoirs.[5] Perhaps the first to supply novels especially for women readers was Werdet, who in the days before his bankruptcy published a *Collection des meilleurs romans français dédiés aux dames* between 1826 and 1829. He started with Madame de Lafayette's works, and included authors such as Madame Riccoboni and Madame de Tencin, and Madame de Graffigny's popular *Lettres d'une Péruvienne*. Later instalments offered Bernardin de St Pierre and, turning at last to more modern writers, Sophie Cottin's *Elizabeth ou les exilés de Sibérie*.[6] Books in his series were illustrated with an engraved frontispiece, and they appeared in the very small in-32o format. Werdet was followed by the *Bibliothèque rose des demoiselles*,[7] Firmin-Didot's *Bibliothèque des mères de famille*, and Gautier-Langereau's *Bibliothèque de ma fille*. The publishers did not assume that women would necessarily be the purchasers of such novels. In fact, as Gautier-Langereau's title implies, the publishers were targeting men who bought reading matter for their wives and daughters.

The publishers' aim in adopting this marketing strategy was to convince the purchaser that the novels in the series contained safe material for susceptible female readers. The objective was to reassure the customer that his female dependants would be profitably entertained but not corrupted by what was on offer. By the second half of the century, such series, specifically directed at women, were obsolete. As a marketing ploy, such labels were, in the long run, confining. Women had been clearly identified as an important part of the fiction market, but they were not the only consumers of novels, and publishers sought the widest possible audience.

Women were considered to be, by their very nature, emotionally vulnerable to romance fiction. In 1843, M.-J.Brisset's novel *Le Cabinet de lecture* presented an image of female fiction-readers which echoed Stendhal's, but far exceeded his in cynicism. The plot, which was set in 1834, opened in one of the Parisian reading-rooms which were one of the main sources of romantic fiction for a public which could hire works by the volume. The establishment was kept by the wrinkled, hunchbacked and bearded Madame Bien-Aimé, discovered in the process of advising an aspiring novelist on the ingredients of a successful potboiler. To impress women readers, she advised him, you need 'some seductive emotional insights, delicious twists of phrase, chaste extravagant thoughts, followed by whirlwinds of passion to sweep you away, wild frenzies and blazing tirades!'[8] Brisset configured female readers as easily moved by wild stylistic excesses.

Two readers enter Brisset's fictional reading-room, observed by the novelist/narrator as they exchange their books. Both are women, each representing one aspect of the author's vision of his female readership. The first is a young seamstress, aged 15 or 16, a *grisette* living on the fourth floor, which was a sign of relative poverty in Paris. She comes to return her copy of Ducray-Duminil's sentimental novel *Victor, ou l'Enfant de la forêt*, in which an *enfant trouvé* eventually marries the daughter of an aristocrat. She asks for another novel in this Gothic-sentimental genre to read after work, 'something really nice (*bien gentil*), with old castles, underground passages, traitors and lovers who get married at the end.'[9] The second reader arrives, this time a fashionable *parisienne*, who disdains sentimental romances and asks for stronger stuff. She professes to be tired of translations of insipid English romances, with heroines who are 'boringly virtuous or stupidly sentimental'.[10] But she cannot escape the anglophile fashions of the period. Madame Bien-Aimé offers her the novels of Walter Scott which she thinks will satisfy her taste. The *parisienne* promises to send her maid to collect the books. The novelist, having watched both these women and finding them attractive, resolves to seduce both the sentimental seamstress and the bored, rich, married woman of fashion. Writing romance fiction, Brisset is suggesting, is a form of seduction. It matters little whether the female reader is sophisticated and restless, or young and poor, for novels play with the emotions of all female readers, arousing them and exploiting their fantasies. Brisset created a fictional protagonist who set out to achieve what actual novelists undertake only metaphorically – the seduction of the female reader. At the risk of spoiling the enjoyment for intrepid readers of Brisset, I can reveal that the narrator succeeds in his double project. Clearly, novelists have their fantasies too.

Many forces came together to define the woman as the quintessential novel reader. There were powerful and consistent attempts to direct and control the reading of women. At the very beginning of the century, Sylvain Maréchal had argued, half-jokingly, half-seriously, that women should be prevented even from learning to read. His provocative pamphlet on this subject was reprinted in 1841 and 1853.[11] His denial of women's intellectual life is especially surprising to modern readers, since the author was a professed atheist and a committed revolutionary, associated with Babeuf's ill-fated Conspiracy of the Equals in 1796. But the democratic left was sometimes just as afraid of female independence as was the clerical right. Maréchal in fact appeared interested neither in what women read, nor how they read. Essentially, he wanted to prevent women from writing. Women's concerns, he argued, were, and should naturally be focused on domestic and marital happiness. Women had no place in the public sphere. 'The intention of good and wise Nature is that women should be occupied exclusively with domestic chores and should find honour in holding in their hands, not a book or a quill, but a distaff and a spindle.'[12] Maréchal believed, like many of his contemporaries, that reading was physically debilitating for women, who were not physiologically prepared for intellectual work. An over-active brain could damage reproductive functions and lead in some cases to early death.[13] His main worry, however, was that women who read might attempt to become authors in their own right. This would lead eventually to female participation in public life, which would violate what he considered to be the natural and reasonable separation of gender roles. Women's reading was to be discouraged because it would generate a desire to play a political role, and thus to trespass on male territory. If women needed to read, there was only one solution: 'Reason desires that heads of households, father and husbands, perform their duty to act as readers for the women.'[14] The values of patriarchy thus remained intact, and no doubt many a bourgeois *paterfamilias* did indeed regard reading to the family as a serious moral duty.

Maréchal's misogynist fantasy of a world with no female readers was an extreme expression of quite common anxieties about what women were reading in the nineteenth century. We can detect traces of it in Daumier's cartoons for *Le Charivari*. In one series of caricatures in the 1840s, Daumier attacked the 'bluestocking' as a new social phenomenon. The underlying theme, once again, was the incompatibility of intellectual work with the obligations of being a housewife. The problem was of course treated in caricature, to extract the maximum humour from this central thesis. In a previous series of 1839, specifically entitled *Marriage Customs* (*Moeurs conjugales*), Daumier had similarly addressed the problem of the reading housewife. An irate husband complains that his trousers have not been mended, while his wife sits in an armchair reading (inevitably) George Sand.[15] He expostulates thus: 'I don't give a damn about your Madame Sand who prevents women from darning trousers, and who is the reason why my stirrups are unthreaded! We should bring back divorce...or else get rid of authors like that.' It must be said, however, that Daumier's humour is subtle and double-edged. The joke is on the spindly-legged husband here, who cuts a bedraggled and ridiculous figure without his *pantalon*.

As gradual industrialization widened the division between home and workplace, so the theory of private and public spheres operated to confine women's reading to romantic and domestic fiction. Women were identified as novel-readers in the nineteenth century, because lack of education was thought to disqualify them from more serious reading matter. The novel was considered entertainment for its own sake, with no important lessons to communicate, and it was therefore suitable for readers of limited education with time on their hands. Newspapers, which connected the reader with the public world of politics and finance, were often seen as a male preserve, read and discussed in the bar or the *cabaret*, those favourite sites of masculine sociability. One part of the newspaper was sometimes considered female territory, and that was the *roman-feuilleton*. Novels, serialized or not, treated the inner, emotional life of their characters, and thus seemed destined specifically for women readers, who were in theory excluded from public life.[16]

At the same time, excessive reading of novels was to be avoided, since they aroused the emotions, played on the reader's inner feelings and could overwork the imagination. Women were held to be volatile and perverse: qualities which were the opposite of the stability and reason appropriated by the bourgeois male. Since women were assumed to be emotionally vulnerable, novels could engender dangerous flights of fancy and indeed stimulate erotic desire. Thus although fiction reading might be interpreted as a typically feminine practice, it was paradoxically highly suspect in men's eyes. For these reasons, women's reading in the nineteenth century in both bourgeois and working-class circles was under surveillance. Parental supervision of reading gave way in adult life to the employer's control of women's reading, until marriage installed the husband as an informal censor of his wife's literary consumption. The practice of reading aloud in the family, usually led by a man, gave him the power to select and edit what women listened to.

Excessive paternalism, however, was always open to ridicule. A good example is provided in Labiche's comedy *Le Voyage de Monsieur Perrichon*, first performed in 1860.[17] The caricatural bourgeois here is Perrichon, a Parisian shopkeeper (*commerçant*), who is about to take his family on holiday to Switzerland. In the opening scenes at the Gare de Lyon, Perrichon goes to the bookstall and asks the *marchande* for suitable reading for the family on the journey. 'Madame', he asks, 'I would like a book for my wife and my daughter... a book with no sexual flirtation (*galanterie*), nothing about money, nothing about politics, nothing about marriage, nothing about death.' The shop has just the book for his exacting criteria: *Les Bords de la Saône*, a descriptive travelogue guaranteed to provide none of the excitement Perrichon fears. But he still asks the bookseller, 'Can you swear there's no rubbish (*bêtises*) in this one?'

The theory of public and private spheres, reinforced by the Catholic hierarchy, as well as the theory of the woman reader as a purely recreational consumer of light fiction, remained just that: theories, which are frequently contradicted by empirical evidence offered by women readers themselves in their journals, diaries and autobiographies. Individual women found ways of resisting controls and negotiating their own reading space. They will be discussed in the next chapter. Women who read had to overcome widespread prejudice against women's reading. The intellectual pursuits of all nineteenth-century women were circumscribed by prevailing notions of their domestic responsibilities, 'artistic' sensibilities and general lack of intellectual capacity.

The dangers of '*bovarysme*'

The female reader, then, was conventionally represented as a consumer of romantic fiction whose imagination was liable to overheat. Solitary romance reading was considered dangerous for young girls, and even for married women, although they were allowed a little more licence. The dominant medical discourse of the nineteenth century, discussed in an English context by Kate Flint, reinforced patriarchal assumptions about the need to 'protect' women and adolescent girls from harmful texts.[18] Women's reading ability, it was thought, was determined by physiological factors. Women had a lower brain-weight than men, and so were considered less fit for intellectual pursuits. The shape of the female brain in this view enhanced woman's intuitive faculties, but limited her reasoning powers, in comparison to those of men. There was a fear that overworked female emotions would prove physically debilitating. High levels of stimulation produced by novel reading could be harmful, causing hysteria and loss of fertility.

It was therefore dangerous to extend the female imagination too much. Romantic fantasies could make readers dissatisfied with their present reality. Romantic fiction could also induce sexual arousal, providing further grounds for male anxiety. Flaubert's Emma Bovary became the best-known representative of the frustrated female reader, looking for a way out of an unsatisfying bourgeois marriage. Emma Bovary was married to a well-meaning but emotionally numb provincial doctor. Her reading fuelled her frustrations and translated them into romantic longing, which drew her into unfulfilling extra-marital liaisons. As a social problem, *bovarysme* was not necessarily an exclusively middle-class phenomenon. *Bovarysme* was a form of escapism, but this escapism was a sign that women refused to be constrained by their allotted roles as mothers, housekeepers and dutiful daughters.

Flaubert, as is well known, was forced to suffer an obscenity trial in 1857 as a result of *Madame Bovary*, which he survived unscathed. Contemporaries may have been offended by the sexual scenes in the novel, such as Emma's adulterous encounter with her lover in a *fiacre* travelling aimlessly with the blinds down across the city. They may have been even more offended by the scene at Emma's deathbed in which Emma amorously embraces Christ on the cross, and Flaubert juxtaposes the administration of the last rites with the memory of Emma's erotic experiences. Perhaps conservatives found Flaubert's detached irony fundamentally the most shocking aspect of all. Flaubert's deadpan prose effaced the presence of the narrator. His studied realism and emotionless descriptions were offensive in the sense that through them, the author was failing to make the correct moral response to his objectionable subject-matter. Although, however, the controversy over *Madame Bovary* is an important part of the context, it is not central to the present argument. What matters here is to consider Flaubert's Emma Bovary as a particular and influential configuration of the female reader. The connection between Emma's reading and her growing *ennui* should be emphasized.

Emma Bovary's romantic reading precipitated her search for fulfilment, her disastrous adultery and descent into bankruptcy, and her eventual suicide. What did Emma Bovary read? Flaubert tells us first that she had read Bernardin de St Pierre's *Paul et Virginie* as a young girl, and dreamed of the tropical island on which it was set. Emma had a convent education, which aimed at preparing her for the life of a dutiful wife. Yet the mysteries of religion generated romantic longings. She was

> soothed by the mystic languor she inhaled from the perfumes of the altar, the chill of holy water and the glow of the candles. Instead of following the Mass, she would gaze in her book at the pious vignettes with their azure borders, and she loved the sick lamb, the Sacred Heart pierced by sharp arrows, or poor Jesus, sinking beneath the weight of his cross.[19]

She surrendered to the sensuality of the Mass, and the melancholy attractions of her religious reading. In order to punish herself, the young Emma tried to impose extra penance on herself. Her romantic disposition, however, was reinforced by a reading of Châteaubriand's *Génie du Christianisme*, with its evocation of the 'lyrical surgings of nature'.[20] Emma, Flaubert tells us, had an emotional temperament, and 'she loved the sea only for the sake of tempests'.

Then Emma became a reader of novels. An old seamstress smuggled romances into the convent and the schoolgirls read them in secret and passed them around among themselves. Emma thus devoured stories of

> love, lovers, loving, martyred maidens swooning in secluded lodges, postilions slain every other mile, horses ridden to death on every page, dark forests, aching hearts, promising, sobbing, kisses and tears, little boats by moonlight, nightingales in the grove, *gentlemen* brave as lions, tender as lambs, virtuous as a dream, always well dressed, and weeping pints.[21]

As she grew older, Emma graduated to more adult forms of reading excitement. She borrowed Walter Scott, and imagined herself the heroine of a historical novel, as a chatelaine awaiting her knight on horseback. She and her schoolmates secretly read the fashionable keepsakes of the period, experiencing a *frisson* of delight as she contemplated engravings depicting lovers embracing or longing for each other in exotic settings. Flaubert's irony ran riot as he fully established the powerful effects of Emma's sentimental reading. He described the engravings she loved, with all their clichés and contradictions. There were

> Tartar minarets on the horizon, Roman ruins in the foreground, then some camels kneeling; – the whole thing framed by a nicely hygienic virgin forest, with a great perpendicular sunbeam trembling on the water, steel grey, with white-etched signs, here and there, for floating swans.[22]

Convent school had taught her the magic of religion but not the doctrine. What she valued in literature was its power to arouse her passions and feed her melancholy.

Emma's romantic reading was not just a passing teenage aberration. Flaubert knew the fashions of middle-class female readers well. Emma became a subscriber to a *cabinet de lecture* in Rouen. She had started with the novel of sensibility, in the form of Bernardin de St Pierre's *Paul et Virginie*. She had moved on to the lyrical themes of Châteaubriand's *Génie du Christianisme*, and then followed the path of Brisset's fictional Parisian woman towards the novels of Walter Scott. Gradually she read more exciting and melodramatic works. Romantic authors continued to shape her experience of life. When her mother died, she 'drifted with the meanderings of Lamartine'.[23] She read Hugo's *Notre-Dame de Paris*, identifying with the heroine Esmeralda to the extent of calling her own pet Djali, after Esmeralda's goat.[24] Later she read unspecified titles by Balzac, and by Eugène Sue, although Flaubert disparagingly suggested that her main interest lay in the details Sue provided of the latest furnishings in the fashionable houses of the *faubourg* St Germain. She is finally described reading George Sand, the novelist most clearly identified by nineteenth-century readers with openly extra-marital relationships and the flouting of the rules of conventional marriage.[25] At the same time, she measured the distance between her aspirations and her husband, who knew nothing of novels, who desired nothing, who excelled at nothing in particular, and who snored into the bargain. Why, asked Emma, 'could she not be leaning out on the balcony of a Swiss chalet, or hiding her sadness in a cottage in Scotland, with a husband wearing a long-tailed black velvet coat, and soft boots, a pointed hat and frills on his shirt!'[26] She became enamoured of the glamorous life of Paris, and subscribed to journals which told her of first nights at the theatre, race meetings, the latest fashions. She dreamed of another life of luxury, balls and fine clothes, fuelled always by her reading:

> She had bought herself a blotting-pad, a writing-case, a pen-holder and envelopes, though she had nobody to write to; she would dust her ornaments, look at herself in the mirror, pick up a book, then, dreaming between the lines, let it fall into her lap. She yearned to travel or go back to living in the convent. She wanted equally to die and to live in Paris.[27]

Emma felt nothing was going to happen in her life: 'The future was a dark corridor, and at the far end the door was bolted.' Her reading and her ambitions had brought her to a dead end. 'I've read everything,' Emma decided in despair.[28]

Flaubert is careful to contrast Emma's reading with the pragmatic reading of her husband Charles, who reads only his medical journal, *La Ruche médicale*. The dangers of women's reading were clearly charted by Flaubert, from the innocent sentimentality of the eighteenth-century novel, via the historical novel of Walter Scott, through the heady melodramas of the 1830s and 1840s, to Sand, the culminating symbol of female sexual freedom. Flaubert led Emma through a Dante-like descent into ruin, which demonstrated the folly of romantic illusions. Novels constituted significant landmarks along the journey.

Emma Bovary's liaison with Léon significantly began with a discussion of the joys of fiction reading. 'You melt into the characters', Léon told her, 'it seems as if your own heart is beating under their skin.' Emma agreed enthusiastically, adding 'I adore stories that push on inexorably, frightening stories. I detest common heroes and temperate feelings, the way they are in life.'[29] Once again, romantic fiction reading provides the vocabulary for Emma's seduction. Léon read her poetry and looked at fashion magazines with her.[30] For Léon, too, his mistress Emma was 'the lover in every novel, the heroine in every play, the vague *she* in every volume of poetry.'[31] In Léon's absence, Emma cannot concentrate. She tried to learn Italian and to read some history and philosophy, but is unable to finish anything she reads.[32] She imagines herself in love and no reading can now rescue her from her moral dilemma. Later, Emma's relationship with the callous seducer Rodolphe is similarly punctuated with references to her reading, as she recalls the heroines from her books, and feels that the dreams they conjured up may at last be realized.[33] Emma's disillusion was inevitable, as she discovered that she was in love not with a man, but an image from her books. Her lover was a shadow. Emma 'was rediscovering in adultery the platitudes of marriage.'[34]

Madame Bovary no doubt deserves its reputation as a landmark in the history of realism. It is usually seen as a novel of bourgeois marriage and female transgression. We may equally read it as a novel about reading itself, and more particularly, about women's reading. It suggests the power of reading to shape the reader's emotional experiences, and to provide the reference points for interpreting the reader's relationships with others. In Emma Bovary herself, Flaubert created a thoroughly consistent representation of women's reading, in which romance reading engendered *ennui* and dissatisfaction with a pedestrian husband and a mediocre provincial existence. Emma's reading led her to seek fulfilment in erotic and passionate affairs. Her reading experience also helped to distort her opinion of the two men with whom she became obsessively involved. Neither of them lived up to the status of romantic hero. Emma Bovary was an archetypal reader who crystallized the problems of what we may call *bovarysme*.

The view of the novel as an aphrodisiac certainly devalued women's literary culture. It assumed their responses could be easily shaped. Women were thought particularly prone to 'surrender' to a novel, because their style of reading rested on a close emotional involvement with the characters. Natural sympathy was an inherent feminine quality, and it produced an identificatory style of reading. There is little doubt, for instance, that female readers of Balzac were very involved with some of his works, because they wrote copiously to the author, sometimes to praise and sometimes to condemn him. Balzac is thought to have received 12 000 letters from female readers, of which unfortunately fewer than 200 survive.[35] He produced a strong reaction from women readers with *Physiologie du mariage* in 1829, and later with *La Vieille Fille* in 1836. Most of Balzac's female correspondents were Parisian, and an unusual number were older women.[36] Perhaps this is not surprising to those familiar with Balzac's personal relationships with women, but it sets him apart from Michelet, for instance, who attracted letters from much younger women after the appearance of *L'Amour* and *La Femme*.[37] Not all women readers had 'surrendered' to Balzac's charm. On the contrary, many wrote because his cynicism had irritated or infuriated them. Whether they loved or hated him, however, a strong bond had been formed between Balzac and thousands of female readers.

The Catholic reading model

In the last 30 years of the nineteenth century, two clear responses to the dangers of *bovarysme* emerged. One of these came from the Catholic Church, and the feminist critique later provided an alternative reading model for women. They will be considered in turn. The Catholic view of women's reading, firstly, must be situated within continuing arguments about the secularization of education in France. For instance, the teaching orders and a number of bishops were mobilized in 1867, when the imperial education minister, Victor Duruy, planned to introduce courses for girls at secondary level. Duruy aimed to abolish 'the intellectual divorce' between husband and wife. The clerical response was led by Monseigneur Dupanloup, Bishop of Orléans, who became a prolific writer on the theme of women's reading.[38] Dupanloup argued that it was unsuitable for young girls to be taught by male professors, and he objected to any kind of instruction which was liable to undermine the Catholic faith. Dupanloup fully subscribed to the dominant domestic ideology. Public affairs, he held, were the male domain, and moreover this was inscribed in the divine order of things. Women had other, more private concerns and the State should not interfere with them.[39] Duruy's attempts to broaden girls' education failed. They met strong resistance in conservative and legitimist circles, and they were dropped when Duruy left office in 1869. The controversy had made clear the Catholic insistence that a woman's literary culture should be subordinated to her role as mother, housekeeper and organizer of charitable works.

Dupanloup, however, saw female education as essential if the Catholic Church was to regain its true position in French society. In 1849, he had been a member of the extra-parliamentary commission set up to prepare the Falloux Law, which promoted the establishment of girls' schools in provincial France. 'Women must be trained [*il faut former les femmes*]', he later wrote, 'especially women who belong to the agricultural and industrial classes, not for science or for public life, but for the household and the inner life.'[40] This could be achieved through intellectual endeavour. Private study, for Dupanloup, could reinforce the woman's sense of domestic duty. Instead of leading women to reject domesticity and to seek an escape from boredom, studying was important in instilling the need to care for a husband, children and the poor. Here was *bovarysme* in reverse: reading would persuade women to accept their domestic destiny, not seek fulfilment elsewhere. Housework, Dupanloup admitted, could be boring; but study was the best consolation.[41] A woman, he thought, should not feel like a servant in the home. In addition, reading would prevent the spread of 'impious doctrines', by which Dupanloup principally meant Darwinism. 'In the divine struggle', Dupanloup pronounced, 'an ignorant woman, however pious, is a useless soldier.'[42]

Too much education, of course, could be as harmful as ignorance. Women should become serious and intelligent without becoming bluestockinged *femmes savantes*. There was no need, for instance, for women to bother themselves with science, which would hardly be within their competence.[43] Men, however, wrote Dupanloup, did not have a monopoly of human intelligence, and a woman's reading should find a *juste milieu*, which would steer her away from frivolous pursuits and idle temptation. Idleness, of course, was a vice of the well-off, and for Dupanloup, the campaign to rechristianize France had to start by reversing the indifference of the rich.

His writings prescribed a programme of reading for women, as well as directions on how to read. Dupanloup's suggestions were entirely orthodox. The Catholic reading model for women placed great emphasis on the classical authors of the seventeenth century. Dupanloup recommended a course of Bossuet and Pascal, the *Lives of the Saints*, Bourdaloue and Massillon, who was ideal for Lent, together with Fénélon, Racine, Corneille, La Bruyère, Molière and Madame de Sévigné.[44] More modern writers could be effectively forgotten, except perhaps for the hardy perennial *Catéchisme historique*, an eighteenth-century work by Fleury. Massillon's *Petit Carême* had fallen out of fashion since the Restoration period, but Fleury's catechism was a familiar bestseller throughout the first half of the nineteenth century.[45] Dupanloup was in this instance recommending the most consulted catechism in France, sold by *colporteurs* and used in primary schools. For Dupanloup, some philosophy was also acceptable, as long as Taine and Renan were avoided. Shakespeare and Milton were recommended, too, but essentially Dupanloup advised a strong dose of pious reading and Christian apologetics. This was to be the antidote to dancing, idle gossip and English romantic novels.

The Catholic reading model, as outlined by Dupanloup, did not confine itself to a list of recommended reading. Dupanloup was equally concerned to advise women *how* to read. Reading was to be undertaken carefully and seriously. The reader should go to bed early, and read the next day when her mind was fresh. In other words, reading should be planned ahead. Superficial or extensive styles of reading were criticized. It was important, Dupanloup advised, 'not to flit [*voltiger*] from book to book, from subject to subject.'[46] Books should be read to the end, not abandoned from lack of interest. Dupanloup emphasized the need for perseverance, suggesting that reading required some intellectual effort if it was to be truly rewarding. Moreover, books should be re-read, so their lessons could be fully appropriated. Re-reading would be difficult for short-term book-borrowers, who needed to return their books to a lending institution. Dupanloup clearly assumed here that he was addressing an audience of book purchasers. This was another sign that he was targeting the wives and daughters of the wealthy bourgeoisie.

Dupanloup's ideal female reader was an active and responsive reader who criticized what she read, taking notes and using a commonplace book to record striking quotations. She was encouraged to read with pen in hand, and to record a summary with personal comments. A reading journal should be taken seriously, otherwise it could easily degenerate into a frivolous diary, a personal *mauvais roman*.[47] Traditional Catholic suspicions of women who wrote were obviously redundant. Keeping a personal journal was now seen as an aid to piety and constructive reflection. Moreover it had a confessional function and it answered important spiritual needs. Dupanloup criticized men who tried to prevent women from writing. He even recommended that women should keep *two* simultaneous journals. One would be a personal *journal intime*, recording thoughts, confessions and presumably the reading notes he had prescribed. The other should be for family purposes, to record the family's activities, memories and visits to places of interest.[48] Although women would put the needs of their marriage first, Dupanloup suggested devoting at least two hours per day to intellectual work. Women could find plenty of time for this, if they would only spend less time talking and dressing.[49] Once again, he was addressing bourgeois women with leisure time to spare.

In many ways, this Catholic reading model constituted a genuine attempt to extend the intellectual horizons of the bourgeois housewife. She was urged to learn more about history, geography, art and literature, philosophy and agriculture, not to please her husband but for her own sake. Dupanloup wanted to give women a more solid intellectual underpinning to the empty rounds of social visits, the theatre, the races and discussions about clothes. He prescribed a more serious and intensive style of reading, which eliminated almost all novels and the 'skimming' style of reading he apparently associated with contemporary fiction. Behind his advice lay the dawning realization that the rechristianization of French society could not be built upon female ignorance. It should instead rest on a return to Bossuet and the Catholicism of the seventeenth century. There was no place in Dupanloup's reading model for contemporary novels, Darwinism or positivist philosophy. Readers were ordered away from these taboo areas.

In formulating this pious Catholic reading model for women, Dupanloup was trying to shape what we might call, following the literary critic Stanley Fish, an interpretive community of readers.[50] A reading community, thus conceived, is not a physical community, since its members may not even know of each other's existence. But the members of a reading community share a common sense of what constitutes literature and what makes it worth while. They have similar preferences for one genre over another, for example in this case they might prefer sermons to *romans-feuilletons*, Bossuet to Eugène Sue. A reading community has a similar view of the hierarchy of literary genres, in this case for example the contemporary novel would be very low on its scale of priorities. Dupanloup was attempting to define the values and common interpretive strategies of the group of readers he was addressing. In a way he regarded this group as a kind of counter-community, formed to resist powerful contemporary trends towards the consumption of sensational novels promoted by unscrupulous, profit-hungry publishers.

The feminist reading model

Thirty-five years later, the feminist press proposed another reading model for women, and outlined the contours of another possible reading community. Although it rarely expressed support for Catholicism, the women's movement had certain things in common with Dupanloup's advice of the late 1860s. For example, feminism took women's reading very seriously, and wanted to use it and direct it in order to minimize female ignorance about the realities of the world. Like Dupanloup's advice, feminist reading models were normally addressed to women of the educated bourgeoisie. There, however, the similarities between them end. For the feminist reader was encouraged to be an independent woman, a 'New Woman', with an active role in the public arena.

La Femme nouvelle, published by Nathan twice a month in 1904–6, encapsulated one ideal of the woman reader of the future. This illustrated journal, which consisted of 64 pages per issue, was written mainly by teachers, many of them men, and its audience was primarily women schoolteachers and *directrices d'écoles*. It also carried a supplement entitled *La Femme universitaire*, which included educational news.

Although the journal did not indulge in any religious or anti-religious polemic, it supported the lay education system, within which it sought a readership. It carried political news, which certainly had not been on Dupanloup's agenda for women's reading, articles on art, education and science, stories and book reviews. It ran a series entitled *Chronique littéraire* which was explicitly feminist, including articles on 'Women in romantic literature', and 'The contemporary woman in the work of George Sand'.[51]

The cover illustration of *La Femme nouvelle* always showed a woman reading. At first her body language was serious and severe. The pale green cover showed a well-dressed young woman sitting on a terrace, reading a book propped up before her on a table. She is seen in half-profile, in a stiff and serious pose, with a very straight back. Later, in 1905, the journal invited readers to propose a new design, and the cover took on a slightly more relaxed character, without however losing its emphasis on the female reader. Instead of green, the cover turned pink, showing a woman from behind, holding a copy of *La Femme nouvelle*, watching the sunset. The rather grave reading posture, which indeed had suggested a schoolmistress, had softened. Was the pink sunset perhaps a concession to romanticism? At any rate, the winning designer, a male reader from the Ecole des Beaux-Arts in Montpellier, won a basket of champagne.

The reading model proposed by *La Femme nouvelle* was one for an independent woman, not necessarily married, who was interested in art and politics, shared the journal's pacifist sympathies and was concerned about issues of sexual inequality. 'What Should We Read?', asked Madame Roy, a teacher from the Nancy *lycée*, in two revealing articles.[52] The reader, she urged first of all, should be discriminating, and directed. A woman should not indulge in casual reading (*lectures hasardeuses*) and should avoid reading hither and thither (*à tort et à travers*). This was the New Woman's answer to *bovarysme*: the unrestrained reading of *romans-feuilletons* was dangerous at a young age, Roy agreed, because it could encourage romantic illusions. Such illusions gave rise to false expectations, and women risked great disappointment later, when the stark realities of married life became apparent. Roy told the cautionary tale of a woman who had been the victim of unrealistic expectations aroused by indiscriminate reading:

> Marriage was like a cold shower to her – now, she is a very down-to-earth matron, incapable of gaiety and inner happiness, a diligent but morose companion to her husband. The contrast between dream and

reality has deadened her soul. – A deplorable outcome, certainly due to intemperate reading in her early youth.[53]

Half a century after the appearance of Flaubert's novel, feminism was still continuing the dialogue with *bovarysme*. This time, however, the remedy was not greater piety, but female independence and a clearer understanding of the world.

For *La Femme nouvelle*, reading could counteract the two traps of ignorance and romanticism. Wrapping sensitive girls in cotton wool would be counter-productive, Roy argued. There was no point in treating adolescent girls like pure and precious darlings (*petites oies blanches*). If deprived of dubious literature, they would simply read it secretly and imbibe false ideas about life.[54] What girls needed was the truth, not a protective cocoon which condemned them to a life of eternal embroidery in a stuffy drawing-room. Roy outlined her own childhood reading, which, surprisingly, overlapped quite considerably with the Catholic reading put forward by Dupanloup. First, when aged between 11 and 13, she had read the gospels and *L'Imitation de Jésus-Christ*. Corneille and Racine had given her a dose of moral heroism in her adolescence. From Pascal, she had learned something of 'the agony of fate' (*l'angoisse de la destinée*). The canonical authors of the seventeenth century were inescapable. Then came a turning-point. At the age of 16, Roy read Quinet's *Histoire de mes idées*, which presented her with a stimulating intellectual challenge, and 'saved' her from romantic literature, as represented by Byron, Lamartine, De Staël, Châteaubriand and Michelet. In Vigny's *Destinées*, she found a more fruitful kind of reading, teaching self-restraint, stoical resistance and moral idealism.

This feminist reading model, then, set itself firmly against the immersion in romantic fiction with which this chapter opened, and which remained the essence of conventional stereotypes of the female reader. The function of reading, in this model, was to open girls' eyes to a world in which they should aim to be active. It should counteract the lure of romanticism. Roy wrote: 'Reading is an extension of social life: just as in society we avoid contact with disease for fear of contagion, so let us also preserve young minds, not yet strong enough, from the contagious heroes of unhealthy novels.'[55]

At different moments in the nineteenth century, therefore, various representations of the female reader competed for her attention. Some representations, like the romance reader ripe for literary seduction, were negative, while others outlined above attempted to mould a more purposeful, godly or self-aware female reader. What these reading models shared was an assumption that women's reading was a social problem. Never before had women's reading attracted so much attention from novelists, publishers and clerics, or from parents, anxious to stop their daughters wasting their time and to protect them from dangerous illusions or erotic excitement. The female reader appeared more frequently in literary fiction, and in Emma Bovary, Flaubert imagined a reader whose presence seemed to hover over all subsequent debate on the dangers of misdirected female reading.

Visual artists also produced frequent representations of women reading. They recur constantly in the work of Manet, Daumier, Whistler and Fantin-Latour. In some cases, nineteenth-century painters described reading as a part of bourgeois female sociability, as in Fantin-Latour's *Les Deux Soeurs* (1859). This much-discussed representation of women reading, however, is itself difficult to read.[56] On one level, the two sisters illustrate a familiar scene of women reading to each other while engaged in sewing. Nathalie may well be listening to her sister Marie reading aloud to her in this painting, but her distracted vacant look may signify that she is not in fact listening at all. We know that Nathalie suffered from schizophrenia and was committed to Charenton not long after this painting was completed. There is therefore an ambiguity about the relationship between Marie, the reader, and her sister Nathalie. Instead of bringing them together, the act of reading may be doing just the opposite – dividing the sisters and isolating one from the other.

Whistler, among others, represented women reading alone. He portrayed his half-sister reading at night with a lamp and a cup of coffee beside her, a very modern image of reading, in a bourgeois environment (*Reading by Lamplight*, 1858). Usually, however, Whistler's female readers adopt a languid pose, as in *The Siesta*, in which the painter's wife is stretched out on a bed with a book on her lap. Reading here seems a casual activity, in which the book may encourage daydreaming, but rarely grips the reader.

It is in the work of Henri Fantin-Latour that we find the most consistently sympathetic portraits of women reading in the nineteenth century. Fantin-Latour also painted women reading alone, concentrated and quietly absorbed by their reading – a pink-covered journal in the case of his *Portrait of Victoria Dubourg* of 1873, which is possibly a copy of the literary and political journal, the *Revue des deux mondes*. In other portraits, such as *La Liseuse, portrait de Marie Fantin-Latour* (1861), and *La Lecture* (1863), the painter represented a serene and focused style of female reading. These women readers are enjoying, it should be said, the kind of peace which was only possible in a well-to-do bourgeois household. They could afford the time to sit down and read in tranquillity. Unlike many artistic representations of women reading, by Renoir, Whistler and other painters, Fantin-Latour's women are not flippant readers, nor does their text send them into a romantic rêverie. Like Charlotte Dubourg, the subject of *La Lecture*, they are active and attentive readers. Portrayals of reading women in visual art reflect the development of individual, silent reading, and the disappearance of oral reading. Paintings of solitary women reading invite us to regard the nineteenth-century bourgeois woman as a pioneer of new notions of privacy and the intimate life, in which private, individual reading was central.

With Manet, men and women reading are represented quite differently. In his *Liseur* of 1861, the artist Joseph Gall is painted in the style of a Tintoretto self-portrait, deep in a large-format heavy volume, in a meditative posture. He is a bearded, paternal figure, absorbed in serious and erudite reading. Manet's *Lecture de l'illustré* of 1879, however, presents a contrasting image of the modern woman reader. A young elegantly dressed woman is sitting on the terrace of a café, flipping through the pages of an illustrated magazine. There is no visible sign of concentration on her face, for she reads purely for recreation and pleasure, her eyes wandering from the page to take in the spectacle of the city street. Here we are not very far away from the enduring figure of the woman as the consumer of light and trivial reading matter. The erudite male reader, the superficial female reader – Manet's prejudices were general and persistent. In the next chapter, some individual examples may suggest how far women readers either accepted or challenged the dominant discourse on the problem of female reading.

5
Reading Women: Defining a Space of her Own

The conventional opinions about women readers discussed in the previous chapter no doubt corresponded in part to the realities of social and cultural life in nineteenth-century France. The reading models reviewed both partially reflected reality and also shaped some of the ways in which women approached their reading. This chapter aims to explore that reality further through the experience of actual readers. It will introduce Catholic readers, romantic-fiction readers and women seeking a distinct space of their own, who all have something in common with those hypothetical images of women readers previously outlined. We will also encounter women who accepted and internalized the notion that there was an inherent conflict between their desire to read and their inescapable household duties. There were women readers, in other words, who seemed to fit the stereotypes. Nevertheless, the individuality of the reader's response must never be overlooked. Women, like other readers, found ways of resisting attempts to control them, as they negotiated their own reading space in a world frequently hostile to their intellectual freedom.

The principal case studies of female reading practices on which the following commentary is based tend to come from the later part of the century. Eugénie de Guérin, who recorded her reading experiences between 1834 and 1841, is the exception. Hélène Legros's correspondence provides another rich case study of a woman reader, covering the period from 1892 to 1898. Louise Weiss offers further insights into women's reading practices between approximately 1890 and the First World War. In addition to this cast of major characters, we will also hear from some anonymous readers who recalled their experiences of childhood and youth in the Belle Epoque. All of them were individual personalities who experienced, in different degrees, the constraints and prejudices surrounding women's reading.

As Janice Radway has reminded us, readers have many ways of subverting the gender norms promoted by mass culture. The romance readers she examined in mid-west America formed their own sustaining community of women readers, for whom romance reading signified a temporary refusal of their reproductive and domestic roles.[1] When they sat down to read, they put aside household tasks and asserted their right to an autonomous space. Instead of focusing solely on the texts of their romance reading, Radway considers the whole context of their reading practices in order to interpret their reading as an act of independence. Silhouette and Harlequin readers were conscious of belonging to a female community of readers, which was broad enough also to include the female writers who created the romances. They bought a brand-name product, but they were also familiar with the names and styles of individual authors who wrote for the genre. Radway was able to suggest that even the practice of reading romance novelettes was a mild form of female resistance. These books were enjoyed by critical women readers, many of them young mothers, who demanded the freedom to withdraw for a time from the physical and emotional demands of husbands and children. We must therefore take account of the autonomy of the reader. Reading is an active process, to which the reader brings interpretive strategies reflecting the cultural capital she has or has not accumulated. The reader re-works and re-imagines what she reads to produce meanings and associations which cannot be predicted in the text itself or in advice literature. This chapter suggests ways in which women readers accepted, subverted or compromised with the many constraints on their reading practices.

The evidence used by Radway came from interviews with 42 women readers, together with their responses to supporting questionnaires. Oral history testimony can also provide us with recollections of reading experiences from the period before 1914. But most of the evidence of nineteenth-century reading practices comes from women's published writing. Various kinds of writing are represented by the main case studies. Eugénie de Guérin wrote a well-known *journal intime*, Hélène Legros maintained a long correspondence with her friend Berthe Willière, while Louise Weiss wrote an autobiography. A few preliminary comments about these sources are necessary.

Most women's correspondence and diaries remain unpublished and inaccessible to us. A great deal of female autobiographical writing was probably destroyed by its authors, because they had never written it with publication in mind. The surviving journals of many adolescent girls come to a halt when they married, and we may speculate that many other women destroyed their previous writings at such moments of personal transition. Most women had little prospect of publishing unless they had an influential male sponsor, or they published at their own expense, as the *communarde* Victorine Brocher eventually did with her memoirs long after she had escaped from France.[2] Women's diaries have also been seen as a kind of safety-valve for the repressed victims of the nineteenth-century bourgeois family.[3] Solitary writing was a retreat into an interior monologue for those who were forced to be silent in public, or who perhaps found communication difficult. Adolescent girls and married women could thus enjoy an emotional outlet which they dared not reveal to fathers or husbands. Diaries were characteristically secret, like the one written by Eugénie de Guérin in hiding and at night to avoid detection by her father. 'My little notebook', she wrote, 'must never see the light of day. This is sacred like the secret of the confessional.'[4] A woman's diary contained a secret life of which her husband was ignorant or perhaps jealous. As Béatrice Didier has suggested, it might even fulfil a masturbatory function.[5] Fear, repression or self-censorship: these were all possible barriers to women writing publicly about themselves. Louise Weiss is the exception to the rule here, because she had a public persona, and her autobiography was far from secret. It went into many editions.[6]

The personal diary or *journal intime* was principally a middle-class genre. Working-class women rarely had the time required to sustain a private diary over a long period. A few wrote autobiographies later in life, like their male counterparts, after they had achieved success as a militant, journalist or teacher. We know far less, therefore, about the reading practices of working-class women, unless they had a political career. The process of cultural appropriation, according to Pierre Bourdieu, depends on the balance between an individual's economic capital, and his or her educational capital.[7] In other words, the cultural goods we consume and cherish are determined by our income level and the level of schooling we have attained. It follows from this formula that most workers were doubly disinherited, being both poor and lacking in educational qualifications. The working-class woman reader, deficient in both inherited and acquired cultural capital, was forced to accumulate it through her own efforts, and by unorthodox means. Excluded from the kinds of cultural consumption enjoyed by the well-off, and even by the male members of her family and class, she inevitably became a usurper of cultural property. She was an interloper who had been denied access to an envied cultural world.

The Catholic reader

Women's reading was often of a devotional kind, associated with traditional Catholic practices. At the same time, women were the guardians of family traditions and rituals. When Pierre-Jakez Hélias recalled his Breton childhood in Plozevet, Finistère, he remembered his mother and her books. The *Lives of the Saints*, he remembered, was part of his mother's *trousseau*. 'In the house,' he wrote in his bestselling memoir,

> besides my mother's prayer books and a few collections of hymns, there were only two important books. One, which always stood in its place on the window-sill, was Monsieur Larousse's French dictionary ... the other was locked away in my mother's wedding chest, which we called 'the press'. It was the *Lives of the Saints*, written in Breton.[8]

Several cultural dichotomies were intertwined here. The *Lives of the Saints*, or *Buhez ar zent* in Breton, belonged specifically to Hélias's mother, and her wedding chest was a hoard of religious knowledge. This contrasted with the Larousse dictionary, which was an emblem of lay culture and reading. One stood for Catholic France, the other for secular republicanism. There was another cultural layer to this duality, connected to the use of the Breton language. Hélias's mother's chest was Breton-speaking territory, whereas the window-sill, with its Larousse, sounds like an altar raised to the French language. Unlike the saints locked away in the chest, the dictionary was by the window, looking out on the world. Thus the contrasts all overlap in Hélias's description between French and Breton, male and female, the secular and the sacred. His mother's reading was traditional, turned towards religion, the family and the local, enclosed world of Breton culture. It seemed not at all connected with public life or the concerns of the outside world.

Eugénie de Guérin, whose journal is one of the main case studies for this chapter, offers a more detailed view of female religious reading. Her world was far removed in social terms from that of the Breton peasantry. She wrote between 1834 and 1841, in her early thirties, on the family property at Le Cayla in the Tarn. Her mother had died when Eugénie was a teenager. Her father was a comfortable farmer (*cultivateur*), with several sharecropping tenants (*métayers*). Her *journal intime*, in which she recorded her reading, shows her to be almost a real-life model of the Catholic woman reader Dupanloup was later to hold up as an ideal. For this reason, it has been reprinted many times, as an exemplar of the spiritual life.

Eugénie wrote her journal firstly for God, but secondly for her brother Maurice. Indeed, her love for Maurice before and after his death informs the whole journal, and makes the later part harrowing to read. This close relationship with Maurice gives it a completely individual character. Eugénie wrote in notebooks and when a notebook was finished, she would edit it and send it to Maurice in Paris. When the journal was interrupted for a few months between July 1837 and January 1838, it was because Maurice was actually visiting Le Cayla and written communication with him was redundant. Eugénie was utterly overwhelmed by Maurice's death from tuberculosis in 1839. She went on writing to him in her journal regardless, vowing she would mourn him eternally, and writing that her journal would become 'a funeral chest, a reliquary where a dead heart is to be found, embalmed with holiness and love'.[9] For a time, her reading helped her to deal with her loss. She turned for consolation to St Augustine's *Confessions* for the section on the death of his friend.[10] She also referred to the *Saints Désirs de la Mort*.[11] At this time, her reading had a specific mourning function. In the light, however, of her continued attempt to commune with Maurice's soul, it is not clear how far reading and writing helped Eugénie accept her brother's death, and how far they were a refuge where she avoided coming to terms with it at all.

This is psychological speculation. Although Eugénie seems to have adopted Maurice's friend, the writer Barbey d'Aurevilly, as a kind of substitute brother, God increasingly filled the void Maurice left in her emotional life.[12] God had never been absent. Her journal and her reading had always had a spiritual purpose. She used the journal to confess her faults. In it, she tried every day to account for her day to God. Through her notebooks and her reading she conducted a solitary conversation with her own conscience. Her writing and reading were the keys to a rich interior life, in which she sought to make her existence useful, to contemplate death and draw nearer to God.

Through the deep religious melancholy of her journal, we can trace Eugénie's reading in detail, both spiritual and secular. In her spiritual reading, she referred constantly to St Augustine, and also to Bossuet. These two authors, above all, were in constant use.[13] She regularly used the *Lives of the Saints*, normally reading the life of the saint of the day. This was a daily source of edification, and Eugénie commented 'These saints' lives are wonderful, charming to read, full of instructive lessons for a believing soul.'[14] She used Massillon as her Lent reading, a conventional choice which once again echoes the ideal reading list later drawn up by Dupanloup, discussed in the previous chapter. Catholic reading followed a seasonal rhythm, as texts were prescribed for specific days and moments in the Catholic calendar. Eugénie read Fénélon's *Lettres spirituelles* and the *Existence de Dieu*.[15] She read works by Père Judde and the abbé le Guillou, and the abbé Quadrupani's *Instructions pour éclairer les âmes pieuses*.[16] Much of her reading, then, consisted of sermons and meditations and was instructional. It was read and re-read, consulted regularly and dutifully at the appropriate time of year. This also emerges from the descriptions Eugénie gave of her own library in 1835.[17] It included St Augustine's *City of God*, although she later wrote that this was too learned (*savant*) for her.[18] Her collection included meditations, reflective monologues, sermons, the letters of St Jerome and of St Gregory, and the writings of St Theresa and St Bernard. She also had Lamennais's *Imitation de Jésus-Christ* and Louis of Blois' *Guide spirituel*. These last works were staples of Didot's *Bibliothèque des dames chrétiennes*, published in the 1820s, but we do not know the precise sources of Eugénie's personal library. These works were the most intimate of her reading, read usually in private in her own room, where she communed privately with God, and wrote her journal.

She read other religious and secular works, too, but sometimes she shared these with her father. Thus she read aloud to him Lingard's *Antiquités de l'Eglise anglo-saxonne*, published in 1806. She read the Gospels, Pascal and Leibnitz's *Confession de la nature contre les Athées*.[19] She read Lamennais's *Essai sur l'indifférence* and the periodical *Annales de la propagation de la foi*.[20] A part of Eugénie's reading therefore was less personal, and included religious apologetics and ecclesiastical history.

So far Eugénie de Guérin has appeared a good example of a pious Catholic reader, for whom reading and writing her journal were integral parts of her private spiritual exercises. But Eugénie also read profane literature, including plays, poems and even novels. This reading, which was not necessarily solitary, brought her closer to her father, with whom she sometimes read novels on long winter evenings. Perhaps her father's presence was a form of protection, a guarantee of the irreproachable moral probity of her reading. In turning to profane literature, and especially to fiction, Eugénie was stepping beyond the norms expected of a devout Catholic woman reader. She was well aware that in so doing she might confront dangerous temptations. The *habitus* of such a profoundly Catholic reader was imbued with spiritual aspirations but threatened by many perils which needed to be resisted. It is interesting to follow her secular reading, in order to define the limits that Eugénie imposed on her own reading both as a woman and a Christian.

Eugénie was interested in Molière's women, and she read *Les Précieuses ridicules* and *Les Femmes savantes*. Unfortunately, we don't know what she thought of them. She even read Voltaire's *Le Siècle de Louis XIV*, although it is interesting that it was her father who acquired this, from the nearby town of Clairac. She was well aware of the implications of dabbling in Voltaire, but she read his historical work 'without too much regret', as she put it.[21] She also read the far more innocuous Bernardin de St Pierre's *Etudes de la nature*.[22] She read romantic poetry, first Lamartine's *Harmonies poétiques et religieuses*, and later some of André Chénier.[23] She read other romantic works, too, by Michelet, as well as Lamartine's *Voyage en Orient*.[24] She enthused over Victor Hugo's *Cromwell* and *Marie Tudor*, and she commented on his work in terms which seemed to mimic Hugo's own love of dramatic antithesis. 'He is divine, he is the devil', she wrote, 'he is wise, he is mad, he is people, he is king, he is man, he is woman, painter, poet, sculptor, he is everything'.[25] Little in the story of Eugénie's spiritual reading prepares us for such an outburst in praise of Hugo. In her mid-thirties, Eugénie read Sainte-Beuve's *Volupté*, Hoffmann's *Contes fantastiques*, and a series of novels by Walter Scott, including *Ivanhoe, Old Mortality (Les Puritains)* and *Waverley*.[26] None of this was seen as a transgression. Rather, Eugénie's personal preoccupations remained constant throughout. What she appreciated most in *Waverley* was the episode of the brother's death at the end.

All the same, novels constituted a form of temptation for the unwary reader. In September 1835, at the age of 29 or 30 (her exact date of birth is not clear), Eugénie had a critical experience, which demonstrated the strength of this temptation and her capacity to resist the forbidden fruit. Wandering through her grandmother's house at Cahuzac, Eugénie stumbled across a case of novels, and was tempted to sample them. The account she wrote of this moment is worth citing in full. Here is what Eugénie recorded in her journal soon afterwards:

> The devil tempted me just now, in a little cabinet where I came across a stack of novels. 'Read a few words of them, I said to myself. Just to look at this one or look at that one', but I didn't like the title at all. It's worthless stuff, and can teach you nothing except the confusions of the heart of which I am sure I know nothing. They are the love letters of a nun, the general confessions of a gallant knight and other highly fragrant tales. Come on, now, I'm not going to read that junk! I am not tempted by them any more now and I will just change the books or even better throw them on the fire so they can't be used for anything. God preserve me from that sort of reading.[27]

It is just possible that Eugénie did in fact read some of these novels, but used her intimate diary to draw away from them and recover her moral equilibrium. Her rejection of this temptation, however, is perfectly consistent with everything else we know about her. I prefer to believe that Eugénie had recognized a clear limit to her reading explorations. Her religious background and her strong Catholic values imposed a taboo on the fiction she identified as trivial or salacious. She was certainly interested and tempted, but she assured her diary on this occasion that she had repulsed the wiles of Satan.

Temptations recurred, however, for Satan never sleeps. She was strongly attracted by her brother's copy of Hugo's *Notre-Dame de Paris*, and clearly dipped into it, for she responded with pleasure, as so many female readers did, to Esmeralda and her goat. She knew that this was dangerous territory, and she wrote : 'these geniuses have an ugly side which is shocking to a woman's eye'.[28] So she stopped reading the book, and confined herself to looking at the illustrations. Somehow she thought the illustrations would not reveal Hugo's grotesque creations to her. Eugénie had clearly been excited by the prospect of this book. She repeatedly contemplated reading it, but could not bring herself to do it. For her brother, it was perhaps permissible, but for Eugénie there were frontiers which women should not cross. Two years later, she attempted Hugo's *Dernier Jour d'un condamné*, but found it too horrible and abandoned it.[29] Then she considered De Staël's *Delphine*, but she had come to the firm conclusion by now that she was not very interested in novels, except for those of Walter Scott.[30]

Reading was vitally important for Eugénie, almost as important as the *journal intime* which dominated her inner life. She wrote 'I always reach for a book or a pen as I get up in the morning, books for praying, thinking, reflecting'.[31] Housekeeping jobs constantly interfered with her reading, and she was very conscious of the demands on her as a woman. 'I am a woman who reads', she wrote one day in frustration, 'but in fits and starts [*à bâtons rompus*]; sometimes it's a key they want from me, a thousand things, often I am fetched in person, and the book is closed for a while'.[32] Duty comes before pleasure, she insisted, especially before non-essential reading.[33] For 'non-essential' reading, assume books other than devotional or spiritually elevating works. Eugénie would sacrifice reading for her needlework and household management, knowing that the work she did was acceptable in the sight of God.

Eugénie de Guérin read therefore as a woman and as a devout Catholic. Reading and meditating upon her reading were essential for her spiritual welfare. Within the reading space that she claimed for herself, she turned constantly to sermons, devotional works, the writings of the fathers of the Church. She read not for enjoyment but for the salvation of her soul. In moments of great suffering, reading helped her to assimilate the death of her beloved brother. This spiritual reading was intimate and solitary. In her more profane reading, she might seek the companionship of her father, and she did not reject contemporary authors, poets and dramatists. As we have seen, some novels attracted her enormously, but she resisted their appeal which she identified with the devil. As she described such conflicts in her *journal intime*, we can see her as a reader adopting firm rules of censorship for herself. Was Eugénie a representative female reader? The answer must be yes and no. Above all, she was an individual whose experiences were unique. We may see her as an ideal type of Catholic reader, but we must not forget her excursions into Voltaire (parental supervision notwithstanding) and modern novels, which were not on the Catholic agenda. On the other hand, Eugénie is a useful corrective to the influential image of the woman as an irrepressible consumer of romantic fiction. To find more convincing female devotees of the novel, we will have to turn to other examples, and to the case study of Hélène Legros.

A female style of reading?

For many women, indeed probably for most women, the space of their own which they desired would be filled not with spiritual reading, as in the case of Eugénie de Guérin, but with fiction. Publishers knew this, Flaubert knew this, and so did the writers of advice literature, whether Catholic, republican or feminist. Women who read novels, however, were not necessarily passive or uncritical readers who derived impossible notions about life from their reading. One such active and critical novel reader was Hélène Legros. She articulated strong preferences for certain authors and certain modes of writing. Her correspondence over the space of a few years in her early twenties reveals a reader for whom reading fiction generated reflection about the role of women themselves.[34] It also offers interesting insights into the role of male relatives in the reading of bourgeois women. Brothers, fathers, lovers and husbands were sometimes supportive, sometimes restrictive, but always present. When individual women such as Hélène Legros attempted to establish a space of their own, they knew they had to recognize and confront the powerful influences of men.

Hélène Legros was born in 1874, the daughter of a country doctor who lived at Barvaux-sur-Ourthe, near the Belgian city of Liège. When her friend Berthe Willière moved to Neuilly-sur-Seine in 1894, the two began a correspondence which was to last a lifetime. Although it seems the two women never saw each other again, they wrote, sent gifts and shared confidences for almost 40 years, until Berthe's death in 1932. This discussion of Hélène, as I will now call her, and her reading, is based on an edited selection of her letters. Unfortunately the published selection has been framed simply as a love story, involving Hélène and her student friend Jacques. As with many surviving collections of correspondence, only one side of the conversation remains, and we have none of Berthe's responses. Their tone and content have to be deduced from Hélène's letters. In spite of these problems, Hélène's letters are a rich source for the history of individual women's reading practices in the late-nineteenth century.

Hélène's mother was dead. She lived with her father and two brothers, both destined for the medical profession, of whom she was very proud but envious. Maurice was six years younger than Hélène, and Robert was two years older than her. Their role in her brief and unhappy love life must first be sketched in order to establish the context of male supervision which Hélène was forced to negotiate. The only love of Hélène's life was Jacques Divelshauvers, a young medical student and a friend of her brother Robert, in whom she had first become interested in 1891. But Hélène only knew Jacques through her brother, and future meetings between the two depended on Robert. It was four years after their first encounter that Hélène dared to make a move. She enlisted Berthe in a complicated intrigue to pass an 'anonymous' letter to Jacques. Eventually, Hélène and Jacques corresponded with each other, although Hélène clearly understood that Jacques did not reciprocate her love for him. She was fully aware that her life and her personal autonomy were at stake in this relationship, and that the experience of love and disappointment was something stronger and more serious than books could ever give her.[35]

The relationship ended when Hélène's father discovered the correspondence and, in Hélène's version of events, called her into his study for an angry scene.[36] Exactly what was unsuitable about Divelshauvers is not clear, but Monsieur Legros gave his son Robert the task of writing to him to order him to stop writing to Hélène. Through a series of letters involving intermediaries, the men of the family succeeded in stifling the relationship. Robert maliciously tore up in front of Hélène the photograph of Jacques which she had kept for years, and threw the pieces onto the fire.[37] Hélène apparently expressed little anger at all this. She seems to have accepted her fate. She had continued to use Berthe as a secret accomplice to obtain news of Jacques, and she secretly opened her brother's mail in order to discover more about him.[38] But she knew there was no way to circumvent the forces of parental and fraternal surveillance. She used the correspondence with Berthe Willière to express her sorrow and disappointment at the collapse of her dreams, and also to vent her jealousy when Jacques ultimately married another woman. As we shall see, even Hélène's reading was subject to the kind of family control which supervised her correspondence.

Hélène's reading firstly illustrates the way in which women often saw their reading as a social experience. Books were to be shared, between friends, either as gifts or simply as topics of discussion. Sharing literature was an important part of the continuing correspondence between Hélène and Berthe Willière. Hélène would ask Berthe to send her a book on Italian painting which Jacques had recommended to her, and Berthe also sent her *War and Peace* as a gift in 1895. This female network also included their former literature teacher, who sent a copy of Manzoni's *I Promessi Sposi* when she found out that Hélène was learning to read Italian.

Books and reading were topics of discussion and reciprocal exchanges between women friends, but access to them depended on male mediators. Hélène's main source of books was always her brothers, who themselves borrowed from friends, or bought books in Brussels or Liège and brought them home. Inevitably, Hélène was at the mercy of their choices, and subject to their censorship of her reading. Occasionally, however, she took their books without their knowledge and she wrote of books 'filched' (*chipé*) from her brother. Hélène's father was also a source of books, for she often came across something interesting in his bookcase. Again, there was something furtive about her taking them. She wrote of books which had to be taken from their hiding place (*déniché*) on the upper shelves. Through a mixture of dependence and subterfuge, Hélène took advantage of her male relatives' privileged access to the city and its books.

Hélène read romantic poetry as a teenager and in her early twenties. She read Lamartine's *Jocelyn* and then *Graziella*, at the time when she thought of visiting Italy.[39] She had portraits of Lamartine and De Musset in her bedroom. She read Leconte de L'Isle and Byron.[40] Reading made her want to write her own poetry. She read the pseudo-Celtic poetry of 'Ossian' in English, knowing that it was the product of a notorious literary hoax, but this simply emboldened her further to write herself.[41] She confessed, however, that reading De Vigny had made her ashamed of her own efforts.[42] She tried writing fiction and drama, without her family's knowledge, and sent Berthe manuscripts to comment on. As Sylvain Maréchal had predicted in 1801, women who read would want to become women who wrote. Hélène's example suggests that, a whole century later, it was still not wise for women to advertise such literary ambitions.

As well as poetry, Hélène read many novels. She read Pierre Loti (*Pêcheur d'Islande* and *Mon Frère Yves*). She read *Manon Lescaut*, and could not understand why it had been considered immoral. She read *Paul et Virginie* and, as she tried to master English, she read two novels of Walter Scott, *The Bride of Lammermoor* and *The Surgeon's Daughter*, simultaneously.[43] She read *War and Peace*, and *Nicholas Nickleby*, possibly in English, commenting to Berthe: 'They drink tea and say the most staggering things [*des choses renversantes*], I am laughing to myself over it all alone'.[44] She read Dumas's *Le Comte de Monte Cristo*, *Le Vicomte de Bragelonne*, and she loved *The Three Musketeers*.[45] As we shall see, other Dumas titles were forbidden her. Hélène was a critical reader who engaged with her reading and expressed strong opinions about it. She appreciated *Werther* enough to denounce Lytton's *Falkland* as a ridiculous copy of it.[46] She thought Loti was a 'poseur' lacking a natural style. She argued with her brother about the role of Marguerite in Goethe's *Faust*.[47] She had distinct preferences, and she was discriminating. Her individual responses could not be taken for granted by her brothers, nor can they be predicted by the historian of reading.

One novel impressed her above all the rest. Hélène's personal masterpiece of masterpieces was Goethe's *Wilhelm Meister*. She first read it aged 18, and immediately re-read it twice. She returned to it again in 1895.[48] She found it a moral book, full of natural observations of people, without, she said, the overblown phrases common in many French novels. Meister was not too worldly, and not too romantic. He offered a balanced model for the ideal life. *Wilhelm Meister* became a yardstick by which she judged other fiction. Hélène classified three kinds of novels in order of preference. First of all, she valued 'those in which the story is not complicated, but which have a mass of reflections, dissertations, short diversions this way and that – of course, that has to be well done and it has to be connected with the theme.'[49] The best example was *Wilhelm Meister*, 'my supreme joy, it's a book you can read a thousand times over.' Second on Hélène's list were novels which proceeded straight towards their goal without reflective asides or deviations, such as those of Mérimée. Finally came purely descriptive novels which said nothing to the reader and which Hélène confessed she would skip-read.

In this brief literary critique of her own fiction reading, Hélène seemed to be outlining the characteristics of what we might call a feminine reading style. She preferred a narrative that was open, not blinkered with its sights fixed exclusively on the race it was about to run. She appreciated reflective interruptions and intelligent diversions. She would probably not have been a devotee of that most masculine of genres, the detective novel, in which the reader may indeed be ambushed by misleading diversions, but remains unaware of them until the conclusion resolves the mystery. Hélène wanted the novelist to take her on interesting excursions along the route, which seemed more important to her than having all aspects of the plot neatly tied up and logically explained.

There were other ways, too, in which Hélène perhaps adopted a distinctly female approach to novels. For example, she had a habit of re-reading them. Some twentieth-century reading surveys have found that women are far more likely than men to return to re-read favourite books.[50] Hélène was no exception. Apart from her frequent readings of *Wilhelm Meister*, she re-read *Pêcheur d'Islande*, and she re-read Taine's *Voyage en Italie* in the *Revue des deux mondes*.[51] Hélène also conformed to the notion that women adopt a strongly identificatory style of reading, engaging and identifying with characters in novels. For example, she imagined the character of Wilhelm Meister and drew his imaginary portrait, which she described as having beautiful black eyes, a high forehead, aquiline nose, witty mouth, a cool look but a good smile, and he blushed easily. And she later admitted the stupidity of feeling this passionate about heroes of novels.[52] In *War and Peace*, she discussed the merits of André and Pierre, and decided she admired André more.[53] Literary appropriation, as Lynne Pearce reminds us, sometimes engages the emotions, and students of the reading process must take account of the reader's pleasures.[54] As in a romance, the reader can be deeply implicated with fictional characters, experiencing devotion, anxiety, and the fulfilment and jealousy associated with romantic love. These ideas seem to fit the way that Hélène entered into her texts. She identified closely with the heroines, admiring those of Goethe above all: 'Dorothy, Charlotte, Marguerite, etc., are admirable; one could not imagine them more perfect, more poetic – and they are all as simple, as naïve, as unlearned as possible.'[55] As this comment suggests, Hélène was no conventional feminist. She rejected the idea of the woman as an intellectual or a scholar. Women, she knew, had special duties, as well as special merits. Goethe more than any other writer had understood this in the natural simplicity of his female characterizations.

As a woman, however, Hélène could not ignore the ways in which the men around her controlled her life. She protested to Berthe that it was no wonder that young girls were keen to be married, 'just to escape the stupid insignificant life they are given almost everywhere'.[56] Hélène's reading, just like her correspondence, was censored by her elder brother and father. Robert locked away Rousseau's *Confessions*, which he did not consider suitable material for young girls. Dumas's *La Reine Margot* was also forbidden her, this time by her aunt.[57] Her reading of *Madame Bovary* provides an interesting case, partly because this was itself a novel about female reading. She read the first part of the novel in a literary journal belonging to her brother in 1893. She expected Robert to be scandalized, but he wasn't, although he had previously forbidden her to read Flaubert's *Tentation de St Antoine*. On this occasion, Hélène had acquiesced.[58] It should be noted that Hélène was then 19 years old and her self-appointed brotherly censor barely two years older. Hélène knew that whatever latitude her brother gave her, her father would certainly be strongly opposed to her reading *Madame Bovary*. Such censorship was not dictated by religious motives: this was a family of anticlerical doctors, who openly discussed Darwinism, and actively supported liberal candidates against the Catholic party at election time. Nevertheless, Hélène's moral purity was a closely guarded family asset. Robert agreed that he would help Hélène on this occasion by procuring her the novel, and leaving it where she could casually read it without anybody else realizing.[59] Hélène consulted her friend Berthe, who disapproved of this plan of deception. Stooping to dishonesty was not the answer. Hélène agreed that Berthe's attitude was the only morally acceptable one, and she resolved not to read a word of *Madame Bovary* unless she had permission.

Once again, Hélène had apparently acquiesced in the parental censorship which she assumed would eventuate. Even with her brother's support, she would not transgress her father's rulings. This was not always her reaction. She defied a family ban on D'Annunzio by reading him regardless.[60] She protested strongly when in 1895 her father 'advised' her to stop reading Dumas's *Les Mohicans de Paris*, at the age of 20. She expressed her fury to Berthe at being treated like a ten-year-old. But she obeyed, saying that although the book was innocent, it wasn't worth fighting over, that it was rubbish and that she had plenty of better ones to read.[61] It's doubtful whether this argument calmed her. Hélène survived by pouring out her rage and humiliation on paper. Her correspondence with Berthe was the outlet for all her domestic frustrations.

Hélène turned to Ibsen. She found him not at all beautiful, but he made her think. While the men in the family were discussing *The Enemy of the People*, Hélène was reading echoes of her own frustrations into *The Doll's House*.[62] Then she read *Wild Duck* in a German translation and found it very beautiful, although she admitted she understood very little in *Brand*.[63] Even though she knew Ibsen was difficult reading, she began to find him indispensable. She told Berthe she was writing an Ibsenian play entitled 'The Slippers' (*Les Pantoufles*) in which there would be plenty of suicides. By 1897, Hélène clearly identified Ibsen with her sense of revolt against her destiny, confined, as the only daughter of the family, to caring for her father and her aunt. The failure of her relationship with Jacques Divelshauvers, as well as the tutelage in which she was held, all contributed to her resentment.[64]

Hélène, I have argued, demonstrated some aspects of what is frequently seen as a specifically female reading approach. She returned often to re-read her best-loved books, which has been statistically shown to be a predominantly female trait. Books and reading were bonds of friendship between herself and her lifelong correspondent Berthe. Reading was a social experience for many women, and exchanging books attached them to networks of female sociability. When Hélène read novels, furthermore, she identified closely with the characters, and it was important to her that she liked or admired them. She also articulated very clearly her preference for novelists who indulged in stimulating asides, rather than those who moved directly to their conclusion by the shortest possible route. Just as her style of reading had feminine characteristics, so did the content. She reflected through her books on her fate and on the social obligations of women. She rejected both the feminist movement and its opposite extreme, the misogyny of Schopenhauer who, she complained, had called women 'this number two of the human species'.[65] In Ibsen's treatment of the issue, she found a writer who challenged her intellectually and, in comparison to whom, her other reading seemed insipid.[66]

At the same time, Hélène was critical and discriminating. In this, she was very far from the vulnerable and easily swayed female reader who figured in contemporary discourse about women's reading. She denounced what was derivative, and she rejected what she found artificial. She expressly distanced herself from romantic exaggerations in her reactions to Goethe. She knew what she wanted in her fiction, but she was always open to new reading pleasures. Like Eugénie de Guérin, her individual responses should not be taken for granted.

The example of Hélène has brought some of the constraints on women's reading in this period clearly into focus. Thwarted in her love life by her father and elder brother, Hélène found that her reading was also restricted, both by them and her aunt. She was subjected to family surveillance which constantly reminded her of her subordinate position in the household. Usually she gave in. She did not wish to anger her father or her brother whom she loved. She depended on them to supply her with books in the first place. She accepted that there were some things she, as a young woman, should not read. On some occasions, she wrote expressing anger or defiance; and on others, she was not entirely above a little ruse. Left entirely alone at home with the housework, on what she called her 'Robinson Crusoe days', Hélène might search her brother's letters for news of Jacques, or dig out a book she was curious about. Resignation, anger and deception were just some of women's possible reactions to men's control. What saved her above all was her correspondence with Berthe. Sometimes Berthe would be enlisted as an accomplice in evading the watchful eyes of her father and brother, as when Hélène persuaded Berthe to write a minuscule message under the postage stamp on her letters, which Hélène would remove with hot water.[67] At other times, the correspondence simply enabled Hélène to express privately what she could never be frank about in public.

The correspondence analysed here illuminates a short period of only about five to six years of Hélène's life. Yet they were crucial years, in which her best friend left for Paris, her search for love failed, and her limited future possibilities became clear. Only with great difficulty did Hélène become accustomed to the obligations her family imposed on her, as the sole carer for her father, her aunt and her brothers. Nevertheless, she did so. In 1895, as if to mark her passage towards this fate, she burned her old diaries and notebooks, and letters from her old teacher, as well as the handkerchief belonging to Jacques which she had kept for several years. 'I felt', she wrote, 'as if delivered of a great weight.'[68] As Hélène accepted all the compromises of female adulthood, her letters to and from Berthe sustained her. Week in, week out, for nearly 40 consecutive years, these two remarkable friends exchanged letters, memories, pressed flowers, books and small gifts. 'It seems', Hélène wrote to Berthe, 'that all the best and the most important part of my life will have been lived through letters, and I regard my right hand as all that is most precious to me.'[69] Berthe Willière died in 1932. A year later, when Hélène was 59, she wrote to Berthe's sister Flore: 'I think quite often of she who was so closely linked with our lives – and sometimes, when the postman comes by in the afternoon, I find myself searching the post as if I still expected to find one of her big blue envelopes.'[70]

Illicit and interstitial reading

The reading experiences of working-class women are far less accessible to us than those of educated women such as Eugénie de Guérin or Hélène Legros. As we have already noted, women of the lower classes were far less likely to discuss reading in their correspondence or their personal diaries, in the improbable event that they wrote such things. Whether we want to consider the reading of working-class women either individually or collectively, therefore, we need to find more ingenious approaches. The techniques of oral history have begun to create a new archive of reading experience, stretching back to the decade of the 1890s.[71] Interviews with elderly readers can produce valuable insights into their reading experiences, and those of their parents' generation.

Their memories are filtered through various lenses: interviewees looking back on their lives often make value judgements which reflect today's priorities rather than past concerns. They are often inclined to report what they imagine the interviewer wants to hear, for each piece of oral history testimony is the product of a process of negotiation between interviewer and interviewee. Informants never recall their experience in a completely transparent or 'authentic' way; they respond to particular questions and their answers are mediated through the process of transcription, editing and publishing. In addition, oral autobiographies tend to revise and re-order the events and perceptions of the past, to make retrospective sense out of a lifetime's confusion and to construct a personal identity out of it. But in this, oral life histories pose the same problems of interpretation as written autobiographies. These reservations, vital though they seem, are not always well remembered by oral historians. Nevertheless, oral testimony does have the power to give a voice to history's silent majority, and it allows us to hear, even in muffled or mediated tones, of the everyday experience of people who have often been marginalized by traditional historiography.

In this perspective, Anne-Marie Thiesse's investigations into lower-class readers before 1914 can help to give a more rounded picture of Frenchwomen's reading. In 1979 and 1980, Thiesse conducted a project on the history of leisure and family life in France between 1900 and 1914. About 100 respondents were interviewed, all born between 1883 and the end of the century. They came from two contrasting locations: a Parisian suburb and the rural, partly mountainous department of the

Ardèche. Their responses illustrated the very wide diffusion of popular fiction, from the point of view of working-class and peasant readers themselves. Thiesse's interviewees testified to a high level of fiction consumption, made possible by newspaper serialization and novels sold in instalments. They also provided clues about women's reading practices which can be compared to what we have already suggested about the reading of bourgeois women.

Just like Hélène Legros and Berthe Willière, the women interviewed enjoyed reading as a social activity, which brought them closer to other women. Books exchanged with friends, or borrowed from them, formed part of the fabric of female networks at all social levels. The *roman-feuilleton*, or serialized novel, was an everyday subject of conversation between women, perhaps in much the same way as conversations about the latest episodes of a television soap opera bring people together today. One shoemaker's daughter, born in the Vaucluse in 1900, reported:

> We passed them [the *feuilletons*] round amongst us women. On Saturday evenings, the men would go to the café, and the women would come round to play cards at our place. The main thing was, that's when we swapped our *feuilletons*, things like *Rocambole* or *La Porteuse de Pain*.[72]

In this way, the popular novel could acquire an enormous 'hidden' readership, going far beyond the purchasers of serialized fiction themselves.

Thiesse's female respondents also made it clear that newspaper-reading practices were determined by gender preferences. Women recalled their fathers reading the political news, while the women were interested in crime reports, *faits divers* and of course the *roman-feuilleton*. In this way, the newspaper could be divided into male and female territories. A woman from the Auvergne, born in 1896, recalled that her father, who was a railway employee, took the socialist *Moniteur du Dimanche*, although he only bought a newspaper once a week since he could not afford it every day. Everyone in the family read the news, the interviewee remembered, but she cut out the *Moniteur*'s *feuilleton* and exchanged it with girlfriends. She recalled 'They were love stories; the *Moniteur*'s serials weren't particularly socialist. My father never read the serial. Oh nooo!'[73] This is not to say, however, that serialized popular fiction was exclusively reserved for women readers. Crime stories such as *Fantomas* were directed towards a male readership, but family dramas and love intrigues had a strong female following.[74]

118 *Readers and Society in Nineteenth-Century France*

The women in Thiesse's survey did not buy books, and usually did not consider reading to have an important educational function, as was more likely to be the case in middle-class households. Their literary culture was borrowed and improvised. Furthermore, there was something secretive about it, as though reading was not a perfectly legitimate activity for working-class women. Several women interviewed reported the practice of cutting out the *feuilleton* from the newspaper every week, and then either sewing or binding together the episodes to form a complete, homemade novel. 'My mother and I', recalled one artisan's daughter from the south-east, born in 1895, 'we would cut the *feuilleton* out of the paper when it was good; we sewed it together to make a little book.'[75] Some journals would encourage this improvised personal library by providing special binders. School prize books were also valued additions to a household library for those who never joined the ranks of the book-buying public. Books could be borrowed from teachers or fellow-workers. The woman from the Auvergne, cited above, explained this:

> There weren't any books in the house: they were too expensive. I had my school prize books from the nuns, but none from the state school. There was a town library; I devoured it, but it didn't have very much. The teachers lent me books for young girls. I used to read on Sunday afternoons, when I went to look after the animals: I didn't have time to read otherwise, because of my lace work. I used to read the serials, the teacher's books, my schoolbooks, or even the Larousse dictionary. I have always read the dictionary regularly. I have even brought it with me to the retirement home.[76]

This reader highlights an enduring problem for working-class women readers: 'I didn't have time to read otherwise', she said, 'because of my lace work.' The demands of work and especially of the home restricted women's reading. This interviewee lived at home with her *patois*-speaking parents, who were small farmers, until her marriage at the age of 28. She worked long hours daily to supplement the family income, giving the finished lace to a dealer who collected her work for a pittance every fortnight. In these circumstances, reading might be a luxury, a furtive pleasure to be enjoyed in moments stolen in the midst of the daily grind. Reading could seem especially illicit when the family was trying to economize on the cost of lighting.[77] The pressure of women's work led many women readers to interpret their own reading activity as reprehensible idleness.

Other oral historians have encountered a similar phenomenon. That is, they have interviewed working-class women who professed a very low opinion of their cultural pursuits.[78] No doubt this is in part a response to highly educated, university-trained interviewers who, with the best intentions, may give interviewees a sense of cultural inferiority. In part, however, it also expresses a common and very real inhibition. Domestic and other work took priority, and women who read may have seen themselves as lazy and indulgent. Women interviewed are inclined to deny that they read at all, although further questioning will often reveal that they read often and regularly. Such readers may have a very clear conception of what constitutes literature, and they define it as something they do not read and have never read. They have a strong tendency to disqualify their own literary culture.

Women's reading thus had to take second place, as it had to compete with other domestic obligations. As we have already seen, even Eugénie de Guérin lamented the fact that her reading was often interrupted by the demands of running her household. As a result, she could read only 'by fits and starts' (*à bâtons rompus*). Working-class women faced this problem even more acutely. They read in the gaps between their work and household duties. Like the Auvergnat woman already quoted, this might mean that they read for a short time on Sunday, or in brief rest periods, or when they were watching livestock. They were forced to use the fragments of time available. Jeanette Gilfedder, in her studies of post-war Italian publishing, has called this 'interstitial reading'.[79] She defines the practice as a particularly modern urban phenomenon, in which commuters devour mini-books produced for consumption on the daily train ride between work and home. Such modern commuters read in the 'interstices' of their busy lives. But we may apply the idea to women's reading as well, as they carved out moments for themselves and their *feuilletons*. Hélène Legros expressed some of the difficulties of women of all social classes, when she complained about having to sandpaper the dining-room furniture all afternoon, to make patés, jams and *boudins* (black puddings), as well as taking tea and coffee to her brothers at whatever time they chose. She understood nothing of their medical studies, but she knew their life, unlike her own, was directed without interruption towards a certain goal, which would give them freedom and purpose. 'I regret not being like them', she wrote, 'and I am furious with my situation as a young girl.'[80] In these circumstances, women's reading, especially in the case of working-class women and housewives, was both illegitimate and interstitial.

120 Readers and Society in Nineteenth-Century France

When the realist painter Bonvin painted peasant women and servant girls reading, as he often did, he showed them briefly interrupting their work to do so. His female subjects are still dressed in their work clothes, their apron and cap, with sleeves rolled up purposefully to address the volume in front of them.[81] Bonvin's paintings have the quality of *reportage*. He takes his figures by surprise, peering over their shoulder from behind, observing their gestures without revealing his presence. His paintings of female readers captured a slice of life, an instant in which they took a break from work. His women are very private readers – inevitably so in the case of the maid spying on her employer's letters in *La Servante indiscrète* (1871). This extreme case perhaps constitutes the 'degree zero' of furtive and illegitimate reading. All Bonvin's working women who read, however, are stealing a moment in the midst of everyday tasks they have interrupted but not completely put aside. They are the ancestors of Gilfedder's interstitial readers on the Milan-Florence express.

The women in Thiesse's survey, she tells us, were 'illiterate readers'.[82] They lacked the kind of critical approach to fiction articulated by Hélène Legros. They rarely remembered the name of the authors of the stories they read. They invested little in their reading. But this is not the whole story. There were those who 'devoured' lending libraries, and who borrowed books eagerly from whatever source they could find. Among Thiesse's own respondents were some women who thought about their reading long enough to feel the need to define a cultural space of their own. One anonymous woman interviewed gave exemplary testimony, and is worth quoting at slightly greater length. She was born in 1899, and lived in a market town in the Somme until just after the First World War. Her background was extremely modest: her father was an agricultural labourer and her mother worked in a hat factory. 'My parents never read books,' she said. But she improvised and borrowed, and she looked back in the following words on those early attempts to acquire a literary culture:

> I went to work in the factory when I was 13. There, when I was about 13 or 14, I swapped little novels with a girlfriend. They were little bound books for 13 *sous* like *Chaste et Flétrie* [*Chaste and Scourged*], *Comtesse et Mendiante* [*Countess and Beggar-Girl*], *Chassée le Soir de ses Noces* [*Thrown out on her Wedding Night*] ... They were little brochures they sold every week, and every story lasted about a year. My girlfriend thought they were wonderful, but I quickly got tired of them ... I was also advised by a friend of my parents, who told me

what books I had to buy. Once he told me to read *Cyrano de Bergerac*. I went to ask for it in a bookshop and they gave me a very difficult book BY Cyrano de Bergerac! Above all, I was given books, during the war, by an officer billeted on us, because we lived in the war zone. He was a Lyon silk-worker who read all day; his supply work was only at night. He used to buy two or three books a day, and he passed them on to me when he had read them; they were novels by Henry Bordeaux, Paul Hervieu, Abel Harmant, Henri Lavedan, Paul Bourget, Marcel Prévost or Gyp. He was careful not to give me sexy books, but I read them secretly! At that time, I also read books by Pierre Loti, Anatole France, Merimée, Hugo...My mother trusted me, and she let me read all I wanted; but all those novels were about the big, wide world, and I missed it. Once I read a novel by Marcelle Tinayre, *La Rebelle*, in which she tells the story of her life. The book caused a scandal, and I was very much criticised by my work-mates because I'd read it. That novel spoke about the emancipation of women, and I liked it a lot'.[83]

We should be wary of such reflections, because unfortunately the voice of the interviewer has been effaced in this transcription of oral testimony. As a consequence, the reader's account may have a more logical and progressive narrative structure than she first provided in answer to questioning. In addition, her testimony relates to the very margins of our period. But nevertheless several features of the reading trajectory she defines seem characteristic of a certain kind of female reading. The first is the exchange of some very familiar popular fiction titles with girlfriends, even though this reader is careful to distance herself from such a reading network. She describes her faltering steps to graduate to something better, and then she acquires a literary capital which is derived purely accidentally, through the intermediary of an army officer who happened to be billeted in her house. She is subject, like so many young women, to the censorship of her reading, both by the soldier and by implication by her mother, too, whose authorization is important. She constructs her reading experience as a steady progression, leading to a greater awareness of the world. Reading novels leads first to the contemplation of horizons beyond her town and her circumscribed life. Her reading leads ultimately, in defiance of the judgement of her peers, to a general consideration of the status of women. Perhaps working-class women who read only serialized pulp fiction, and who rarely if ever bought a book, were unsophisticated readers. This did not mean that their reading was necessarily passive or purely escapist. Examples of individuals who used reading to explore unexpected intellectual paths warn us to hesitate before accepting such general categorizations of women readers.

A space of her own: the problems of a *fille savante*

Some women who rejected traditional female roles turned to escapist reading, as Flaubert's Emma Bovary had done. A few women, however, who established a career in journalism, teaching or in political movements, used their reading differently. Their reading experience was neither introspective nor subjective. Instead, it could ensure their integration into a wider, public culture. Reading helped to introduce women into public or political life. This was increasingly the case in the last 20 years of the nineteenth century, and at the beginning of the twentieth. Of those who left a record of their reading and autobiographical experiences, Suzanne Voilquin became a St Simonian, Victorine Brocher was condemned to death as a *pétroleuse* in the Paris Commune, and Jeanne Bouvier became a unionist.[84] The careers of such pioneers ranged from political agitation to a life in the service of God. They adopted very different paths, but all these careers led women readers into the public arena.

Working-class women autodidacts laboured under multiple handicaps, among them hostile parents, a background of domestic violence and the lack of formal education. In addition, they encountered (but overcame) the exclusion of women from intellectual and public life. They remind us that there were at least two faces of the working-class woman reader. At times, she was a very private reader of romantic and historical fiction. Her reading was subjective and solitary and it nurtured sentimental fantasies which she later rejected. At other times, we find women turning to socialist philosophy, history and political journalism. Women's reading did not always lead them to an interior world of romance, imagination or religious devotion. Instead it could introduce them to political life and revolutionary militancy. At first, for example, Suzanne Voilquin tells us that she enjoyed novels, chiefly those by female authors such as Madame Cottin, Madame de Genlis and Madame de Staël. Like many women readers, she tended to place a higher value on fiction than did men. Voilquin recalled evenings when she read to her mother from novels borrowed from the local *cabinet de lecture*. 'These different works', she wrote, 'exalted love and became accomplices of nature, by stirring up my imagination and filling my heart with unknown longing.'[85] Looking back in her autobiography, however, she would distance herself from this phase of her reading. She felt that all she had derived from this experience were misleading ideas.[86] Voilquin was born in 1801, the daughter of a radical but illiterate hatworker. She worked as a poor *brodeuse* until her marriage in 1825. She joined the St Simonians, in spite of their ambiguous position on female equality.[87] She had a high opinion of motherhood and its moral power, but was constantly frustrated in her own attempts to have a child. She eventually had a child in Egypt, but the baby only survived a few days. Her repeated miscarriages may have been connected to the venereal disease which her husband passed on to her. They separated in 1833 (he left for America with his lover) and Voilquin followed the leader of the St Simonian group, *père* Enfantin, to Egypt, where she learned midwifery. Her personal ambitions thwarted, she could at least assist and nurture other women's children. Like her father, Voilquin had no formal education. Her literary culture had been acquired from her brother, who was a defrocked seminarist, and her first lover, a medical student who introduced her to philosophical literature. She had read Voltaire, Rousseau and Volney as well as St Simonian literature. In spite of her impoverished background and lack of formal education, Voilquin had given herself a political education. In condoning her husband's departure and joining Enfantin, she put into practice her unorthodox ideas on marriage and socialism. She became, within the St Simonian movement, an 'apostle' of female emancipation.

Such women succeeded in blurring conventional distinctions between the public and the private. They resisted and negotiated with fathers, priests and employers, many of whom were threatening and a few inspiring. Some channelled their private rebellion into personal diaries and novelistic fantasies. Reading drew others into thinking about public affairs and social issues.[88] Reading and writing showed the way to personal emancipation, but they also had a socializing function. Reading and writing gave them entrance into organizations in which they could exercise leadership and assume broader social responsibilities. The act of writing an autobiography was sometimes one further step in their struggle to find a voice.

The growth of education eventually gave women of the rural and industrial working classes the opportunity to move into clerical or service-trade jobs. With some schooling, they could become shop-girls, and later typists and teachers, too. They could escape manual labour to graduate into white-collar or professional occupations. French schoolteachers of the Third Republic were particularly good examples of the 'social mutant' as Lejeune called them.[89] Very often from peasant or artisan backgrounds, they took advantage of new educational opportunities to enlist in the expanding state education system. Mademoiselle L., for example, born in the Cher in 1868, related that when the local teacher recommended that she should prepare for a teaching career, her parents could not believe their luck. Her reading and studying had paid dividends for her family. Although rural teachers were still miserably paid, this meant the chance of a permanent release from peasant drudgery. 'My poor parents', Mlle L. recalled, 'must have seen the gate of heaven opening for them. They stuck their foot in the doorway so that it wouldn't slam shut again. For me, it was a kind of fairy tale.'[90] The *instituteurs* and *institutrices* were an upwardly mobile group, whose autobiographies looked back not just on the progress of French education, but also on their personal transition between different social strata.

At this point the story of women's reading and intellectual effort becomes part of a narrative of late-nineteenth-century social mobility which was by no means confined to women. At the same time, reading is also central to the struggle to promote women's social and political interests generally. This chapter closes with a brief case study which develops this connection: the case of Louise Weiss. Weiss's autobiography is a multi-volume work covering the political history of the entire first half of the twentieth century. In the first volume, she describes her education and youthful reading, and it is with this section that we are concerned.[91]

Unlike peasant women who became schoolteachers, Louise Weiss came from a very wealthy background. Born *circa* 1890, she grew up in the household of a rich public official who originated from Alsace. This was a cultured, bourgeois and pro-Dreyfusard milieu. Yet even at this level, as we shall see, Louise encountered some prejudice against women's intellectual work. She enjoyed every possible social advantage. She was educated first at the Lycée Molière in Auteuil, on the extremely comfortable western fringes of the capital. Then she was sent to a boarding school at Bexhill, where she learned and performed Shakespeare. This education of a daughter of the élite was completed by a period in a finishing school in Baden. Louise was well equipped to occupy a place of her own at the most privileged social level.

Not only did she enjoy a rich girl's education, but also it was above all an international education, partly French, partly English and partly German. This cosmopolitan, or at least European, perspective inspired the career she was later to establish. When Louise wanted to improve her English for the *agrégation* examination, which would qualify her to teach, she was not satisfied with half-measures. She went to Oxford to learn the language properly. It was in Oxford in the years immediately before the outbreak of war that Louise experienced an improbable baptism into left-wing political philosophy. There, in student discussions, she discovered socialism and Karl Marx. But she still had plenty to learn: when she later met Léon Blum, she was amazed to find a socialist eating *foie gras*. She visited the Middle East and the Holy Land, her experiences framed by literary references. 'We were living the Arabian Nights,' she wrote.[92] In 1912, she visited Spain in comparative luxury, travelling by car.

Internationalism and foreign travel, as well as her reading, were crucial to her future careers. She became a radical journalist, at first unpaid, but she could well afford it. She was involved in welfare work for disabled soldiers. She was a supporter of post-war Czech democracy, and supported the independence of eastern European states through the journal *L'Europe nouvelle*, for which she became increasingly responsible. She travelled to the Soviet Union and interviewed Trotsky. She rejected Leninism, however, and devoted herself to the public promotion of the League of Nations, which embodied all her internationalist hopes. As she put it, she preferred Geneva to Moscow. Then she devoted herself to one further cause: women's suffrage. At an obvious level, Louise Weiss's careers as nurse, journalist and political campaigner were failures. In the late 1930s, internationalism was a lost cause, and votes for women had to wait until after the war which was Europe's major preoccupation. The death of Louise's lover in combat in 1940 meant the end of her personal as well as her political ambitions. Her autobiography understandably transformed her lover's death into an act of heroic patriotic sacrifice. She joined the Resistance doubly defeated.

On another level, however, Louise Weiss was an unmitigated success. She had taken her place as a woman, if not at the epicentre of European political life, then at least in the forefront of those who commented upon it professionally and who sought to influence its direction. Through *L'Europe nouvelle*, she was involved in *avant-garde* literary and artistic circles which included Cocteau, Picasso and Apollinaire among others. This would have been impossible without her reading and her studies. At home, she had a rich library to draw on. She remembered reading Rousseau's *Confessions*, Châteaubriand's *Mémoires d'Outre-Tombe* and stories for children by the comtesse Ségur. She also discovered the more recent novels of Erckmann-Chatrian, which may have had a particular resonance for a family from Alsace. Her reading tastes were by no means confined to French literature. She read selections from Keats, and she became familiar with Shakespeare while at school in England. She read Tolstoy's *Resurrection*. But what inspired her most of all was the poetry of Emerson. She was the natural reader of the family, and would read aloud to her blind grandfather.

In spite of her eclectic and multi-lingual reading, Louise was not in any way trained for an intellectual career. She, too, struggled to overcome the problems of a *fille savante* in a milieu which systematically obstructed the tortuous path to female independence. In this respect, as Louise's example shows, women from high-status families faced similar difficulties to those from less fortunate backgrounds. Louise left boarding school at the age of 17 with an armful of school prize books. When she arrived home, however, her mother warned her not to advertise her intellectual achievements. Louise recalled her mother's advice many years later in her autobiography:

> When you get in [her mother reportedly said] hide your books. No point in your father seeing them. He is already unhappy enough that the *lycée* turned you into a *fille savante*, whereas your brothers, in their classes, didn't come top in everything. Because you are good at your studies, you are like him and he probably can't bring himself to forgive you for it.[93]

So Louise was sent to Baden, to an Ecole Ménagère which trained young ladies to cook and to keep house. Not only her father but also her mother compared her scholarly progress to that of her brothers and found it inappropriate that she should surpass them. Looking back on this, Louise represented her identity at this stage of her life as a struggle to find an acceptable career in defiance of her family's preconceptions. She rejected everything that the young ladies' finishing school in Baden represented about her future.

At this point, Louise enlisted an ally. She was guided by a former schoolmistress from her years as a *lycéenne*. The female mentor is a familiar figure in the reading biographies of many middle-and upper-class women. The sympathetic schoolmistress recurs in their stories as a powerful role model of an independent, intellectual woman. So it was for Louise who, supported by her teacher's advice, continued her studies in Paris at the Bibliothèque Nationale and resolved to prepare for the highest qualifying test as a secondary teacher: the *agrégation*. Meanwhile, she was still inspired by Emerson, whose work she now read in the original. Before long, Louise was to outgrow both Emerson and her teachers. Yet when Louise expressed an interest in journalism, her aunt was horrified at the thought, crying out: 'A profession! What for? Stay with your mother. The journalism you are dreaming about will degrade you [*te déclassera*].'[94] Once again, a female relative tried to dissuade Louise from studying and looking for a job.

In 1914, Louise achieved the greatest ambition of her youth, passing the *agrégation*. Using the family's money, but through her own efforts and studies, she had scaled the academic heights and a professional life now beckoned. But by now she was more than a match for the education system. When assigned a teaching post in what she regarded as a contemptible provincial town, she arrogantly refused to accept it. This time, in a reversal of attitude for which her autobiography does not prepare us, her father opened a bottle of champagne to celebrate the success of the daughter who apparently resembled him so much. The war of 1914–18, in which many of her friends and acquaintances were slaughtered, marked the end of Louise Weiss's 'première vie'.

Intellectual emancipation demanded a break with the Church. This was the case for militant socialist women like Suzanne Voilquin in the 1830s, and it was true again for Louise Weiss. If religion played any significant part in her life, her autobiography does not show it. Although she was half-Jewish, this too was not important for the story of herself that Louise wished to tell. Louise's reading and upbringing were profoundly secular. The title of her memoirs – *Souvenirs d'une enfance républicaine* – was intended to emphasize this. Later on, Louise significantly became an acquaintance and supporter of the Radical leader Edouard Herriot, whose party made the defence of the secular state one of its central dogmas.

The lives of our three main individual case studies, Eugénie de Guérin, Hélène Legros and Louise Weiss, cover a broad period from the 1830s to the First World War. They describe a wide range of different women's reading practices during and immediately after the nineteenth century. Eugénie de Guérin was a devout and introverted Catholic reader, for whom reading and writing were spiritual exercises through which she identified, confessed and repented her faults, and subordinated her life to God. Hélène Legros, on the other hand, who lived half a century later, was a critical novel reader for whom reading and writing were means of confronting her own destiny as a woman and becoming reconciled to her limited future. Louise Weiss, blessed with many social advantages, went one step further, to defy conventional obstacles and follow a profession. She read widely in different languages and she read and studied in order to establish an independent career.

Each one's account of her reading is embedded in a different kind of historical source. Neither Eugénie de Guérin nor Hélène Legros wrote with publication in mind. Eugénie wrote for God and her brother; Hélène corresponded with a friend whose voice unfortunately remains silent. Furthermore, only an edited selection of her letters has been made available. Louise Weiss's autobiography demands even greater care. There are lacunae and inconsistencies in it. She is reticent about her first, failed marriage, for instance. The role of her father, who makes his first entrance as a tyrannical patriarch but then gladly toasts his daughter's success, remains shadowy. Had he been won over by Louise's brilliance and persistence? Was he reassured by her refusal to take a provincial posting? Had Louise exaggerated his original antagonism towards her plans in order to throw her personal determination into greater relief? We cannot tell. Like all autobiographers, Louise edited and reordered her life, to read it as a consoling narrative of her independence, post-war achievements and the subsequent collapse or postponement of her internationalist and feminist aspirations. The triumphs were her own. The despair was that of a blinded and corrupt world.

The stories of all three women superficially vindicate some arguments of the conventional wisdom on women's reading in the period. The example of Eugénie de Guérin was itself enlisted to define and reinforce Catholic discourse on women's reading in the second half of the century. The unrestrained consumption of fiction by Hélène Legros, and the independence of Louise Weiss, immersed in political debates, also echoed competing reading models of the period. Yet ultimately their reading trajectories challenge broad generalization. There is a core of individuality in each case which remains irreducible, and their practices and responses fail to fit neatly into designated patterns. Through their reading and writing, we can follow them as they extended the scope of their inner dialogue in unexpected directions. Each one tells us something about the difficulties and temptations surrounding female reading practices, which they met with cunning or with compromise, with resignation or with determined resistance, as each in her own way sought to occupy a place of her own.

6
Reading Peasants: the Pragmatic Uses of the Written Word

The landed classes of the early nineteenth century expected peasants to be submissive and to know their place. So the very devout Eugénie de Guérin, on her family's estate in the Tarn, was horrified in 1837 when a labourer dared to argue with the local *curé* about the significance of the Council of Trent.[1] The peasant reader was a new phenomenon. He (such peasants were usually men) constituted a potential challenge to the landowners' traditional perceptions of the social hierarchy, in which the peasant's deference and intellectual dependence had seemed natural and permanent. Then, in the Second Republic, the liberal bourgeoisie registered the alarming progress which socialist, legitimist and bonapartist literature had made amongst the newly enfranchised subordinate classes. Substantial peasant support ensured Louis-Napoleon's comfortable election to the presidency in December 1848. Three years later, rural resistance in the south-eastern departments challenged the bonapartist seizure of power in the name of 'La République démocratique et sociale'. The 1848 Revolution produced a mass experience of political participation which did not turn out as the liberals expected. The 'excesses' of the 1848 Revolution were frequently blamed on the diffusion of obscene and anarchistic tracts amongst the susceptible masses. Peasant reading had become an important political issue.

Peasant readers must therefore be situated within the context of a struggle for control, which engaged Catholics and legitimists, secular republicans, socialists and bonapartists. Contemporaries in various camps, however, discussed and 'read' peasant cultural practice from a distant point of observation, as though it was either a closed universe, speaking barbaric and corrupt dialects and much in need of enlightenment, or else a folkloric curiosity soon destined to disappear. Whether they idealized the countryside like George Sand, or saw it rather as a jungle of rampant greed and violence, as Balzac and Zola tended to do, their discourse remained at one remove from the realities of rural life. The historian, too, is very often obliged to fall back on indirect sources, such as the clues offered by normative texts concerned to prescribe rather than describe peasant reading. Official questionnaires on rural readers, such as that of 1866, are valuable sources, even though their responses were completed not by peasants, but by schoolteachers, *commissaires de police* and sub-prefects.

Only quite late in the century do peasants speak to the historian with a voice of their own. Rare peasant autobiographers such as Henri Norre, Emile Guillaumin, Antoine Sylvère and, even later, Pierre-Jakez Hélias give the historian more direct means of access to the history of cultural practices in the countryside. Even some of these peasant 'autobiographies', however, are indebted to an educated intermediary who initiated, transcribed and edited them. Peasants were more ready to *speak* their lives to other writers, than to write them themselves. Thus, Alexandre Merlaud allowed Gérard Coulon to collect his reminiscences[2] and Grenadou similarly allowed Alain Prévost to make use of their interviews together.[3] For the period immediately before 1914, oral historians and ethnographers have assembled oral testimonies which further enrich the store of evidence on French rural culture. Peasant voices therefore rarely reach us, except in muffled tones and except at the very end of the period. In the case of rural readers, we cannot 'interrogate the audience' as freely as we have done with articulate women readers and worker-autobiographers. This chapter thus relies heavily on those who 'read' the peasants, and not so heavily on individual reading peasants.

The question of peasant reading is important for the ongoing debate about the social and political 'integration' of the peasants. Underpinned by many assumptions of modernization theory, the study of the integration process seeks to elucidate its mechanisms, its precise geography and its timing. It has appeared far less concerned to analyse possible resistance to the process, except perhaps to underline its archaism.[4] In its crudest manifestations, modernization discourse outlines the 'dissemination' of literature in the villages, the 'penetration' of rural areas by urban cultural forms and the consequent 'opening up' of the countryside, previously a (virginal?) victim of its own *cloisonnement*. In the third volume of the *Histoire de la France rurale*, covering the nineteenth century, rural France is penetrated twice by the railways, is further penetrated by ideas of social revolt, and experiences a fourth penetration by the city, 'its institutions, its models, its attractions (*appâts*)'.[5] The sexual imagery of these concepts would probably have comforted nineteenth-century progressives.

The issue nevertheless remains a real and an important one. In studying the peasants' encounters with print culture, we are examining the meeting of peasant civilizations with an expanding national culture. As Roger Chartier has recently reminded us, we should not conclude too hastily that the result of the encounter was necessarily a new and more powerful cultural homogeneity, nor that nationalizing forces left rural culture defeated and in a state of dissolution. Historians have written the obituary of popular culture so often in the past that we must begin to wonder how there could be any of it still left in nineteenth-century France to repress or to integrate. For Chartier, 'the historiographical fate of popular culture is thus always to be stifled, bruised and rejected, and at the same time always to rise again from its ashes.'[6] Popular culture is reborn phoenix-like, adapting to new conditions and formulating new means of expression. The historian must once again respect the autonomy of the reader, the variety of possible responses to what is read, and the reader's capacity to reject imposed ideologies. Individual readers assimilate what is read into pre-existing interpretive frameworks. As Janice Radway reminds us in a different context, 'opportunities still exist within the mass-communication process for individuals to resist, alter, and reappropriate the materials designed elsewhere for their purchase.'[7]

The changing dynamic of the relationship between peasants and print culture cannot be divorced from broader developments which transformed French agrarian life during the nineteenth century. These include the gradual formation of a national economy, and the growth of specialized agricultural production for national and international markets (wine-growing is an obvious example of an agricultural sector with international horizons). As Roger Thabault realized as he summarized the history of his own village, increasing contact with the world of the book was a function of agricultural change and developing connections with a diversified exchange economy.[8] The process of industrial concentration also had an effect on rural life: it resulted in the de-industrialization of the countryside, which accelerated the rural exodus already under way in the July Monarchy. In addition, the advance of minimal standards of reading competence, indicated by the growing number of spouses and conscripts able to sign their name, is clearly relevant. The advance of literacy, however, must not be confused with the spread of primary education, which obeyed a different rhythm as it responded to local demand. As Chapter 1 suggested, the achievement of mass literacy *preceded* the introduction of Jules Ferry's legislation in the 1880s, designed to make primary schooling free, compulsory and universal.[9]

The history of reading in the countryside is inevitably connected to these wider trends. For this reason, it is logical that its basic chronology should reflect the division into periods adopted by Maurice Agulhon and his colleagues in their overview of the rural history of France.[10] In the first half of the century, print culture remained something largely foreign to the peasant world. Under the Second Empire, however, and in the early years of the Third Republic, there is evidence of the increasing presence of books and newspapers in rural France. In this second phase of the century, the growing availability of printed matter coincided with rising anxiety among the élites about their own ability to control and channel the cultural life of the rural population. The presence of print in this period, however, does not necessarily imply that peasant readers always welcomed it, or had learned how to use it for their own ends. Many of them remained on the margins of literacy. In a third phase, however, rural readers began to show a greater mastery of print and written culture. This phase is relatively recent; its origins are to be found in the last 20 years of the nineteenth century. This simple chronological schema obscures regional and gender differences, as well as other aspects of uneven development. The broad argument of this chapter, however, is that from the 1880s onwards, a decisive transformation occurred. The peasant was no longer a stranger to the printed and the written word, and at the same time, he or she was no longer a victim of its all-embracing power.

Peasants on the margins of book culture

The linguistic diversity of France, together with the difficulty of gaining access to primary schooling, helped to keep peasants on the margins of book culture, especially in the first half of the nineteenth century. Although the Guizot Law of 1833 proposed an ambitious plan for a school in every commune, this was only partially implemented. School attendance still depended on its affordability; even when it became 'free', school nevertheless deprived families of the income of potential young wage-earners. Attendance in rural areas was intermittent, and subordinate to the economic needs of peasant families. At harvesttime, for example, the schools were deserted. In practice, they could only hope to offer tuition in the winter months, when the seasonal demands of agricultural work were less intense.

Landowners and employers frequently discouraged the intellectual ambitions of their tenants and labourers. In *La Vie d'un Simple*, Tiennon encountered powerful bourgeois hostility towards his desire to give his children a basic knowledge of reading, writing and accounting.[11] At Le Cayla, Eugénie de Guérin thought it her duty to teach Miou, the miller's daughter, to read. As long as peasant reading was supervised, it was presumably innocuous. In other circumstances, the presumption of peasant readers shocked her. She noted in her diary in 1840: 'Much better rosary beads than a book in a labourer's pocket! Let them cultivate the fields, and let others cultivate knowledge.'[12]

Historians have often turned to inventories of deceased estates (the estates of deceased persons – *inventaires après décès*) to investigate levels of book ownership in individual households. Most studies, unfortunately, of the presence of books in post-mortem inventories have had an urban location. One rare investigation in a rural setting was conducted by the anthropologist Suzanne Tardieu for the Mâconnais.[13] The result suggested a very feeble presence of books in rural households. Out of 58 inventories analysed between 1790 and 1909, only seven recorded the presence of books (12 per cent). Four of these private libraries were owned by urban residents of Mâcon, and another by a businessman (*négociant*) from Lyon, so that only two strictly qualified as rural bookowners. The *cultivateur* of the Mâconnais had little time or space to read books or to amass a private library.

It would, however, be dangerous to conclude from the inventories of deceased estates that the book was a foreign object to the peasant. It may simply have been that the books they owned were not of sufficient value to merit a listing in a deceased estate inventory. We know, from Tardieu again, that peasant homes might contain almanacs which, like other household objects, would hang from the ceiling by a nail.[14] Similarly, in the Rouergue, the *bibliothèque paysanne* would consist of a piece of wood, suspended over the main table, on which would be stored the family's reading matter: some almanacs, perhaps a newspaper or an old missal.[15] In the centre of France, too, the almanac was an object which would hang in the principal room, like a kitchen utensil, for family use.[16]

Newspapers were comparatively rare acquisitions in many areas until the end of the century. Emile Guillaumin recalled that only the bourgeois read newspapers in the Bourbonnais in the 1840s.[17] The almanac, in contrast, features regularly in descriptions of the peasant household, and the fact that it hung in such a prominent position, and in a place used together by the whole family, suggests that it was in frequent use by the family group. Works of piety, too, were essential works of reference in a peasant family but, if the family owned any number of books, they were likely to be stored apart from the rest. The Mâcon *cultivateur* who left 27 devotional works and a copy of the Code Napoléon at his death in 1823 stored them in different places.[18]

Peasants frequently attributed magical properties to the printed word, which was a symptom of the rarity of the book in the countryside, of the threat that it seemed to pose, and the peasants' failure to master it. The book was frequently associated with supernatural and religious powers. It provided mysterious strength to those individuals who consulted it. These individuals were the local priest, and the village wise man (or woman), who might well be the two most literate members of the village community. The book was sometimes considered a source of occult power, *Le Grand Albert* and *Le Petit Albert* being perhaps the two most popular magic books, important accessories of the sorcerer.[19] Their popularity only encouraged the critics of *colportage* literature to denounce the spread of superstition and irrational beliefs.

Just as incantations and oft-repeated formulæ were invoked in occult magic, so too, written signs and messages were endowed by the illiterate with supernatural strength. The wizard of St Pompon, in the Périgord, was apparently capable of curing rabies, and his fame spread to the villages of the Lot and the Dordogne. The Académie de Médecine offered him a large sum to reveal the composition of the mixture he prescribed. In spite of the wizard's reluctance to divulge an ancestral secret, the experts did eventually analyse his pills. Inside each one, they discovered a miniscule fragment of paper. His followers, it is reported, were not at all dismayed by this revelation:

> This did not undermine the conviction of the witnesses to his healing. It was rather strengthened since tradition asserts that harm is transmitted in the form of writings, wrapped up in wax and swallowed by the patient. What had caused harm in one case could, in benevolent hands, work an improvement![20]

Henry Massoul remembered another local cunning man, who read the almanacs of Mathieu Laensberg on his doorstep, and dispensed remedies from a big, old book.[21] Books were the sources of remedies and curses. In the Berry, some priests would attribute illnesses or accidents to the reading of a *mauvais livre*, and if they could identify the accused volume, they would burn it.[22] Rural priests who felt threatened by 'diabolical' literature sometimes became experts in texts on sorcery, and built up substantial libraries specializing in the occult sciences.

Magic, like the *veillée* and *colportage* literature, was forbidden or suspect in the eyes of both church and state. Such taboos helped to make books a special attraction for those who were excluded from access to them at school. This exclusion applied particularly to women, who were usually on the margins of school-based literacy until well into the twentieth century.

Magical books such as *Le Petit Albert* had a physical effect on their reader, and could induce a trance-like or convulsive state, no doubt intensified by the fact that this was illicit reading. Reading forbidden magical works was a sign of madness and diabolical possession, as illustrated by oral testimony collected by Daniel Fabre in Roussillon: 'A woman from Laforce turned the famous page of *Le Petit Albert*, and the devil appeared. It took possession of her [*se logea en elle*] and paralysed both her legs. Only a pilgrimage to Lourdes could cure her'. Another interviewee gave the ethnologist a story about *Le Petit Albert*: 'I heard my grandparents say that there was a woman schoolteacher who read it, and when she was reading she saw little mice running by with lighted candles.'[23] Both these recollections significantly concerned women readers, the second perhaps conveying a common distrust of an independent woman intellectual.

The book's powers could be tamed, however, by copying it. Private peasant *cahiers* of the pre-war period which survive are anthologies of different kinds of wisdom which could be put to practical use. They typically contain remedies for ailments, recipes, the words of songs and special prayers. The most remarkable author of such a *cahier* was Jean-Pierre Baylac, the young shepherd from the Hautes-Pyrénées, born in 1900. He read cheap novels, almanacs and old books he picked up at local fairs. He borrowed Michelet, Proudhon, Lamartine and Ponson du Terrail from the local schoolteacher's library. In the ancient tradition of shepherds, he could read, use and invoke magical signs.[24] Before his death from pleurisy at the age of only 20, Baylac had filled 60 handwritten notebooks, in which he had recorded comments on his reading and his work as a shepherd, news of the First World War, his sexual episodes of masturbation and bestiality. He also recorded the punishments he inflicted on himself when, on his lonely hillside, he gave in to such temptations. Baylac had not merely flirted with literacy but, in spite of his humble social status, had mastered its powers for the most secret purposes.[25]

The winter *veillée* has sometimes been seen as an event where peasants read stories and popular legends to themselves. I have argued elsewhere that there is very little evidence from the nineteenth century to support the contention of Robert Mandrou that collective readings of texts of the Bibliothèque Bleue normally occurred in the *veillée*.[26] The nineteenth-century clergy were anxious about the *veillée*, not only because they linked it to the reading of superstitious folk tales and other profanities, but also because they saw it as an occasion for licentious dancing and sexual rendezvous. Their investigations into it, however, did not reveal widespread reading in the *veillée*. When, in 1845, Monseigneur Rendu questioned his *curés* in the diocese of Annecy (Savoie du Nord) about peasant cultural practices and superstitious beliefs, only one reply out of 122 made a clear reference to the habit of reading at the *veillée* (and this was a reference to a catechism).[27] The very existence of a winter *veillée* could only be definitely confirmed in about a third of the parishes in Rendu's diocese. A similar episcopal enquiry in 1859 in the Versailles diocese also revealed that the *veillée* survived in only 35 out of 107 parishes.[28] Nor did the scattered evidence about surviving *veillées* assembled by Le Play mention reading in this context.[29] In the very last decade of the century, reading may possibly have infiltrated the *veillée*, as more fiction (Hugo, Dumas, Verne, Maupassant) was available in the local school library.[30] For most of the century, however, the *veillée* is best seen as a traditional form of peasant sociability centred on work, which retained elements of collective celebration, in which oral transmission had little need of books.

The festive qualities of the *veillée* were under attack. It was accused of fostering immorality, and was suspected by the clergy and others of allowing the unrestrained consumption of liquor, free intercourse between the sexes, and the propagation of dangerous superstitions. The clergy would paradoxically have liked to introduce reading into the *veillée*, in order to 'rescue' the practice from moral degeneracy. But its real offence was probably to express the values of an autonomous peasant civilization, impervious to dominant ideological persuasions. The village in late-nineteenth-century France is conventionally portrayed as an arena of conflict between the priest and the schoolteacher, the agent of the lay republican state. This traditional view has tended to obscure all that the priest and the *instituteur* had in common: as representatives of print culture in the countryside, they both criticized *mauvais livres*, and what they considered as peasant vulgarity and irrationality. The cultural battle in the village was not simply a duel between two rival partisans of education and print culture. The contest was in fact triangular. The peasants were more than pawns in the struggle; they had distinctive cultural practices to defend in the face of the disapproval of both Church and school.

Even those who could not read had access to print culture as listeners. Books would often be read aloud, in the evening, and *en famille*. Not only was reading a family occasion, but for the peasants, listening to the sound of the spoken word was a special pleasure to be relished. Hélias, who learned to read with *La Vie des Saints*, found that his services as a reader were in demand in the village. Families asked him to come and read *La Vie des Saints*, or the *Fables* of La Fontaine, 'to listen to the sound that it made' (*pour écouter le bruit que ça fait*).[31] Every farmhouse would have its *Lives of the Saints* (*Buhez ar Zent*), and family ritual required the youngest child present to read aloud after dinner.[32] Perhaps this is surprising in an area (Basse-Bretagne), which the statistics describe as one of dire illiteracy. Many young Breton readers probably did not attend school regularly in the nineteenth century, and officially, they were indeed illiterate – in French. But official figures take no account of reading competence in Breton.

In Eugene Le Roy's version of peasant life in the Périgord in mid-century, the young hero Hélie reads Ledru-Rollin's paper *La Ruche* aloud to his uncle. In the 1860s, his grandfather would occasionally buy a few books at a local fair or auction. They would no doubt have ended up as tobacco-wrappers, if Hélie had not rescued them, and read them aloud to admiring and astonished rustic companions. 'That is how,' the author remarked, 'where we lived, in remote Périgord country, you learned about the Greeks and the Romans, who normally the peasants had never even heard talk of, let alone wondered what such people could be like.'[33] Reading aloud, amongst friends and family, was an important means through which officially illiterate, or semi-literate peasants, came into contact with books. In this way, the printed word was assimilated into oral forms of communication and culture.

There were other occasions, too, when the written word reached a much wider audience than circulation figures might suggest. During the Second Republic, the authorities were greatly disturbed by the ease with which socialist doctrines were being propagated in the countryside. Their dissemination was limited neither by illiteracy nor by the expense of a newspaper subscription. In small Provençal towns, *La Voix du Peuple* was read aloud in the main square (*sur la place publique*). In St Gaudens (Haute-Garonne), in 1849, *L'Emancipation* was read publicly, and local mayors would subscribe out of public funds to make this possible.[34] In the *chambrées* of Provence, group readings occurred in the framework of a social institution which officials gave up hope of transforming. As one report from Aix-en-Provence complained in 1851, 'all the discontented join the *chambrées*. The members of these *chambrées* subscribe to an opposition journal and it is read out loud for illiterate peasants to hear.'[35]

Testimony of this kind underlines the danger of relying on the statistics of literacy as a guide to reading and writing in the countryside. Although the evidence of the signature test has immense value as a national benchmark of literacy in French, the historian of reading must adopt more subtle procedures to analyse the uses of reading and writing in rural society. Distinctions must be maintained as far as possible between, for example, reading-and-writing literacy and reading-only literacy, which was more widespread but at the same time less visible. In addition, those who could neither read nor write still had opportunities to develop a creative contact with the world of print. Even those who listened to their texts were involved in what De Certeau called a process of silent production.[36]

Rural readers confront the world of print and of writing

After mid-century, and increasingly during the Second Empire, the rural population became familiar with the ubiquitous demands of printed and written culture. Even if peasants were themselves illiterate, there were always intermediaries in the village who could read and write: the local mayor might read newspapers to villagers, or write letters for them to higher authorities. For instance, when in 1855 a policeman's widow from Loupiac (Gironde) wanted to exempt her son from paying school fees, she approached the mayor to draft the necessary petition.[37] Rural teachers, too, were involved in extra-curricular activities which included mediating between the local population and written culture. Many of them were town clerks, in which capacity they might give advice on mortgages and wills, or write letters for local inhabitants. They often gave agricultural advice, distributing pamphlets on the treatment of animal diseases, like the *instituteur* at Piriac (Loire-Atlantique), who was secretary of the local farmers' co-operative, the *mutuelle de bétail*. Other teachers offered evening classes on writing business letters, as did the *instituteur* at La Regrippière (Loire-Atlantique), in 1895.[38] In this phase, the rural population became increasingly familiar with the world of print, although it was often dependent on literate mediators, such as the mayors, teachers and postmen of village society.

The household surveys organized by Frédéric Le Play in mid-century have already been discussed in Chapter 3 for their data on urban working-class readers. Le Play's investigations also included a few peasant families, and several of them possessed books and writing materials.

Often the peasants' books were limited to catechisms, works of devotion and school texts, which was the case of the Provençal peasant-soap worker observed in 1859.[39] Perhaps his status as a worker-peasant was exceptional, as he was a member of the 'urban peasant' communities peculiar to lower Provence with which the researches of Maurice Agulhon have familiarized us. The Basque peasant, however, observed by Le Play's disciples in 1856, also owned some school books, and the family budget of peasants in Lavedan (Béarn) in 1856 included an item for their daughters' writing materials.[40] This family displayed many of the characteristics which Le Play had identified as important ingredients of social stability – it obeyed the Ten Commandments, respected paternal authority, was responsibly trying to save a little capital and had inherited a little property of its own. Even Le Play's *bordier* from Champagne owned an *Almanach Liégeois*, and could handle his accounts competently – another form of (arithmetical) literacy on which statistics are silent.[41] These are isolated examples, but they suggest the existence of a peasantry which by the 1850s was no longer a stranger to written culture.

It was during the 1850s, in the aftermath of the 1848 Revolution, that the imperial government and its supporters showed a heightened sensitivity towards the evils of *colportage*, or chapbook literature. Consequently, traditional *colportage* literature went into decline, partly because the government took active steps to suppress it. First novels entered the sack of the *colporteur* alongside the almanacs, and then the railway and local bookshop made the *colporteur* himself redundant. The accessibility of cheap popular newspapers such as *Le Petit Journal*, and the spread of the bookshop network, reinforced the presence of print in the countryside, and helped to transform the cultural geography of France.

Before the second half of the nineteenth century, the itinerant *colporteur* had been a familiar and regular visitor to most parts of rural France. The typical long-distance professional came from the Pyrenees, and travelled up to 30 km a day on foot, carrying a spare shirt, and a basket of 40 kg of books.[42] On the eve of the 1848 Revolution, over 3000 *colporteurs* were authorized in France. Their trade supported several specialist publishers, and they put into circulation over nine million volumes of pamphlets, brochures and almanacs. Among their wares were the chapbooks which made up the Bibliothèque Bleue, so called because of the coarse blue sugar-paper in which they were often bound. The Bibliothèque Bleue contained a traditional literary corpus which had sustained the popular imagination of rural France for centuries.

A large proportion of popular titles were on religious subjects – over a quarter of them, according to Mandrou.[43] They included catechisms, Christmas carols, works of piety and devotion, lives of the saints, and meditations on death which had a medieval origin. The Bibliothèque Bleue also included almanacs, prophecies, tales of chivalry and romance, and historical legends. Stories such as *Les Quatre Fils Aymon* romanticized a social universe in which the leading role of a chivalrous aristocracy was never questioned. But popular reading was not all piety, chivalry and fantasy. It had a spontaneous if coarse sense of humour, based on farce and burlesque. Parodies of confessions, wills and drunken sermons recurred constantly, ridiculing cuckolds, hypocrites and pedants. Their taste for vulgar celebration and orgiastic horseplay continued a long tradition dating from the Middle Ages, which Bakhtin identified as a specifically medieval comic idiom.[44]

Such literature did not have an exclusively popular origin. Its anonymous authors and editors plundered learned texts by authors such as Boccaccio and Quevedo, adapting them for a popular audience, as Chartier has demonstrated.[45] The Bibliothèque Bleue was composed *for* the people, not *by* the people. The main target for nineteenth-century publishers of the Bibliothèque Bleue, however, were those who read a little and rarely. The geography of *colportage* in the Second Empire suggests that itinerants may have deliberately avoided areas where the population was illiterate or else ignorant of French. Itinerant pedlars rarely reached the interior of Brittany, or the Massif Central. The northeast was also forbidden territory to them, perhaps for the opposite reason, namely that this was a very literate area. Between these two extremes of high literacy and illiteracy lay the chosen realm of the *colporteur*, Normandy, the centre, south-west and south-east regions of France, and the Mediterranean Midi.[46]

In the nineteenth century, the readership of the Bibliothèque Bleue had for the first time become almost exclusively rural. The peasant consumer of almanacs and catechisms was the last remaining bastion of popular literary traditions, abandoned by nobility, bourgeoisie and urban readers as a whole. The Bibliothèque Bleue had catered for a world on the margins of book culture itself. As the book spread its influence socially and geographically, through serialized novels and illustrated magazines, the world of *colportage* literature correspondingly shrank. In the second half of the nineteenth century, it disappeared altogether.

It did not, however, disappear of its own accord. It was the victim of active suppression in the early years of the Second Empire. It had always been officially regarded as a dangerous medium, which might encourage the politicization of the masses. Under the Restoration, officialdom had blamed *colportage* for disseminating subversive Voltairean doctrines. One administrator of the department of the Mayenne complained in 1828:

> Impious and obscene books are proliferating in a frightening manner, they are printed in their thousands and peddled everywhere. Before the Revolution, the works of Voltaire and other impious writers were rare and costly: even under the reign of the usurper [i.e., Napoleon], these works were not widely known...Under the reign of the beloved son of the Church, whose virtues are so admirable [i.e., Charles X], it is distressing to find the poison of impiety on sale so cheaply in every corner of France.[47]

A certain amount of bonapartiana and royalist literature had been absorbed into *colportage* literature, but in the 1850s there was a strong reaction against any kind of politicization in the literature of the Bibliothèque Bleue. Critics such as Nisard reacted with moral revulsion against brochures on the occult sciences, or against the obscene humour of much popular entertainment.[48] The spread of blasphemous obscenities and socialist propaganda amongst the masses, it was thought, had created support for the Revolution of 1848. Thus, *colportage* literature had to be purged for political reasons.

The almanac had indeed become politicized in 1848. Plon produced a Fourierist *Almanac phalanstérien*, and Schneider an *Almanac de l'Ami du Peuple*, a title with a Maratist echo. There was an *Almanac démocsoc*, an *Almanac du proscrit*, an *Almanac des opprimés*, not forgetting the splendidly defiant *Almanac de la Vile Multitude*. In publicizing the Jacobin calendar of 1793, this literature helped to sustain a tradition of revolutionary radicalism. The radical almanacs, however, were ephemeral and had very small print-runs. Only the *Almanach populaire de la France*, which survived from 1840 to its suppression in 1851, with a print-run of 25 000 in 1847, seems to have been destined for a widespread rural sale.[49] The songs of Béranger, and miniature versions of Eugène Sue had found their way into the basket of the *colporteur*, which reinforced official suspicion of the itinerants. Agulhon has suggested that official repression was also motivated by the need to stamp out copies of the Belgian-produced editions of Hugo's *Napoléon le Petit*.[50]

After 1849, the machinery of censorship and control was set in motion. Prefects were empowered to issue permits to *colporteurs* in

1849, and since the permits were only valid in the department where they were issued, itinerants were compelled to seek a whole series of prefectoral authorizations in order to complete their journeys.[51] This exposed the *colporteurs* to police and bureaucratic harassment. In 1852, a censorship commission was established, and its stamp of approval was necessary to legalize the sale of *colportage* literature. The critic Nisard was one of its early members. These measures effectively ruined the publishing industry of Troyes, which had been the main provincial production centre for the Bibliothèque Bleue. Production declined, and the number of *colporteurs* declined, too, as hundreds every year were condemned for infringing the regulations in the 1850s.[52]

The arrival of the railway, which brought newspapers such as *Le Petit Journal* into the heart of the countryside, pushed the remaining *colporteurs* into the remotest rural areas of France. *Le Petit Journal*, founded in 1863 as a cheap, small-format daily, selling for five centimes, was the first daily newspaper to conquer a provincial readership. By 1887, it had a print-run of 950 000, which made it the largest daily in the world.[53] In contrast to its predecessors, *Le Petit Journal* had very few subscribers: it sold directly to readers through a national network of outlets. It was sold at Hachette's new railway kiosks, and distributed from depots set up in small towns. Itinerant vendors on bicycles, who were paid employees of the paper, collected it from station depots, then took it into the countryside.

The rise of *Le Petit Journal* coincided with the emergence of the press magnates, such as Solar, the Pereire brothers and Mirès, the model for Saccard in Zola's novel *L'Argent*. These changes in the press and its readership are attributable not to some vague, impersonal process of modernization, but to the investment priorities of such entrepreneurs. The daily press extracted huge revenue from selling space to banks and financial consortia, who aimed to tap the savings of gullible small investors. Links between banks and the press were such that by 1880 Soubeyran, vice-governor of the Crédit Foncier, controlled the financial copy of 64 provincial newspapers.[54]

Le Petit Journal relied on a regular dose of *romans-feuilletons* by authors such as Ponson du Terrail, and devoted considerable space to nonpolitical *faits divers*, such as the exploits of the notorious murderer, Troppman. Sales shot up almost three-fold to 594 000, on the day of Troppman's execution in 1869.[55] If *Le Petit Journal* did venture into politics, as in the Wilson affair of 1887, it was only because it saw a chance to slaughter a rival: Wilson, son-in-law of President Grévy, implicated in a scandal over the sale of medals and decorations, was the owner of the regional daily, *La Petite France*, which was forced into liquidation in 1889. By this time, sophisticated distribution methods had made the itinerant pedlar obsolete. In reporting events like Troppman's execution, the daily press absorbed one of the staple genres of *colportage* literature. The retail bookshop allowed even the peasants to buy literature on market days in small towns. By the 1870s, *colportage* literature included illustrated versions of novels by Paul de Kock, Dumas and Sue.[56]

To describe what kinds of literature were available to rural readers, however, is only to give half of the story. It may indeed help us to understand the role of print in peasant culture and some of the reasons why élites were moved to control peasant reading. It is equally important to suggest the uses which readers made of this material, so as to try to outline the interpretations and responses which determined the reception of such texts in the countryside. The scarce autobiographical material available suggests that rural readers were looking above all for practical knowledge which would improve cultivation and the performance of familiar agricultural tasks. Henri Norre, for example, was a peasant-autobiographer from the Allier, born in 1859. The son of illiterate peasants, he filled several notebooks with details of crops, agricultural implements and instructions to his fellow-peasants. While he was ill with consumption *circa* 1891, his reading introduced him to the wonders of superphosphate. As he wrote, 'I learned, by reading an almanac published in Limoges, the role of chemical fertilisers. Then I took out a subscription to the *Gazette de village* in which I found much useful information'.[57] He went on to establish a shortlived Syndicat des Agriculteurs in his commune. For Norre, reading had an essentially utilitarian purpose; it provided information on prices, land for sale, and agricultural improvements. Norre's severely utilitarian approach was echoed by Alexandre Merlaud in the Berry, who attended evening classes in 1907 at his local school, without being completely convinced that they were worthwhile. His scepticism was dispelled, however, when he realized that book-knowledge could teach him how to estimate the weight of a bull, from a few simple measurements.[58] This pragmatism was one of the hallmarks of late-nineteenth-century peasant approaches to reading. Such examples of respect for books, and in a few cases of the mastery of the written word, become more frequent after mid-century. They should balance the image of archaic traditionalism which has too frequently conditioned our appreciation of rural culture in the nineteenth century.

Attempts to control peasant reading and the questionnaire of 1866

After the Second Republic, liberal and secular reformers increasingly perceived peasant reading as a political problem. They wanted to provide an antidote to what they saw as the harmful influences of clericalism, Bonapartism and socialism. Many, like the republican Jules Simon, felt that one constructive answer to the problem was better library provision.

The dangers which popular libraries could counteract were outlined in a prize essay produced by a teacher for the Société académique de la Marne in 1857.[59] The essay was a long diatribe on the progress of immorality in the countryside since 1789, and especially under the July Monarchy. The advance of irreligion, argued the author, had been furthered by the diffusion of Volney, Rousseau, Diderot and Voltaire, and abetted by the *roman-feuilleton* of Eugène Sue. The spread of novels in the countryside had been a social and religious disaster, corrupting the young, especially inexperienced females, encouraging idleness and libertinage, emptying the churches and breaking up the family. The best remedies were stronger laws against prostitution, laws to compel workers to save for a pension, and better popular education. The reader will by now be familiar with the tone and direction of such polemics about popular reading.

For Léon Curmer, the *colporteurs* were 'messengers of evil'.[60] When Charles Robert analysed the replies of 1200 schoolteachers to a questionnaire on the need for popular libraries in the countryside, the most common answer was that libraries would undermine 'l'influence des mauvais livres', and this was usually accompanied by an attack on *colportage* literature.[61] *Colportage* was dying out in the 1860s, but *mauvais livres* had not been eradicated. Charles Robert summarized thus his replies from the Seine-et-Oise:

> If, at the back of a smoke-stained cupboard, you discover a few old books, you groan at the realisation that they are the most immoral in existence; under our last regime, unlimited *colportage* flooded our countryside with these corrupt writings that one is embarrassed to name and which form the peasant's entire library. Today the reading of cheap novels penetrates everywhere and is destroying the good sentiments of the rural population. Cheap serialised fiction, publications by instalment are flooding and poisoning our countryside.[62]

From the Charente came complaints that *colportage* was a dangerous leprosy, and that an *instituteur* who had seized copies of Paul de Kock and the story of Mandrin from his students had almost come to blows with their parents.[63] The dissemination of cheap popular fiction had indeed made great inroads into the countryside by the 1860s, although not all Charles Robert's correspondents regarded this as an irreversible process. The demand for recreational literature was increasing much faster than the reformers' ability to direct it into safe channels. The masses knew *how* to read; popular libraries had to show them *what* to read, in the interests of social and political harmony. The attempt to establish social literacy thus took the form of an attack on two of the most familiar characters in the world of popular culture: the *colporteur* and the *cabaretier*. As Jean Hébrard has shown, governments between 1860 and Jules Ferry placed their hopes in the local school library, as a source of books for adult readers in the countryside.[64] By the end of the Second Empire, 25 per cent of all primary schools had a library, and by 1882 this percentage had risen to 37. In spite of this expansion, school libraries were small, and their contents paternalistic. In the long run, the cost to the government of renewing and maintaining a stock of books in every French commune made the notion unrealistic. Nevertheless, the *bibliothèques scolaires* advanced the process of the peasant acculturation to the printed word.

The government questionnaire on rural reading habits, organized by the Ministry of Education in 1866, was motivated by the push to develop a framework of school libraries.[65] The minister asked all prefects to list the works most popular with their readers, so that schools could acquire those titles with a guaranteed readership. In addition, the minister's circular specifically asked what works were distributed locally by the *colporteurs*.

This official attempt at market research is potentially a very revealing document, informing us of what peasant readers all over France were actually reading in the 1860s. Once again, however, the historian of popular culture is reliant on secondhand assessments, this time from the prefects. As a result, we must moderate our enthusiasm. The prefects gathered their information from a variety of local sources: sub-prefects, *commissaires de police* and local mayors were asked to contribute information, and occasionally a prefect would consult schoolteachers and local bookshops. Their reports, digested by the prefect, were then relayed to Paris. The archive of responses to the questionnaire therefore consists of third- or even fourth-hand information, sifted through

146 *Readers and Society in Nineteenth-Century France*

several layers of the administrative hierarchy. It would be risky to regard it as a fresh and immediate *sondage* of peasant reading.

The government received a mixed response. There were geographical deficiencies in the replies : there are important lacunæ in the Massif Central, and the extreme west, Burgundy and parts of the north. The prefects realized the purpose of the questionnaire, and adapted their responses accordingly. Rather than report what peasants were reading, they tended to give their own views of what a *bibliothèque scolaire* ought to stock. Prefects' replies fell into four categories. Firstly, there were those who reported that no popular reading matter whatsoever was worthy of a place in a school library, and consequently, they gave no details at all about peasant reading. In Tours, for example, the prefect felt that it was hardly worth enquiring what the peasants read, since

> People read little in rural areas, the peasants have hardly anything except almanacs. It is not the same with the working class, with whom the taste for reading is very widespread, and they read bad novels and often immoral books which pedlars manage to slip past the censor's stamp.[66]

Secondly, and only marginally more helpfully, some prefects agreed that what the peasants read was completely worthless, but they nevertheless condescended to give their own suggestions as to what a good local library should contain. This attitude was adopted by the prefect in Périgueux, who deplored the fact that 'ignorance and bad taste too often dictate the choice of these books, and the administration should be concerned to reform this taste rather than to conform with it.'[67] Thirdly, a few prefects argued that some popular reading matter could safely be included in a school library, and they therefore provided the government with a partial list of peasant readings from which undesirable titles had been carefully 'purged'. This was the strategy adopted for example by the prefect of the Creuse. A fourth and very helpful group of prefects took the view that what peasants read was deplorable, gross and immoral, but like obedient *fonctionnaires* they decided to give the minister a list of it anyway, as he had requested.

The prefects' replies illustrate the decline of *colportage* during the Second Empire. From Blois, the prefect reported that *colportage* sales had fallen in the last few years, and that *colporteurs* sold only almanacs, songs, fairy tales and works of piety. 'Competition from little illustrated papers', he added, 'at five or ten centimes, has been disastrous for itinerant book sales,' and *colporteurs* were even selling 'insignificant brochures' made up of reports of *faits divers* cut from newspapers.[68] The local police *commissaire* from Montereau (Seine-et-Marne) reported that no *colporteur* had been sighted there for over two years, and similar reports were received further away from Paris.[69] In Bourges, the public was avid for new newspapers such as *Le Petit Journal*, and all were familiar with 'the whole series of reputedly more or less futile novels by Alexandre Dumas and son, Victor Hugo, George Sand, Gauthier, etcetera etcetera'.[70]

In some areas, *colportage* literature was already extinct. Newspapers and cheap novels had won over the urban populations, and were spreading quickly into the countryside. From the Eure, the Ardennes, the Indre, the Loire and elsewhere, came reports of the popularity of cheap illustrated novels sold by instalment, as well as of 'petits ouvrages' celebrating the military campaigns of Napoleon I and III. Where *colportage* literature was still sold, the most popular titles were the *Thousand and One Nights* and the *Quatre Fils Aymon*, together with *La Clef des songes* and *L'Oracle des dames* (see Appendix B, pages 164–5). Prefects were nearly unanimous in deploring the bad taste of readers everywhere.

There was one exception to this. They suggested that bonapartist literature was very popular with the reading public of the 1860s, and here it is particularly hard to decide how far the prefects were suggesting titles which they considered politically correct, rather than reporting what was actually read. In Meaux, the police *commissaire* did make this distinction, recommending that the study of French history up to 1815 should become compulsory, 'in order to maintain the present generation in the feelings of affection and sympathy which the masses show for the imperial dynasty.'[71] In the Puy-de-Dôme it was clearly the population, and not just the prefect, who valued stories of the First Empire.[72] The *commissaire* of Fontainebleau also reported that the Crimean and Italian wars had made history books popular in the countryside.[73] No fewer than 24 reports mentioned the popularity of Loudun's *Les Victoires de l'Empire*, and others mentioned the *Histoire populaire de Napoléon 1er* (23 mentions), *Souvenirs du 1er Empire* by Kermoysen (19 mentions), the *Oeuvres* of Napoleon III (19 mentions), and the *Campagnes de la Crimée et d'Italie* (19 mentions). Perhaps there was an element of sycophancy in these reports, and perhaps the police *commissaires* were doing what they have often tended to do, namely tell the authorities exactly what they thought they wanted to know. Twenty-one reports mentioned the popularity of Duruy's *Petite histoire de France*, which would certainly have pleased the Minister for Education, who was none other than the author!

The prefects' reports suggest the enduring popularity of the classical playwrights of the seventeenth century, and also of La Fontaine's *Fables* (24 mentions), which has been identified elsewhere as one of the French bestsellers in the *longue durée*.[74] Preferences for the works of the eighteenth century also seem to have varied little over time. The prefects mention old favourites such as *Paul et Virginie* (18 mentions), Lesage's *Gil Blas* (13 mentions) and the *Fables* of Florian (14 mentions), as though they were reading the bestseller lists of the 1820s. They resorted to recommending standard school texts such as *Télémaque*, Lhomond's *Grammaire* or Hachette's histories. Their ideal libraries for the people excluded potentially controversial authors such as Rousseau, George Sand or Voltaire, except in carefully selected *morceaux choisis*, just as they ignored the popularity of works of piety in the countryside. In their résumé of the popularity of nineteenth-century fiction, however, the emergence of a new brand of popular novelist can be seen. Leading the field by a clear margin was Alexandre Dumas (23 mentions), followed by Paul de Kock (13 mentions), Eugène Sue (15 mentions), and Victor Hugo (10 mentions), together with the surprising addition of Châteaubriand (16 mentions). Here the prefects were probably reporting accurately, since except for Châteaubriand, these were novelists which they almost universally deplored.

In the field of foreign literature, however, tastes were again very traditional, for the two most popular foreign novels, according to this source, were *Robinson Crusoe* and *Don Quichotte* (not forgetting *Swiss Family Robinson*, which apparently had a large Protestant readership).[75]

Works of history were popular, according to the prefects, including those relating to the First Empire already listed. Various versions of the life of Joan of Arc, by Michelet, Lamartine and others, had a considerable readership. Thiers' *Histoire de la Révolution française* was mentioned in 14 reports, and it was particularly popular in the east and the Parisian region. One report, however, described it as a work chiefly for bourgeois consumption.[76]

Prefects recommended a wide range of titles of a didactic nature, on personal hygiene, horticulture, popular science and the individual's obligations to the Patrie. Raspail's health manual was recommended by just three prefects; their colleagues tended to prefer the many works of Barrau, author of *Conseils moraux et hygiéniques aux ouvriers des villes et aux habitants des campagnes*, *Les devoirs des enfants envers leurs parents*, and *La morale pratique*, among others.

Appendix B lists the 30 titles most favoured by responses to the 1866 questionnaires, together with the number of departmental responses in which they were mentioned. It remains difficult to distinguish prefects' preferences from peasant practices; but responses give the impression that these practices were changing. Colportage literature was almost extinct, now replaced by cheap, illustrated novels and magazines. Rural readers liked military memoirs, works on agriculture, and the *romans-feuilletons* of Sue and Dumas. Through the *bibliothèque scolaire*, the imperial government hoped to provide a secular mixture of modern novels, and classics of French and European literature. The government clearly wished to make available to rural readers works which presented a bonapartist view of French history, and manuals offering practical advice and lessons in civic duties.

From the 1880s to 1918: Peasant readers make independent use of the medium

A multitude of sources therefore illustrate the frequency of contact betweeen rural France and the print medium in the second half of the nineteenth century. They also reveal how this transformation was perceived as a problem. As we have seen, rural readers of the Second Republic and Second Empire were no longer 'on the margins of literacy'. Rather, they enjoyed an expanding range of possible means of access to print culture. Railway bookstalls made literature available for rural readers. Local urban booksellers would leave books for sale with village shopkeepers, in the grocer's shop or the *marchand de vin*. Novels were now accessible in five- or ten-centime weekly instalments.[77] Government concern in the 1860s to channel and control rural reading practices was one important sign that peasants were already familiar with book culture before 1870.

Eugen Weber argued that the period of the Third Republic between 1871 and 1914 was the crucial period in the cultural integration of the peasantry. He drew heavily on sources from the more remote areas of France – Brittany, the Pyrenees and the Massif Central – which almost inevitably highlighted the persistence of traditional cultural practices. In one respect, however, Weber was correct to underline the importance of the last quarter of the nineteenth century, and the years before and during the First World War. What changed in this period was not so much the frequency of contact between rural readers and written culture, but the ways in which peasants began to make use of their long-established familiarity with print and with writing. They were becoming less dependent on intermediaries, and more able to adapt written culture for their own ends. These ends might be purely personal, as in the growth of personal correspondence, or they might be more collective, as in the use of journals to organize the first *syndicats des agriculteurs*. It was no coincidence that the schoolteacher who lent Augustine Rouvière Tolstoy's *Anna Karenina* also introduced her to the local Mutualité.[78]

This chapter has taken a slightly different approach to the problem of the 'new readers', in comparison with the previous discussions of women readers and working-class readers. The main reason for this is simply the relative scarcity of autobiographical testimony from peasants themselves. As a result, the chapter has given greater weight both to the hostility of élites to peasant reading, and to the issue of the social integration of the nineteenth-century peasantry. Official attempts to control and direct 'new' peasant readers, by censoring *colportage* literature or by establishing school libraries, had serious limitations. They were in any case powerless to alter profound social and economic changes in the countryside. Regardless of official reactions to peasant reading, the gradual economic integration of France was having irresistible cultural consequences. One was the slow decline of *patois* and regional languages. Another was the gradual absorption of peasant readers into a more homogeneous national reading public. At the end of the nineteenth century, even rural readers shared the national taste for mass fiction by Dumas or Verne, Ohnet or Ponson du Terrail.

A national reading public was emerging, but it was one in which peasant readers increasingly took their own initiatives, improvising their own literary culture and adapting the use of print and the written word for their own practical ends. This section will review a few examples of independent peasant uses of written culture between the 1880s and the First World War.

Rural readers did not need to be book-buyers in order to be consumers in the expanding world of illustrated magazines and cheap mass fiction. The peasant women from the Ardèche, for example, encountered in Chapter 5, described how, in the 1890s, they and their parents cut out the *roman-feuilleton* from the newspaper, and sewed the instalments together to fashion a continuous home-made book.[79] Such personal *feuilleton*-booklets were the subject of everyday conversation between the women, and they were lent and borrowed through informal female reading networks. Of the peasants interviewed by Anne-Marie Thiesse, only one in five came from a household where the newspaper was purchased daily at the turn of the century,[80] but buying the paper was only one way of obtaining access to the news. Antoine Sylvère, recalling life in and around Ambert in 1890s, remembered *Le Petit Journal*. He didn't have to buy it or even borrow it, because its pages were spread out on display in the windows of local *marchands de tabac*.[81] Local borrowing networks could be exploited by rural readers. According to Augustine Rouvière, even the novels of Tolstoy were read in the peasant heartland of the Cévennes, when a keen *institutrice* decided to share her literary enthusiasm with local pupils.[82] As Rouvière put it, this represented 'a real cultural revolution' (*une véritable révolution dans les moeurs*) in her village of Sainte-Croix-Vallée-Française.

A further example is the increasing use of letter-writing by peasant families. A recent study of the history of private correspondence shows that whereas rural areas were hardly touched by written culture in midcentury, they were much more accustomed to writing and receiving letters by 1914–18. Even the introduction of a universal 20-centimes postage stamp in 1849 did not alter the fact that letter-writing was then still chiefly an urban phenomenon, and that the channels of epistolary communication tended to run in one direction only: from the towns to the countryside. The postal enquiry of 1847 showed that in rural communes outside the *chef-lieu du canton*, individuals received on average less than one letter per day.[83]

Increasingly, however, there were occasions when peasants needed to correspond with friends or family members in writing. Migration was one such occasion. Migrant workers from the Limousin needed to send money home, and to keep in touch with the management of their farms, while they spent a season or more on the building sites of the capital. As a result, seasonal migrants were much more familiar with letter-writing than those who stayed behind in the village.[84] Above all, the two wars of 1870 and 1914–18 made letter-writing an essential skill for peasant conscripts. In the First World War, four million letters circulated daily between the front and the rear.[85] This unprecedented epistolary flood constituted a completely new kind of 'popular literature'.

Sometimes, peasant soldiers still needed to enlist one of their number to act as a scribe. Alexandre Merlaud wrote letters home for his fellow-conscripts in 1903, even though they knew they were very unlikely to receive a reply.[86] Repeatedly using a third party to write letters was risky: the writer enlisted tended to recycle a small stock of conventional phrases, and he might also censor the text dictated to him. Thus when Antoine Sylvère wrote for his family to his father, absent cutting wood as *scieur de long*, he was not prepared to transcribe all the insults that his mother wanted to heap upon her husband.[87] In spite of the use of intermediaries, younger peasants, forced by the necessities of war and conscription, gradually mastered the art of correspondence. Augustine Rouvière even recalled that her younger sister Anna received love letters from the young man who courted and married her in 1916.[88]

The correspondence of the peasant *poilus* reveals how far the new primary education system had succeeded in inculcating a national republican ideology, through its principal medium, the French language. The world of the peasants was still a local world. They wrote from the front for news of their family and their crops. They wrote, too, to give advice on bringing in the harvest and the best time to sell the produce. As they fought for France, they thought of their own village and their own fields. A soldier in the Second Army wrote instructions home in June 1916 in typical fashion: 'You have got it straight. First the cattle, then the patch of lucerne, then the garden. You've got six days' work there.'[89] An umbilical cord still tied the peasant soldier to his family and his native *pays*. Soldiers dreamed of going on leave to assist with crucial agricultural tasks. As Grenadou recalled, 'Right through the war, I dreamed at night that I was back at Saint-Loup. I dreamed I was harvesting, I dreamed I was at the plough.'[90]

Yet it is clear from peasant writing that, in spite of these local territorial loyalties, wider issues were also important. For the most part, this wartime 'popular literature' was written in French, even if at times the writer's competence in the national language wavered. There were many mistakes in peasants' written French. The language of the schoolroom was mixed up with local languages in the letters of many southern peasants. They wrote in a hybrid of 'franco-occitan' or 'franco-catalan'.[91] Ferry's educational reforms had done their work but it was still not quite complete. The influence of local languages was still important. They had a patriotic sense of Germanophobia, according to Annick Cochet, for their writings described the enemy as the bestial 'Boche', as vermin, bandits or pirates – a vocabulary which implied that the *revanchiste* lessons of primary school had been well learned.[92] In accepting their patriotic duty, peasant writers from the front incorporated much of the official rhetoric about imminent victory against a stereotyped hereditary enemy. The official discourse and school textbooks had had an impact on peasant written culture. But perhaps the most striking development was the very existence of the correspondence itself, and its extraordinary volume.

In other ways, too, the national education system changed the peasant's cultural horizons. It enabled the brightest readers and writers to leave a life of drudgery and become socially mobile. The educational system itself provided an opportunity to escape one's origins and become a teacher, albeit a miserably paid one. Reading and writing could thus demonstrate tangible, practical benefits for previously sceptical rural readers. They provided new opportunities to be grasped. Reading and writing had important uses in the growth of peasant trade unionism. The peasant-biographer Henri Norre was the founder of a *syndicat des agriculteurs* in his commune in the Allier. Reading was also linked to militancy in the better-known case of Emile Guillaumin, whose reading trajectory is worth considering more fully.

Guillaumin's experience suggests that rural reading had diversified enormously. On one level, his reading was that of any peasant interested in local affairs, which he learned of through the local press, the *Journal de l'Allier*. At the same time, his reading reflected his interests as a militant unionist. He recommended to his fellow-peasants militant periodicals such as *Le Paysan*, the monthly paper of the Fédération des Travailleurs Agricoles du Midi, *Le Travailleur de la terre*, *La Voix du peuple* and *Les Annales de la jeunesse laïque*.[93] He urged young readers to educate themselves by reading a selection of literature, both fiction and non-fiction, which he described as 'livres de documentation sur la classe ouvrière et paysanne'. These included Zola's *Germinal*, Nadaud's memoirs, Eugène Le Roy's *Jacquou le Croquant* and *Le Moulin du Frau*, as well as George Sand's *François le Champi*.

Not only the peasant reader with regional horizons, and the reader as militant, but the model of the schoolboy reader also exerted an influence on Guillaumin's literary culture. It was school that introduced him to Mayne Reid, Dickens's *David Copperfield* and the almost universal *Uncle Tom's Cabin*.[94]

Finally, there was also in Guillaumin the model of the discriminating reader of national literature, in touch with new publications, journals and novels. The *colporteur* was no longer the medium through which the peasant acquired his or her limited reading matter. By the turn of the century, as has been shown, there were other means of obtaining access to sources of general literature. There were local study groups and reading circles, even in Guillaumin's small community at Ygrande.[95] Nothing now prevented the young rural reader from making direct contact with Parisian literary culture. Guillaumin was familiar with the novels of Jules Verne, Loti's bestseller *Pêcheur d'Islande*, and more predictably, with Zola's novel of peasant life, *La Terre*.[96] In 1890, Guillaumin spotted an advertisement in the local paper for Challeton's *L'Abbesse de Montauger*. He wrote to the publisher, who sent him not only the book, but also a copy of his catalogue, which put a whole undreamed-of array of recreational literature within Guillaumin's reach. He saved up to order more novels, including *Notre-Dame de Paris*, and in 1891, aged 18, he took out a subscription to *Annales politiques et littéraires*. He had become a member of a national reading public. His father did not know what to make of his son's progress. 'Your reading', he warned, 'I don't know if in the end, it will make you smart or stupid'.[97]

Conclusion

After the 1880s, then, to take an approximate date, a younger generation of peasants began to make more use of reading and writing than their fathers and mothers, grandfathers and grandmothers had ever been able to do. The young Antoine Sylvère read the *feuilleton* from the *Moniteur de Dimanche* to his illiterate mother.[98] In Guillaumin's memoirs, old Tiennon would buy a newspaper at the local fair in the 1880s for his grandchildren to read aloud to him.[99] New skills acquired by the young were a valuable family resource.

Thabault traced the change at a microscopic level in his home village of Mazières-en-Gâtine. Here was a closed economy, and a *patois*-speaking community, which the postman visited on foot once a week. The first primary school, established prematurely in 1835, had not been a success. After the 1850s, iron ploughs started to win the struggle against gorse and bracken. More land was cleared for pasture, which meant that there was more manure available as fertilizer. Cereal production started to accelerate. By the 1890s, new crops such as Jerusalem artichokes had been introduced, a co-operative dairy had been formed, and local produce travelled by rail to be sold in Paris.[100]

As a result of the introduction of cash crops and expanding opportunities for the sale of local produce in distant markets, cultural life changed too. Peasants already knew the uses of literacy. They needed to calculate the value of goods and transactions, and they needed occasionally to write contracts and business letters. Sometimes they wrote down useful recipes. But after 1880, their contacts with the printed word expanded dramatically. In 1880, a local café started a newspaper stall, and between 1884 and 1895 the school library expanded its stock to an all-time maximum of 400 volumes, where children borrowed Dickens, About, Erckmann-Chatrian and *Uncle Tom's Cabin*.[101]

Print culture was present in the village from Second Empire onwards, even if many still lived on its margins. Newspapers were available to the villages of Roussillon studied by Daniel Fabre, such as *Le Courrier de l'Aude*, and the more left-wing *Fraternité*. By 1900, villagers' horizons were wider still, and they could read *Le Dépêche de Toulouse*, and even Parisian magazines such as *L'Illustration*.[102] At first, there was a limited élite of rural readers, consisting of the schoolteacher, the postman and the *garde-champêtre*. Villagers would seek the advice of this élite on legal and other matters. After the 1880s, they were increasingly able to exploit print and literacy for their own ends. Weber underestimated the degree of familiarity with print culture which rural readers had acquired before 1870. Moreover, the 'impact' of print and attempts to regulate it cannot be fully understood without some analysis of the *uses* of literacy in the countryside. Only from this perspective can rural readers be rescued from modernization theory, which condemns them to a passive or merely obstructive role. Peasants were not helpless creatures on which outside forces – the forces of library reformers and of Parisian print culture – made a fatal 'impact'. They reacted to, and interacted with the world of print. At first, perhaps, they saw print as an instrument of the powerful, to be respected and revered. By the last 20 years of the century, however, they were taking control of the medium, as it was absorbed within a dynamic and ever-changing rural culture.

7
Reading Classes and Dangerous Classes

Louis Chevalier entitled his well-known book on early nineteenth-century Paris *Classes laborieuses et classes dangereuses*, suggesting that workers were dangers to bourgeois civilization in the eyes of administrators, authorities and writers. In the same style, the present book might have been called 'Reading Classes and Dangerous Classes'. It started with the premise that the reading of workers, women and peasants was perceived as a threat to the dominant position of the patriarchal, property-owning bourgeoisie in nineteenth-century France. At the same time, it was a source of anxiety for the Catholic Church. In the nineteenth century, literature became freely accessible to members of the lower classes for the first time. First, they could hire books by the hour from a reading room (*cabinet de lecture*). Then literature, particularly fiction, was produced ever more cheaply as publishers such as Calmann-Lévy, Garnier, Hachette and Flammarion exploited a rapidly expanding market. The serialization of fiction in the press and its publication in cheap weekly or monthly instalments broadened the reading public even further. From the 1860s onwards, illustrated magazines and mass popular dailies like *Le Petit Journal* appeared, and new methods of distribution, depending on the railways, took them to the small towns and villages of France. The reading public was growing as 'new readers' joined it in unprecedented numbers. The democratization of reading was a process that could not be stemmed or reversed. Instead, the dominant classes tried to contain it and influence the direction of its flow.

The barometer of bourgeois and clerical anxiety obeyed a fluctuating rhythm, and its symptoms evolved in the course of the century. The fear of reading was at its most intense in what we might loosely call the century's post-revolutionary moments. After 1815, for example, the Catholic Church's attack on *mauvais livres*, and its promotion of literary antidotes to lingering Jacobinism were part of a systematic effort at spiritual reconquest. The 1848 Revolution caused another major alert about popular reading, not only because of the popular insurrection of June 1848, but also because the introduction of universal male suffrage had led to huge bonapartist successes. In the last quarter of the century, the terms of the debate shifted again. Popular reading then became an arena in which clerics and liberal republicans battled for ideological supremacy. In these different ways, popular reading became an important social and political issue. The fear of popular reading lay at the heart both of the Church's fear of secularization, and of the bourgeois fear of democracy. At the same time, untutored women's reading challenged bourgeois patriarchal assumptions, and it also undermined the Catholic clergy's enormous female constituency.

I hope it has become apparent that the history of reading thus conceived is not merely an esoteric branch of literary history, but a topic capable of throwing light on some central social developments. The history of reading practices connects with the broad history of class relations in the period, as the dominant classes attempted to neutralize social conflict, through reading advice and the creation of appropriate cultural institutions. We have seen that lending libraries were more successful in integrating the *petite bourgeoisie* than the working classes – and here the story of the lending library looks like the epitome of the history of the Third Republic as a whole.

I hope, too, that the history of reading practices has illustrated some aspects of nineteenth-century gender relations. Reading models proposed for women by male novelists, Catholics and feminists suggest some of the ways in which gender differences were constructed. Various representations of the female reader competed with each other, but they all seem to have shared certain fundamental characteristics. They believed that women readers were particularly given to a very emotional mode of literary appropriation. Women were therefore considered especially vulnerable to the evil influences of romantic pulp fiction.

The history of reading practices converges in these ways with other histories – histories of social antagonisms and gender representations. Perhaps this is uniquely true of the nineteenth century, because of the growing importance of print culture in the century before 1914. Print culture had by that date acquired a mass audience amongst a universally literate population, and it was as yet unchallenged by radio, cinema or any electronic medium of communication. Print was, for a brief historical moment, supreme, and debates about its uses were debates about the nature and the workings of society itself.

158 Readers and Society in Nineteenth-Century France

I am very much aware that the story presented here is incomplete. One omission deserves to be underlined. I plead guilty to leaving out a fuller discussion of the French educational system. Clearly, one of the most successful answers to the problems of republicanism discussed here was the introduction of Jules Ferry's educational reforms. The new state primary schools and their almost missionary cohort of *instituteurs* and *institutrices* set out to fashion a national consciousness founded on loyalty to the bourgeois Republic. But a full account of the school reading experience in the nineteenth century lies outside the scope of this history of reading. Other historians have already treated it, whereas the history of reading practices is a relative newcomer to the discipline. I have chosen to concentrate on adult readers rather than children, in the belief that, until the 1880s at the earliest, the apprenticeship of many new readers took place outside the schoolrooms which they only briefly and intermittently attended.

There can be no history of reading practices without a history of readers. Nor, for that matter, can the history of literature be complete without a history of readers. We do not need them merely as the disembodied audience of a novelist's imagination, the intended targets of a clerical diatribe, or items in librarians' faceless statistics. We need to encounter individual readers, to recognize their human presence and appreciate the diversity of their reading experiences. Sometimes, their reading strategies absorbed elements of the reading models and advice that were embedded in nineteenth-century discourses about reading. At other times, they forged their own independent literary culture. Their individual stories are indispensable to an understanding of reading in past societies. The presence of Eugénie de Guérin and Hélène Legros, of the illiterate Norbert Truquin and of the peasant women of the Ardèche interviewed by Anne-Marie Thiesse are essential. Our analysis rests on them and without their company our historical journey would be dull and one-dimensional.

The stories of these individual readers are available to us in their correspondence, diaries and interviews, and above all, in their written autobiographies. As always, we must beware of these sources. They can fudge details, censor what does not correspond to the desired version of the self, or present a highly manicured image for public exhibition. In the case of militants' memoirs, they can be adopted to construct a martyrology in celebration of proletarian struggles. Recollections of country life can be infused with a 'peasantist' nostalgia for France's authentic rural roots – a tendency intensified by their gradual disappearance in the new rural exodus which has taken place since the 1950s. All autobiographies are fictional, and they are likely to tell us much more about how the authors represent themselves and their reading than what they actually read. But how they 'image' themselves as readers constitutes priceless information in itself. In our own time, the vogue for autobiography has met a commercial demand for nostalgia, but it also has more profound political implications. Life-stories of workers who 'made good' by escaping from abject poverty can be recruited by right-wing ideologists. According to a Thatcherite reading of their work, they advertise the enduring relevance of nineteenth-century values such as self-help. More importantly, such autobiographies succeed in historicizing poverty itself. They place hardship and material difficulties firmly within a sepia-tinted past from which we have all by now supposedly emerged. Hunger, poor housing and oppressive employers appear as relics of the early industrial revolution. Working-class autobiographies can thus be exploited to put poverty at a distance, and to make welfare systems seem obsolete.[1]

Usually, however, the nineteenth-century autobiographies discussed here were not published to promote a twentieth-century revival of Victorian values. The majority appeared within the author's lifetime. Most of those considered were published in book form in Paris, or perhaps locally in a journal. Publication was frequently difficult, if Agricol Perdiguier's experience is anything to go by. His first attempt to publish *Mémoires d'un compagnon* was rejected by *La Presse*, whose editor Girardin told the author his work was of no interest. It was eventually published as a book, but with a print-run of only 500 copies.[2] For women, there were even greater obstacles. The nineteenth-century publishing industry did not welcome independent women authors. Women's autobiographical writing only saw the light of day through the intervention of a male intermediary. Marguerite Audoux, for example, was 'discovered' and published on the recommendation of the writer Octave Mirbeau. Such sponsors, however, were not always fully appreciative of their protégées. Jeanne Bouvier, the seamstress and unionist, had her manuscript cut, but since she had never believed she was capable of writing enough material for a book, she innocently took this as a compliment, remarking proudly: 'I who thought myself unable to write a book because I didn't know with what words to compose it, I had passed the page limit.'[3] Oral autobiographies, too, are mediated through the dynamics of an interview and through the questions and priorities of the interviewer. It is regrettable that some interviewers do not publish their questions. Perhaps in hoping to efface themselves from the process of gathering information, they are hoping to give a heightened illusion of detachment. The interviewer's disappearing trick should not delude us into thinking the informant's voice is producing purely spontaneous and unedited testimony. Yet despite these various pitfalls of political slanting, nostalgia and the fallacy of the transparency of oral testimony, we must plunder such autobiographical sources if the history of reading is to have a human face.

Readers are subject to all sorts of social and cultural pressures. In spite of this, there remains an irreducible autonomy in the responses of any individual. The process of dialogue between reader and text often conspires to undermine the intention of the author, the warnings of the priest or the subtle signposts erected by the publisher. An individual may read the canon in order to subvert its authority, or an atheist tract in order better to refute it. As soon as we consider the question of reader response, we must be prepared for a few surprises. Individual readers, however, are never entirely autonomous. Their individuality is constrained, in Bourdieu's conception, by their cultural and economic capital. In other words, their wealth and social status on one hand, and their educational qualifications on the other, place readers in distinct categories, whose cultural practices conform to discernible sociological patterns. Their reading is thus the expression of a common *habitus*, as in the case of the worker-autodidacts, whose reading was part of a *habitus* of frugality, social ambition and self-distancing from the frequently drunken mass of workers who surrounded them. These readers both read and wrote in a common context. They identified their lack of educational opportunities as a source of oppression. Their desire to read reflected a personal ambition to transcend their situation, but it also brought a broader awareness of social inequalities. They did not necessarily share the classical education which had formed the western European middle class. They were not familiar, in Bourdieu's phrase, with the 'cultural capital' which the nineteenth-century middle class had inherited, although many of them proved eager to claim their share of that cultural legacy. This group of exceptional working-class readers constituted an informal community of readers, bonded by a common anticlericalism and with similar ideas about what for them constituted good literature.

The 'new readers' discussed used different methods of appropriation. The autodidact workers conceived their reading as emancipatory. 'Brisons nos idoles', as Arnauld urged in the rhetoric of the age of enlightenment. 'We must smash our idols, and henceforth consider only our common happiness; let us read Jean-Jacques Rousseau, let's read Lamennais, Victor Hugo and Châteaubriand; these great men will revive our souls and clarify our judgment'.[4] Peasant reading tended to be more pragmatic. Peasants searched for practical, useful information which would either improve the productivity of their land or allow them to leave it altogether. The women readers selected for this study placed a higher value on fiction, and favoured a more emotional or spiritual relationship with the text. As individuals and as members of informal reading communities, they were part of a struggle throughout the nineteenth century for independence and for autonomy. Workers sought self-emancipation and a self-sustaining working-class reading culture; the women readers sought a place of their own, free of male censorship and family tutelage. For all of them, reading could bring a greater awareness of the possibilities for liberation.

Appendix A
Popular Uses of the Book in Early-Twentieth-Century France

The following individual testimonies are translated from Anne-Marie Thiesse, *Le Roman du quotidien: Lecteurs et lectures populaires à la Belle Epoque*, Paris: Chemin Vert, 1984, pp. 62–3 and 65–6. They are discussed in Chapter 5 above.

A woman born in 1896

I was born at A., in the Auvergne. We lived in an isolated house, a kilometre from the village. My father had a little land, and three or four cows. He had been to school and he wrote very well. He was very intelligent. My mother could read, too, and even my grandmother could. Everyone there was quite well-educated. In my family, the children were better at their studies than at manual work; but there were five children, and then there were the grandparents, as well as an aunt to feed, and of course you would have had to leave the village to continue your studies, so we didn't get beyond the certificate. My father had gone to Paris for ten years, working on the railways, but he was forced to return to take over the farm when his father was too old to go on. It was a pity, because otherwise, we might have gone on with school.

My parents spoke dialect to each other, but they spoke French to the children, and forced them to speak French. I went to school with the nuns up to 1904, after that, there was the separation [of church and state], and I went to the state school. After that, I stayed with my parents until my marriage when I was 28. I worked as a lace-maker, all day long, and even in the evenings. A dealer came by to pick up the work every fortnight and I earned 18 *sous* a day, at the most!

My father bought the paper once a week. He couldn't afford to take it every day. He took *Le Moniteur du Dimanche*: it was a socialist newspaper; my father was a socialist, and he was a candidate in every municipal election, but the poor man was never elected. You had to fetch the paper from the village, from the store, a kilometre away, but the children never had to be asked twice about going to get it! Everyone devoured the paper, for the market news, and politics. My parents also took the *Almanach of the Drôme*: there were stories in it in French, the eclipses, etc. It was a favourite. I used to cut out the serials from the *Moniteur*, and sew them together, and I exchanged them with other girls whose parents took *La Croix*. They were love stories; the *Moniteur*'s serials weren't particularly socialist. My father never read the serial. Oh nooo!

There weren't any books in the house: they were too expensive. I had my school prize books from the nuns, but none from the state school. There was a town library; I devoured it, but it didn't have very much. The teachers lent me books for young girls. I used to read on Sunday afternoons, when I went to look after the animals; I didn't have the time to read otherwise, because of my lace work. I used to read the serials, the teacher's books, my school books, or even the

Larousse Dictionary. I have always read the dictionary regularly, I have even brought it with me to the retirement home.

When I was in the village, I never went to the theatre or the cinema. I went when I got to Paris with my husband. What I remember most is when I saw electricity for the first time, the day I passed my certificate at the cantonal centre in 1906. It dazzled me. And when I came to Paris, I was very happy, I was in my element.

A woman born in 1899

I was born in V., in the Somme; it was a market and industrial town. My father was an agricultural worker, my mother worked at the hat factory. I was an only daughter. My father could read and write, my mother read and wrote very well. As for me, I went to school until I was about 12. We were Catholics, but not practising. My father even slapped me when I sung the hymns. I lived with my parents until 1918, when they separated, and we left the Somme, because of the war, to live in Normandy and later in Paris.

My parents took the *Progress of the Somme* every day; my father read the serial, me too, I started to read very young. My mother hardly ever read the paper, she had too much work to do. My father also used to buy little illustrated children's books. They cost two or three *sous*. My parents never read books, but there was a library I could borrow from at school. The teachers and headmistress pushed the kids very hard, and they would give extra evening classes to prepare for the certificate.

I went to work in the factory when I was 13. There, when I was about 13 or 14, I swapped little novels with a girlfriend. They were little bound books for 13 *sous* like *Chaste et Flétrie* [Chaste and Scourged], *Comtesse et mendiante* [Countess and Beggar-girl], *Chassée le Soir de Ses Noces* [Thrown Out on Her Wedding Night]. They were little brochures they sold every week, and every story lasted about a year. My girlfriend thought they were wonderful, but I quickly got tired of them. I was also advised by a friend of my parents, who told me what books I had to buy. Once he told me to read *Cyrano de Bergerac*. I went to ask for it in a bookshop and they gave me a very difficult book BY Cyrano de Bergerac! Above all, I was given books, during the war, by an officer billeted on us, because we lived in the war zone. He was a Lyon silk worker who read all day; his supply work was only at night. He used to buy two or three books a day, and he passed them on to me when he had read them; they were novels. He was careful not to give me sexy books, but I read them secretly! At that time, I also read books by Pierre Loti, Anatole France, Merimée, Hugo. My mother trusted me, and she let me read all I wanted; but all those novels were all about the big wide world, and I missed it. Once I read a novel by Marcelle Tinayre, *La Rebelle*, in which she tells the story of her life. The book caused a scandal, and I was very much criticized by my work mates because I'd read it. That novel spoke about the emancipation of women, and I liked it a lot.

I have always been a great reader, but I stopped two years ago because my eyes got too bad.

Appendix B
Thirty Works for Peasant Readers

This list consists of 30 most-cited titles, taken from prefects' responses to the Ministry of Education questionnaire on rural reading, 1866. The prefects were asked the following question by the Minister:

> I am currently conducting detailed and in-depth investigations into the choice of books destined to form our new school libraries. At the point when I draw up the list of works which seem to answer best the needs of our urban and rural population, it is very important that I should know which books today enjoy a certain popularity and have a guaranteed success amongst country readers. I therefore request you to kindly provide me at your earliest convenience with the principal titles which have a wide sale by pedlars or at local fairs.[1]

Archives Nationales F17.9146, Ministerial Circular to Prefects, 27 June 1866.

Title	Number of times mentioned in departmental responses
Robinson Crusoe	28
LaFontaine, *Fables*	24
Loudun, *Victoires de l'Empire*	24
Histoire populaire de Napoléon 1 er	23
Alex. Dumas père, novels	23
Wyss, *Swiss Family Robinson*	22
Duruy, *Petite histoire de France*	21
Kermoysen, *Souvenirs du 1er Empire*	19
Napoléon III, *Oeuvres*	19
Campagnes de la Crimée et d'Italie	19
St Pierre, *Paul et Virginie*	18
Fénélon, *Télémaque*	16
Chateaubriand, *Oeuvres*	16
Molière, *Oeuvres*	15
Eugène Sue, novels	15
Berthoud, *Les Soirées d'hiver*	15
Thiers, *Histoire de la Révolution française*	14
Mulloid, *Histoire de Napoléon III*	14
Florian, *Fables*	14
Mille et Une Nuits	14
Barrau, *Le Morale pratique*	14
Barrau, *Conseils aux ouvriers*	13
Barrau, *La Patrie*	13
Les Quatre Fils Aymon	13
Don Quichotte	13

Appendix 165

Paul de Kock, *Oeuvres* 13
Lesage, *Gil Blas* 13
Racine, *Oeuvres* 13
Corneille, *Oeuvres* 12
Dessieux, *Entretiens sur l'hygiène* 12

Notes

1 The new readers of nineteenth-century France

1 Martyn Lyons, *Le Triomphe du livre: une histoire sociologique de la lecture dans la France du 19e siècle*, Paris: Promodis, 1987, p. 28.
2 Mona Ozouf, *L'Ecole, l'Eglise et la République, 1871–1914*, no place cited, Cana/ Jean Offredo, 1982, p. 221.
3 Arnould Frémy, *Comment Lisent les Français d'aujourd'hui?*, Paris: Calmann-Lévy, 1878, pp. 7 and 67–92. '...un immense bazar de faits, d'intérêts et d'idées où les plus graves questions contemporaines se trouvent journellement coudoyées par les plus futils détails de l'existence usuelle.'
4 Lyons, *Triomphe du livre*, p. 100.
5 Jean-Yves Mollier, *L'Argent et les lettres: Histoire du capitalisme d'édition, 1880–1920*, Paris: Fayard, 1988, p. 478.
6 Lyons, *Triomphe du livre*; and 'Towards a National Literary Culture in France', *History of European Ideas*, vol. 16, nos 1–3, 1993, pp. 247–52.
7 This is not the place to debate the merits of the signature test as a measure of literacy. But its value as an indicator of reading ability has been well supported by Roger Schofield, 'The Measurement of Literacy in pre-industrial England', in Jack Goody, ed., *Literacy in Traditional Societies*, Cambridge: Cambridge University Press, 1968, and by François Furet and W. Sachs, 'La Croissance de l'alphabétisation en France, 18e–19e siècle', *Annales-économies, sociétés, civilisations*, vol. 29, 1974, pp. 714–37.
8 M. Fleury and A. Valmary, 'Les Progrès de l'instruction élémentaire de Louis XIV à Napoléon III d'après l'enquête de Louis Maggiolo (1877–79)', *Population*, 12, jan–mars 1957, pp. 71–92.
9 François Furet and Jacques Ozouf, *Reading and Writing: Literacy in France from Calvin to Jules Ferry*, Cambridge: Cambridge University Press and Maison des Sciences de l'Homme, 1982, pp. 5–9 and chapter 1. This is an abbreviated translation of *Lire et ecrire: l'alphabétisation des français de Calvin à Jules Ferry*, Paris: Editions de Minuit, 1977.
10 Furet and Sachs, 'La Croissance de l'alphabétisation'.
11 F.Furet and J. Ozouf, 'Literacy and Industrialisation: the case of the Département du Nord in France', *Journal of European Economic History*, vol. 5:1, spring 1976, pp. 5–44.
12 Daniel Roche, *The People of Paris: an essay in popular culture in the 18th century*, Leamington Spa UK: Berg, 1987, p. 199 and p. 203.
13 Furet and Ozouf, *Reading and Writing*, pp. 166–91.
14 Raymond Grew, Patrick J. Harrigan and James Whitney, 'The Availability of Schooling in 19th Century France', *Journal of Interdisciplinary History*, XIV, summer 1983, pp. 25–63.
15 R. Grew and P. J. Harrigan, *School, State and Society: the growth of elementary schooling in 19th century France – a quantitative analysis*, Ann Arbor: University

of Michigan Press, 1991, p. 47. But see also the critical debate in *Annales-éc6nomies, sociétés, civilisations*, vol. 41: 4, 1986, pp. 885–945.
16 Robert Gildea, *Education in Provincial France, 1800–1914: a study of three departments (Nord, Gard, Ille-et-Vilaine)*, Oxford: Clarendon Press, 1983, pp. 211–6.
17 Grew and Harrigan, *School, State and Society*, p. 47 and pp. 55–6.
18 P. Butel and G. Mandon, 'Alphabétisation et scolarisation en Aquitaine au 18e siècle et au début du 19e siècle', in Furet and Ozouf, *Lire et Ecrire*, vol. 2, pp. 32–3; Y.Pasquet, 'L'Alphabétisation dans le département de la Vienne au 19e siècle', in Furet and Ozouf, *Lire et ecrire*, vol. 2, p. 263.
19 Linda Clark, *Schooling the Daughters of Marianne: textbooks for the socialization of girls in modern French primary schools*, Albany NY: State University of New York Press, 1984, p. 11; and see Laura S.Strumingher, *What Were Little Girls and Boys Made Of? Primary education in rural France, 1830–1880*, Albany NY: State University of New York Press, 1983.
20 Grew and Harrigan, *School, State and Society*, cited p. 128.
21 Paul Lorain, *Tableau de l'instruction primaire en France*, Paris: Hachette, 1837, pp. 2–5.
22 Jean Hébrard, 'Ecole et alphabétisation au XIXe siècle', *Annales-économies, sociétés, civilisations*, vol. 35:1, jan–fév 1980, pp. 66–80. And see Antoine Prost, *Histoire de l'enseignement en France, 1800–67*, Paris: A. Colin, 1968.
23 G. Duveau, *La Vie ouvrière en France sous le Second Empire*, Paris: Gallimard, 1946; G.Duveau, *La Pensée ouvrière sur l'éducation pendant la Seconde République et le Second Empire*, Paris: Domat Montchrestien, 1948.
24 Martin Nadaud, *Mémoires de Léonard, ancien garçon maçon*, intro. by Maurice Agulhon, Paris: Hachette, 1976, pp. 67–80 (first published at Bourganeuf by Duboueix in 1895).
25 André Armengaud, *Les Populations de l'Est-Aquitain au début de l'époque contemporaine: recherches sur une région sous-développée vers 1845–1871*, Paris: Ecole pratique des hautes études, 1961.
26 Nöe Richter, *Les Bibliothèques populaires*, Le Mans: Plein Chant, 1977, p. 6.
27 Furet and Ozouf, *Reading and Writing*, p. 242.
28 Maurice Agulhon, ed., *Histoire de la France urbaine, tome 4, La ville de l'âge industriel: le cycle haussmannien*, Paris: Seuil, 1983, pp. 458–9.
29 Lyons, *Triomphe du livre*, pp. 73–5.
30 Charles-Augustin Sainte-Beuve, 'De la littérature industrielle' (1839), in *Portraits contemporains*, Paris: Calmann-Lévy, 5 vols., 1888–89, vol. 2, pp. 444–71.
31 J.-Y. Mollier, *Michel et Calmann Lévy, ou la naissance de l'édition moderne, 1836–91*, Paris: Calmann-Lévy, 1984, pp. 265–8.
32 Mollier, *L'Argent et les Lettres*, and his 'Histoire de la lecture, histoire de l'édition', in Roger Chartier, ed., *Histoires de la lecture: un bilan de recherches*, Paris: IMEC/Maison des Sciences de l'Homme, 1995, pp. 207–13.
33 Octavio Paz, *The Labyrinth of Solitude*, Harmondsworth UK: Penguin 20th Century Classics, 1985, pp. 65–7.
34 Louis Chevalier, *Classes laborieuses et classes dangereuses*, Paris: Plon, 1958.
35 M. Ozouf, *L'Ecole, l'Eglise*, p. 83.
36 Martyn Lyons, 'Fires of Expiation: Book-burnings and Catholic missions in Restoration France', *French History*, vol. 10:2, June 1996, pp. 240–66.

168 Notes

37 Ibid., p. 247.
38 Anne-Marie Chartier and Jean Hébrard, *Discours sur la lecture, 1880–1980*, Paris: Bibliothèque publique d'information, Centre Georges Pompidou, 1989, pp. 22–9.
39 Mgr Turinaz, évêque de Tarentaise, *Les Mauvais Lectures: la presse et la littérature corruptrices (Lettre pastorale)*, Paris: Librairie de la Société Bibliographique, 1881.
40 Zechariah, chapter 5, verses 1–4. In the King James Authorized Version: 'I see a flying roll... This is the curse that goeth forth over the face of the whole earth.'
41 Chartier and Hébrard, *Discours sur la Lecture*, p. 46 and chapter 3.
42 Ibid., cited p. 50.

> Qu'on n'oublie pas que certains lecteurs ou plutôt certaines lectrices, surtout à la campagne et dans les milieux qui fréquentent les bibliothèques paroissiales, n'ont qu'un bagage de lecture très restreint et seront facilement choquées par une peinture un peu réaliste, quoique discrète, de la vie réelle ou par des illustrations un peu libres: ceci est une affaire d'habitude et d'éducation.

43 Abbé Louis Bethléem, *Romans à lire et romans à proscrire*, Cambrai: Masson, 4th ed., 1908, pp. 20–2.
44 Ibid., pp. 26–7 and 29.
45 Ibid., pp. 34–5.
46 Ibid., pp. 37–40.
47 Ibid., p. 169 and pp. 209–11.
48 Ibid., pp. 291 and 331–2.
49 M. Ozouf, *L'Ecole, l'Eglise*, pp. 8–11.
50 Chartier and Hébrard, *Discours sur la lecture*, cited p. 242. 'Apprendre à lire est un bienfait illusoire ou un présent dangereux si vous ne rendez pas vos élèves capables de comprendre et d'aimer les lectures sérieuses. C'est par là qu'il faut les mettre à l'abri des séductions.' Bréal was a linguist, who took over from Ernest Renan in charge of oriental manuscripts at the Bibliothèque Nationale. He was Inspecteur-général de l'Instruction publique pour l'Enseignement Supérieur from 1879 to 1888.
51 Ibid. Translation of this phrase is given in the extract on page 15.
52 Michel De Certeau, *The Practice of Everyday Life*, Berkeley: University of California Press, 1984.

2 Reading workers: Libraries for the people

1 Espérance-Augustin de L'Etang, *Des Livres utiles et du colportage comme moyen d'avancement moral et intellectuel des classes rurales et ouvrières*, Paris: Maillet, 1866.
2 Charles de Rémusat, *Mémoires de ma vie*, ed. C. Pouthas, Paris: Plon, 1958–67, vol. 3, p. 420. 'Les ouvriers tailleurs, formés par les lectures qu'ils entendent en se livrant à leur travail sédentaire, avaient en général des opinions avancés.'

3 Frédéric Le Play, *Les Ouvriers européens: études sur les travaux, la vie domestique, et la condition morale des populations ouvrières de l'Europe*, 2nd ed., 6 vols, Tours: Mame et fils, 1877–79, vol. 6, pp. 408–9 and 438–9.

La plupart d'entre eux, surtout dans les ateliers, lisent beaucoup les ouvrages à bon marché qui renferment des connaissances historiques, et ces notions, plus ou moins exactes, servent d'aliment à leurs préoccupations politiques... Les ateliers, par les lectures qui s'y font, le [the apprentice tailor] familiarisent avec la plus révoltante obscénité, ou suscitent jusqu'à l'exaltation les haines politiques et les passions envieuses dirigées contre les classes élevées. Souvent les ouvriers d'un même atelier se cotisent pour payer un soldat invalide qui vient leur faire la lecture à haute voix, à raison de 0f40 ou 0f50 par heure. A défaut de cette ressource, chaque ouvrier lit à tour de rôle. Parfois, l'un des ouvriers, beau parleur d'atelier, leur raconte de grossières facéties ou des lambeaux d'histoire arrangés à son gré, et empruntés souvent au plus sanglantes époques de la révolution française. En résumé, l'apprentissage coïncide avec un véritable enseignement de la débauche et des idées que la société peut à bon droit redouter.

4 Michelet to Béranger, 16 June 1848, cited in Maurice Agulhon, 'Le Problème de la culture populaire en France autour de 1848', *Romantisme*, no. 9, 1975, p. 60.

La Presse n'atteint pas le peuple. En effet, vous le voyez, elle est, en ce moment, d'un côté, et les masses de l'autre. Elle laisse un grand nombre d'hommes bonapartistes (c'est-à-dire idolâtres), la majorité des femmes idolâtres ou catholiques. Les masses ne savent pas lire et ne veulent pas lire, parce que c'est un fatigue pour l'homme peu habitué. Il faut que la République agisse sur ces masses, pour exiger la lecture, qui est impossible aujourd'hui. Les journaux, les bibliothèques circulatoires, écoles d'adultes, etc., agiront, mais à la longue.

5 François Delessert, *Opinion dans la discussion sur le budget de l'Instruction publique, 13 mai 1836*, Paris: Chambre des Députés, 1836; and see Richter, *Bibliothèques populaires*, p. 72.
6 Léon Curmer, *De l'Etablissement des bibliothèques communales en France*, Paris: Guillaumin, 1846.
7 Charles Louandre, 'La Bibliothèque royale et les bibliothèques publiques', *Revue des Deux Mondes*, vol. 13, 15 mars 1846, p. 1055. 'Le peuple est avide de lecture, mais il lit au hasard, au rabais, des rapsodies qui l'abêtissent ou le dépravent.'
8 Charles Robert, 'La Lecture populaire et les bibliothèques en 1861', *Bulletin de la Société Franklin (BSF)*, vol. 4, no. 45, 1er avril 1872, p. 105. 'Par les bibliothèques on combattrait les cabarets et les cafés, les deux plus fatales institutions de la prétendue civilisation des classes ouvrières.'
9 Ibid., p. 107.

En Ecosse et en Suisse, les paysans se délassent de leurs travaux le soir et les jours de fête par la lecture. Les nôtres vont généralement dépenser leur argent au cabaret. Comment voulez-vous qu'ils fassent autre chose? L'Eglise, l'école, les maisons du village d'où puissent venir l'influence

morale sont graves, presque sévères. Tandis que chaque village a cinq ou six cabarets où l'on est si gai!
10 Nadaud, *Mémoires de Léonard*, pp. 140–1.
11 Pierre Pierrard, *La Vie ouvrière à Lille sous le Second Empire*, Paris: Bloud et Gay, 1965, pp. 284–9.
12 Maurice Agulhon, 'Les Chambrées en Basse- Provence: histoire et ethnologie', *Revue historique*, no. 498, 1971, pp. 337–68.
13 Frémy, *Comment lisent les Français*, p. 7.
14 Ibid., pp 74–8.
15 Lyons, 'Fires of Expiation', pp. 240–66.
16 Ibid., p. 247.
17 Ibid., p. 248.
18 Ibid., pp. 253–5.
19 Nöé Richter, *L'Oeuvre des bons livres de Bordeaux: les années de formation, 1812–1840*, Bernay: Société d'histoire de la lecture, 1997.
20 Richter, *Bibliothèques populaires*, pp. 18–9.
21 Maurice Pellisson, 'Les Lectures Publiques du Soir, 1848–50', *La Nouvelle Revue*, vol. 30, 1er octobre 1904, pp. 317–26; Richter, *Bibliothèques populaires*, pp. 49–54.
22 *L'Atelier: Organe des intérêts moraux et matériels des ouvriers*, Paris: EDHIS facsimile reprint, 1978, 3 vols, with introduction by Maurice Agulhon.
23 *La Ruche populaire: Journal des ouvriers rédigé par eux-mêmes (sous le direction de Vinçard)*, Paris, 1839–49.
24 A.Cuvillier, *Un Journal d'ouvriers: L'Atelier, 1840–1850*, Paris: Felix Alcan, 1914, p. 51.
25 Jean-Louis Lerminier, 'De la Littérature des Ouvriers', *Revue des deux mondes*, 1841, vol. 4, p. 576. 'Le démon de l'orgeuil est venu heurter à la porte de l'artisan ... L'ouvrier rêve la gloire des lettres; il aspire à un but qu'il ne peut atteindre'.
26 Cuvillier, *Un Journal d'ouvriers*, pp. 156–62.
27 Alain Faure and Jacques Rancière, eds., *La Parole ouvrière, 1830–1851*, Paris: Union Générale d'Editions, série 10/18, 1976, pp. 12–22 and 208–12; and see Duveau, *Pensée ouvrière*, pp. 50–64.
28 *L'Atelier*, 7e année, no. 8, mai 1847; 5e année, no. 12, sept. 1845.
29 *L'Atelier*, 4e année, no. 2, novembre 1843. 'Un poison qui fausse notre intelligence, qui stimule et débilite tour à tour notre âme'.
30 *L'Atelier*, 4e année, no. 4, jan.1844 and no. 7, avril 1844, which carried an extract from *Le Magasin pittoresque*. This weekly magazine was launched in 1833 by Edouard Charton, who later became a supporter of the Franklin Society. It was sparsely illustrated, carried articles on travel, science, architecture and history, as well as the sayings of great writers. Its highly instructive contents also tried to dispel some common 'erreurs et préjugés'.
31 *L'Atelier*, 6e année, no. 6, mars 1846.
32 *L'Atelier*, 4e année, no. 2, novembre 1843.
33 Cuvillier, *Un Journal d'ouvriers*, pp. 232–4.
34 Jules Simon, 'L'Instruction populaire et les bibliothèques populaires', *Revue des deux mondes*, vol. 47, 15 septembre 1863, pp. 364ff.
35 Pierrard, *La Vie ouvrière à Lille*, pp. 267–8. 'C'est une manière de sanctuaire où les blouses et les sabots sont fort mal vus'.

36 Jean Hassenforder, *Dévéloppement comparée des bibliothèques publiques en France, en Grande-Bretagne, et aux Etats-Unis, dans la seconde moitié du 19e siècle, 1850–1914*, Paris, 1967.
37 Richter, *Bibliothèques populaires*, pp. 45–6.
38 Simon, 'L'Instruction populaire', p. 375.
39 Archives Nationales, F1a 632.
40 Richter, *Bibliothèques populaires*, pp. 41–2. '..une députation de contre-maîtres, d'ouvriers, d'employés d'usine, de cultivateurs et d'artisans était venue lui demander de signaler les principaux ouvrages propres à figurer dans une bibliothèque de 4 à 500 volumes bons pour amuser et instruire, et étrangers à la politique ainsi qu'à la controverse religieuse.'
41 *BSF*, vol. 1, no. 1, 15 juillet 1868, pp. 13–15 and vol. 1, no. 6, 15 décembre 1868, p. 108.
42 *BSF*, vol. 1, no. 7, 15 janvier 1869, pp. 113–6.
43 *BSF*, vol. 1, no. 1, 15 juillet 1868, p. 7.
44 Archives Nationales F1a 632; M.Carbonnier, 'Une Bibliothèque populaire au XIXe siècle: la bibliothèque populaire protestante de Lyon', *Revue française d'histoire du livre*, 47e année, no. 20, juillet-août-septembre, 1978, pp. 628–9.
45 Arlette Boulogne, 'L'Influence de Pierre-Jules Hetzel, éditeur, sur les institutions de lecture populaire', in Christian Robin, ed., *Un Éditeur et son siècle: Pierre-Jules Hetzel, 1814–1886*, Paris: ACL, 1988, pp. 255–67. Taking catalogues published by the Franklin Society up to 1878, Boulogne found a slightly higher proportion of novels and literature in the ideal library (42 per cent).
46 E. Marguerin, 'Du Choix des Romans', *BSF*, vol. 1, no. 6, 15 déc.1868, pp. 105–6.

> La vie réelle ne se prête pas avec complaisance à ces velléités romanesques. De là, des déceptions, des dégoûts, des misères morales sans nombre. Quand on a vu de près les ravages causés par les romans honnêtes dans les existences simples et laborieuses, on est effrayé de la responsabilité que l'on prend en provoquant ces sortes de lectures.

47 *BSF*, vol. 1, no. 11, 15 mai 1869, pp. 204–7.
48 Archives Nationales, F. 17* 3236, p. 21, 30 juin 1882.
49 Lyons, *Triomphe du livre*, pp. 182–3 for this section.
50 Denis Poulot, *Question sociale: Le sublime, ou le travailleur comme il est en 1870 et ce qu'il peut être*, ed Alain Cottereau, Paris: Maspéro, 1980 (first published 1870), pp. 135–6 and 195.
51 Maurice Pellisson, *Les Bibliothèques populaires à l'étranger et en France*, Paris: Imprimerie Nationale, 1906, p. 169.
52 Richter, *Bibliothèques populaires*, p. 31.
53 Archives Nationales, F.17* 3236, p. 86, 11 mai 1883. 'On ne doit pas oublier que la plupart de nos habitants...ne sont, au point de vue intellectuel, que de grands enfants; et l'on ne nourrit pas les enfants exclusivement de gros pain et d'aliments chargés.'
54 Martyn Lyons, 'La Transformation de l'espace culturel français: le réseau des librairies et des bibliothèques, 1870–1914' in Jacques Girault, ed., *Ouvriers en banlieue, xixe et xxe siècles*, Paris: Editions de l'Atelier, 1998, pp. 390–407.
55 Katherine Auspitz, *The Radical Bourgeoisie: the* Ligue de l'Enseignement *and the origins of the Third Republic, 1866–1885*, Cambridge: Cambridge University Press, 1982.

172 *Notes*

56 Philip Nord, *The Republican Moment: Struggles for democracy in 19th-century France*, Cambridge MA: Harvard UP, 1995.
57 Duveau, *Pensée ouvrière*, p. 41; Richter, *Bibliothèques populaires*, p. 7, quoting article by Macé in *Courrier du Bas-Rhin*, 25 avril 1862.
58 Jean Macé, *Morale en action: Mouvement de propagande intellectuelle en Alsace*, Paris: Hetzel, 1865.
59 Auspitz, *Radical Bourgeoisie*, pp. 72–5.
60 Macé, *Morale en action*, pp. 26–7, 55–6, 131–7.
61 A. Audiganne, *Les Populations ouvrières et les industries de la France: Études comparatives*, 2 vols., New York (Franklin reprint) 1970, I, p. 199 (first published in 1860).
62 Ibid., II, pp. 334–5 and 373.
63 Philip A. Bertocci, *Jules Simon: Republican Anticlericalism and Cultural Politics in France, 1848–1886*, Columbia USA: University of Missouri Press, 1978.
64 Marcel Boivin, 'Les Origines de la *Ligue de l'Enseignement* en Seine-Inférieure, 1866–71', *Revue d'histoire économique et sociale*, vol. 46, no. 2, 1968, pp. 225–6.
65 Poulot, *Question sociale*.
66 Ibid. p. 188.
67 Ibid., pp. 195 and 203.
68 Ibid., pp. 133–6.
69 Ibid., pp. 143–4.
70 Macé, *Morale en action*, pp. 139–70.
71 Nöe Richter, *Lecture populaire et ouvrière: Lecture et travail*, Bernay: Société d'histoire de la lecture, 1998, pp. 13–14.
72 Ibid., p. 16.
73 Boivin, '*Ligue de l'Enseignement* en Seine- Inférieure', pp. 207–8.
74 Auspitz, *Radical Bourgeoisie*, p. 99; and Abel Chatelain, 'Ligue de l'Enseignement et éducation populaire en Bourgogne au début de la Troisième République', *Annales de Bourgogne*, vol. 27, 1955, pp. 104–14.
75 Auspitz, *Radical Bourgeoisie*, p. 108.
76 Ibid., pp. 157–8.
77 Archives Nationales BB18.1449, dossier 3160, circular from Ministry of the Interior, 6 September 1849.

> Le caractère le plus commun des écrits que l'on s'efforce de répandre en ce moment et auxquels on donne la forme la plus populaire, c'est de diviser la société en deux classes, les riches et les pauvres, de représenter les premiers comme des tyrans, les seconds comme des victimes; d'exciter l'envie et la haine des uns contre les autres, et de préparer ainsi dans notre société, qu'a tant besoin d'unité et de fraternité, tous les élémens d'une guerre civile.

3 Reading workers: Improvisation and resistance

1 Jonathan Rose, 'Rereading the English Common Reader: a preface to the history of audiences', *Journal of the History of Ideas*, vol. 53, no. 1, 1992, p. 70.
2 Richard Hoggart, *The Uses of Literacy: Aspects of working-class life*, Harmondsworth UK: Penguin, 1958.

3 Hamish Graham, 'How did 19th-century Workers get into Frédéric LePlay's "Bad Books"?', *Australian Journal of French Studies*, vol. XXIII, no. 1 (4th George Rudé Seminar issue), 1986, pp. 130–44.
4 Frédéric LePlay, *Les Ouvriers européens: Études sur les travaux, le vie domestique et la condition morale des populations ouvrières de l'Europe*, Paris: Imprimerie Impériale, 1855. A second edition was published with the same title in six volumes by Mame et fils in Tours, 1877–79. Then appeared F. LePlay, *Les Ouvriers des deux mondes: Études sur les travaux, le vie domestique et la condition morale des populations ouvrières, 2e série, vol. 1*, Paris: Firmin-Didot, 1887.
5 Frédéric Barbier, 'Livres, lecteurs, lectures' in Dominique Varry, ed., *Histoire des bibliothèques françaises, vol. 3, Les Bibliothèques de la Révolution et du xixe siècle, 1789–1914*, Paris: Promodis/Cercle de la Librairie, 1991, pp. 581–2.
6 Le Play, *Ouvriers européens*, 1st ed., pp. 272–3, *Chiffonnier de Paris*, information collected by Cochin and Landsberg in 1849 & 1852.
7 Le Play, *Ouvriers des deux mondes*, vol. 1, monograph 52, *Pêcheur-Côtier, maître de barque à Martigues, Bouches-du-Rhône*, 1879, pp. 303–4.
8 Le Play, *Ouvriers des deux mondes*, vol. 1, monograph 55, *Gantier de Grenoble*, 1865 and 1886–7, p. 470.
9 Le Play, *Ouvriers des deux mondes*, vol. 1, monograph 49, *Charron des forges de Montataire, Oise*, 1884, p. 148.
10 Ibid., p. 150.
11 Le Play, *Ouvriers des deux mondes*, vol. 1, monograph 50, *Faiencier de Nièvre*, 1864, p. 184.
12 Barbier, 'Livres, lecteurs, lectures', pp. 615–18.
13 Archives Nationales F1a.632; Carbonnier, 'Une Bibliothèque populaire', pp. 628–9.
14 *BSF*, vol. 3, 1871, pp. 59–60. Total loans = 2,425.
15 *BSF*, vol. 3, 1871, p. 76. Total loans = 1,905.
16 *BSF*, vol. 5, no. 67, 1er mars 1873. Total loans = 2,214.
17 E. de Saint-Albin, *Les Bibliothèques municipales de la ville de Paris*, Paris: Berger-Levrault, 1896, pp. 60–1 and 262; Lyons, *Triomphe du livre*, pp. 183–92.
18 Saint-Albin, *Bibliothèques municipales*, pp. 60–1.
19 Edward Lillie Craik, *The Pursuit of Knowledge Under Difficulties*, new, revised and enlarged edition, London: George Bell, 1876.
20 Nöe Richter, *La Lecture et ses institutions: la lecture populaire, 1700–1918*, Le Mans: Eds. Plein Chant and l'Université du Maine, 1987, pp. 20–2.
21 Jean Hébrard, 'Comment Valentin Jamerey-Duval apprit-il à lire: un autodidaxie exemplaire', in R.Chartier, ed., *Pratiques de la lecture*, Marseilles: Rivages, 1985, pp. 38–43.
22 Jacques-Louis Ménétra, compagnon vitrier au XVIIIe siècle, *Journal de ma vie*, ed. Daniel Roche, preface by Robert Darnton, Paris: Albin Michel, 1998, pp. 300–2. First published Paris, Montalba, 1982.
23 Norbert Truquin, *Mémoires et aventures d'un prolétaire à travers la Révolution, l'Algérie, la République argentine et le Paraguay*, Paris: Librairie des Deux Mondes, 1888, p. 14. For more about Truquin, see Michel Ragon, *Histoire de la littérature prolétarienne en France*, Paris: Albin Michel, 1974, pp. 100–3; Michelle Perrot, 'A Nineteenth-Century Work Experience as Related in a Worker's Autobiography: Norbert Truquin', in Steven J.Kaplan and Cynthia J.Koepp, eds, *Work in France: Representations, meaning, organization and practice*,

174 *Notes*

Ithaca and London: Cornell University Press, 1986, chapter 10; Paule Lejeune, introduction to the 1977 edition of Truquin's *Mémoires et aventures*, published by Maspéro in Paris; Mark Traugott, ed., *The French Worker: Autobiographies from the early industrial era*, Berkeley, University of California Press, 1993, chapter 5.
24 Truquin, *Mémoires et aventures*, pp. 144 and 231.
25 Ibid., pp. 72–3.
26 Ibid., pp. 225–7 and 235–6.
27 Ibid., pp. 294–5.
28 Ibid., pp. 447–8.
29 Ibid., p. 451.
30 Antoine Sylvère, *Toinou, le cri d'un enfant auvergnat, pays d'Ambert*, preface by P.-J.Hélias, Paris: Plon, 1980, pp. 121–5.
31 Sylvère, *Toinou*, pp. 157, 199 and 210.
32 Nadaud, *Mémoires de Léonard*: 'Un livre de bonne foi qui ne les égarera pas dans des subtilités fausses et mensongères'.
33 Gabriel Gauny, *Le Philosophe plébéien*, ed. Jacques Rancière, Paris: La Découverte/Maspéro, 1983, p. 27.
34 Nadaud, *Mémoires de Léonard*, pp. 67–80.
35 Jean-Yves Mollier cites this often and with relish, and I am grateful to him for reminding me of it. See his 'Le roman populaire dans la bibliothèque du peuple', in Jacques Migozzi, ed., *Le Roman populaire en question(s)*, Paris: PULIM, 1996, p. 587. The phrase opens chapter 5 of the novel, but in chapter 4 *père* Sorel had already hurled Julien's copy of *Le Mémorial de Ste Hélène* into the stream.
36 Jean-Baptiste Dumay, *Mémoires d'un militant ouvrier du Creusot (1841–1905)*, ed. Pierre Ponsot, Grenoble: Maspéro, 1976, pp. 116–18.
37 Dumay, *Mémoires*, p. 298.
38 Ibid., pp. 302–12.
39 Pierre Bourdieu, *La Distinction: Critique sociale du jugement*, Paris: Editions de Minuit, 1979, p. 378.
40 Nöé Richter, *La Conversion du mauvais lecteur et la naissance de la lecture publique*, Marigné: Editions de la Queue du Chat, 1992, pp. 9–22.
41 Gauny, *Philosophe plébéien*, pp. 99–111.
42 Xavier-Edouard Lejeune, *Calicot, enquête de Michel et Philippe Lejeune*, Paris: Montalba, 1984, pp. 104–5.
43 Lejeune, *Calicot*, pp. 117–20.
44 Lejeune, *Calicot*, p. 120–1. 'Ainsi que les flots tumultueux d'un torrent déchaîné à travers les roches, ces choses nouvelles faisaient irruption en mon jeune cerveau et y formaient un chaos que nulle méthode ne pouvait régler.'
45 Sebastien Commissaire, *Mémoires et souvenirs*, 2 vols, Lyon: Meton, 1888, vol. 1, p. 121.
46 Autobiography of A., in Jean Peneff, ed., *Autobiographies de militants CGTU-CGT*, Nantes: Université de Nantes, cahiers du LERSCO, 1979, p. 18. I am grateful to Jacques Girault for bringing this work to my attention.

A sept ans, on a supprimé l'école totalement! Les jeunes ne se rendent pas compte quelle était la situation, il y a 50, 60, 80 ans. Ils vous disent:

'Comment vous avez appris à lire? comment vous avez pu...?'...y avait alors les vieux militants guesdistes... C'étaient de bons instituteurs qui faisaient l'école le soir pour nous apprendre à lire et à écrire. Ils nous faisaient des cours. Ils nous apprenaient les problèmes, le calcul. Ils nous faisaient une demi-heure de théorie sur ce qui s'était passé, sur les révolutions, l'action, et puis alors évidemment, à ce moment- là, c'était très riche au point de vue social. Mon père était né en 1852 et il nous a élevés dans le souvenir... il nous parlait de la Commune. Il était adhérent au parti socialiste et naturellement, il nous parlait de Louise Michel. On a été élevé, vous savez, avec cet état d'esprit de gens qui s'étaient révoltés contre l'injustice.

47 Claude Genoux, *Mémoires d'un enfant de la Savoie suivis de ses chansons*, preface by Béranger, Paris: Le Chevalier, 1870; Richter, *La Lecture et ses institutions*, pp. 123–7.
48 Duveau, *Pensée ouvrière*, pp. 302–7.
49 Henri Tolain, 'Le Roman populaire', *La Tribune ouvrière*, vol. 1, no. 3, 18 juin 1865, pp. 9–10.

Comme un champignon vénéneux, le journal-roman foisonne. Au grand jour ou clandestinement, il s'étale orgueilleux ou se glisse furtif sous le toit du pauvre. Si papa le proscrit, par hasard, comme une nourriture malsaine, Lise le cache dans son corsage. Le tyran n'y peut rien, et sa défense ajoute à l'intérêt palpitant du drame l'âcre saveur du fruit défendu'.

50 Duveau, *Pensée ouvrière*, pp. 291–2, taken from Perdiguier's *Livre du compagnonnage*, Paris, 1857.
51 Duveau, *Pensée ouvrière*, pp. 290–8.
52 Edgar Leon Newman, 'Sounds in the Desert: the socialist worker poets of the Bourgeois Monarchy, 1830–1848', *Proceedings of the Third Annual Meeting of the Western Society for French History, December 1975* (USA), 1976, pp. 269–99.
53 Cited in Jean Briquet, *Agricol Perdiguier, compagnon du Tour de la France et représentant du peuple, 1805–1875*, Paris: Rivière, 1955, pp. 187–9.
54 For Perdiguier's difficulties with publishers, see Briquet, *Agricol Perdiguier*, pp. 359–65.
55 Agricol Perdiguier, *Mémoires d'un compagnon*, Moulins: Cahiers du Centre, 1914.
56 Perdiguier, *Mémoires*, p. 137.
57 Rose, 'Rereading the English Common Reader', p. 64.
58 Martyn Lyons, 'The Autodidacts and their Literary Culture: Working-class autobiographers in nineteenth-century France', *Australian Journal of French Studies*, vol. XXVIII, no. 3, 1991, pp. 264–73 gave a short preliminary answer to this question.
59 Roger Chartier, *The Order of Books: Readers, authors and libraries in Europe, between the fourteenth and eighteenth centuries*, Stanford: Stanford University Press, 1994.
60 Stanley Fish, *Is There a Text in This Class? The authority of interpretive communities*, Cambridge, MA: Harvard University Press, 1980.
61 Nadaud, *Mémoires de Léonard*, pp. 140–1.
62 Genoux, *Mémoires d'un enfant de la Savoie*, p. 275.

176 Notes

63 Joseph Benoît, *Confessions d'un prolétaire*, Paris: Editions Sociales, 1968, first published Lyon, 1871, pp. 56–7 and 73–4.
64 X.Egapel (pseudonym of Constant Lepage), *Soixante Ans de la vie d'un prolétaire*, Paris: Vanier, 1900, p. 34.
65 Louis-Arsène Meunier, 'Mémoires d'un ancêtre ou tribulations d'un instituteur percheron', *Cahiers percherons*, 65–6, 1981, pp. 38–44. Meunier's memoirs were first published as supplements to the teachers' journal *L'Ecole nouvelle* in 1904.
66 Victorine B. (Brocher), *Souvenirs d'une morte vivante*, preface by Lucien Descaves, Paris (Maspéro), 1976, p. 34.
67 Suzanne Voilquin, *Souvenirs d'une fille du peuple ou la Saint-Simonienne en Egypte*, ed.Lydia Elhadad, Paris: Maspéro, 1978, p. 65 (first edition 1866). 'Je puisais dans ces romans des notions fausses sur la vie réelle'. For more on Voilquin's relations with the Saint-Simonians, see Susan Grogan, *French Socialism and Sexual Difference: Women and the new society, 1803–44*, London (Macmillan Press, now Palgrave), 1992.
68 Egapel, *Soixante Ans*, pp. 178–80.
69 Lejeune, *Calicot*, p. 101. 'Avec quelle ardeur, quelle passion je lus et relus ce chef d'oeuvre immortel de poésie et de style! Je puis dire que mon esprit borné et enfermé jusqu'alors s'ouvrit soudain aux choses sublimes de la nature et à des horizons intellectuels que je n'avais jamais connus.'
70 Victorine B., *Souvenirs*, p. 62.
71 Cécile Dufour, ouvrière en modes, 'A M. de Lamartine', *La Ruche populaire*, sept. 1839, pp. 15–18, and see Lamartine's unimpressive response in the November issue.
72 Genoux, *Mémoires d'un enfant de la Savoie*, e.g. pp. 99, 107, 133.
73 Lejeune, *Calicot*, pp. 13–14.
74 Archives Nationales, BB$_{18}$.1374, no. 6342.
75 Roger Bellet, 'Une Bataille culturelle, provinciale et nationale, à propos des bons auteurs pour bibliothèques populaires', *Revue des sciences humaines*, vol. 34, 1969, pp. 453–73; Charles-Augustin Sainte-Beuve, *A propos des Bibliothèques populaires* (speech in Senate, 25 juin 1867), Paris, 1867; Lyons, *Triomphe du livre*, pp. 367–9.
76 Archives Nationales F1a 632, 10 février 1863.
77 Saint-Albin, *Bibliothèques municipales*, p. 31.
78 Pascale Marie, 'La Bibliothèque des Amis de l'Instruction du IIIe arrondissement', in Pierre Nora, ed., *Les Lieux de mémoire – 1, La République*, Paris: Gallimard, 1984, pp. 323–51.
79 Marie, 'Bibliothèque des Amis de l'Instruction', p. 342.
80 Fernand Pelloutier, *Histoire des Bourses du Travail*, Paris: Publications Gramma/Gordon and Breach, 1971, pp. 141–3, (first published in 1902). See entry on Pelloutier in Jean Maitron, ed., *Dictionnaire biographique du mouvement ouvrier Français*, vol. XIV, 3e partie, 1871–1914, Paris: Editions ouvrières, 1976, pp. 231–3.
81 Pelloutier, *Histoire des Bourses du Travail*, p. 180.
82 Juliette Spire, 'La Bibliothèque de la Bourse du Travail à Paris: Étude des acquisitions de 1898 à 1914', unpublished *mémoire de maîtrise*, Université de Paris-1, 1985, chapter 4.

Notes 177

83 Jacques Julliard, *Pelloutier et les origines du syndicalisme d'action directe*, Paris: Seuil, 1971, pp. 243–4.
84 Pelloutier, *Histoire des Bourses du Travail*, pp. 130–3.
85 Julliard, *Pelloutier*, p. 257.
86 Daniel Rappe, 'La Bourse du Travail de Lyon des origines à 1914', unpublished *mémoire de maîtrise d'histoire contemporaine*, Université Lumière, Lyon-2, 1997.
87 Spire, 'La Bibliothèque de la Bourse du Travail', p. 135.
88 Pelloutier, *Histoire des Bourses du Travail*, p. 181.
89 Spire, 'La Bibliothèque de la Bourse du Travail', p. 83.
90 Ibid., chapter 6.
91 Ibid., pp. 26–8.
92 Ibid., p. 105.
93 Bourdieu, *La Distinction*, pp. 91–2.

L'autodidacte d'ancien style se définissait fondamentalement par une révérence à l'égard de la culture qui était l'effet d'une exclusion à la fois brutale et précoce et qui conduisait à une dévotion exaltée et mal orientée, donc vouée à être perçue par les tenants de la culture légitime comme une sorte d'hommage caricatural.

94 Alphonse Viollet, *Les Poètes du peuple au xixe siècle*, ed. M. Ragon, Paris: Librairie française et étrangère, 1846; François Gimet, *Les Muses prolétaires*, Paris: Fareu, 1856.
95 Benoît Malon, 'Fragments de Mémoires', *Revue socialiste*, vol. XLV, janvier-juillet 1907 (several parts).
96 *Grand Dictionnaire Larousse*, 1866 ed., I, p. 979. Quoted by J. H. Buckley, *The Turning Key: Autobiography and the subjective impulse since 1800*, Cambridge, MA: Harvard University Press, 1984, p. 38.
97 Philippe Lejeune, 'La Côte Ln27', in *Moi aussi*, Paris: Seuil, 1986, pp. 264: 'le développement maladif et monstrueux du MOI'.
98 My rough classification seems in no way to contradict the ideas of Traugott, *The French Worker*, pp. 27–8.
99 Jacques Laffitte, *Mémoires de Laffitte, 1767–1844*, ed. Jacques Duchon, Paris: Firmin-Didot, 1932.
100 Victorine B., *Souvenirs*, pp. 113–6.
101 Jacques Rancière, 'The Myth of the Artisan: Critical Reflections on a Category of Social History', in Kaplan and Koepp, *Work in France*, pp. 317–34.
102 Joseph Voisin, dit Angoumois, *Histoire de ma vie et 55 ans de compagnonnage*, Tours: Imprimerie du Progrès, 1931.
103 J. B. E. Arnaud, *Mémoirs d'un compagnon du Tour de France*, Rochefort: Giraud, 1859, e.g. pp. 50, 65, 223, 300 and on p. 226: 'Brisons nos idoles pour ne plus nous occuper que de notre bonheur commun'.
104 Philippe Lejeune, *Le Pacte autobiographique*, Paris: Seuil, 1975; and his *On Autobiography*, ed. P. J. Eakin, Minneapolis: University of Minnesota Press, 1989.
105 Dumay, *Mémoires*, p. 75: 'J'ai la grande satisfaction intime de pouvoir me dire que j'ai poussé dans la mesure de mes forces au char du progrès humain'.
106 Rémi Gossez, ed., *Un Ouvrier en 1820: Manuscrit inédit de Jacques-Etienne Bédé*, Paris: Presses Universitaires de France, 1984, pp. 45–9.

178 Notes

107 Gossez, *Un Ouvrier en 1820*, 1984, p. 73. See the review by Michael Sonenscher in *History Workshop Journal*, 21, summer 1986, pp. 173–9.
108 Among them Traugott, *The French Worker*, pp. 47–8.
109 Philippe Lejeune, 'En Famille', in his *Moi aussi*, Paris: Seuil, 1986, pp. 199–200.
110 Perdiguier, *Mémoires*, p. 87.
111 Dumay, *Mémoires*, pp. 302–3: 'Ma maison était considérée plus que jamais comme la maison d'un pestiféré'.
112 Arnaud, *Mémoires*, p. 50.
113 Nadaud, *Mémoires de Léonard*, 1976 ed., p. 282: 'Il s'était formé dans chaque corps de métier, des groupes parmi les ouvriers les plus fiers et les plus intelligents, qui aiguillonnaient les masses et leur faisaient honte de leur indolence et de leur apathie'.
114 Benoît, *Confessions*, p. 32:

> Au sein de cette foule, de ces masses compactes, il y avait des coeurs généreux à qui les secrets de l'avenir avaient été sinon dévoilés, mais révélés dans leur conscience inquiète et tourmentée par les problèmes qui les cachaient encore à leurs investigations laborieuses. Mais ces hommes étaient en petit nombre et isolés au milieu de cette masse confuse comme dans un désert.

115 Cited in Ragon, *Histoire de la littérature prolétarienne*, p. 99.
116 Traugott, *The French Worker*, pp. 28–30.
117 Cited in Ragon, *Histoire de la littérature prolétarienne*, p. 82: 'J'aime mon état, j'aime mes outils et alors même que j'aurais pu vivre de ma plume, je n'aurais pas voulu cesser d'être ouvrier serrurier.'
118 Truquin, *Mémoires et aventures*, p. 273:

> Il est urgent que tous ceux qui travaillent et souffrent les vices de l'organisation sociale ne comptent que sur eux-mêmes pour se tirer de l'affaire et se créer un présent et un avenir meilleurs par la solidarité. Il importe donc que chacun d'entre eux apporte sa pierre à l'édifice commun, en publiant ses notes, ses cahiers, ses mémoires, en un mot tous les documents qui peuvent contribuer à détruire les iniquités de vieux monde et à hâter l'avènement de la révolution sociale.

4 Reading women: from Emma Bovary to the New Woman

1 Letter to M.le Comte..., Aquila, 18 October 1832, in *Correspondance de Stendhal (1800–1842)*, ed. A. Paupe and P.-A. Chéramy, Paris: Bosse, 1908, vol. 3, pp. 89–93.
2 On the popularity of Scott, see Martyn Lyons, 'The Audience for Romanticism: Walter Scott in France, 1815–51', *European History Quarterly*, 14:1, 1984, pp. 21–46.
3 *Bibliographie de la France*, vol. 7, no. 41, 11 juillet 1818, p. 397; vol. 8, no. 7, 13 fév.1819, p. 91; vol. 8, no. 17, 24 avril 1819, pp. 209–10.
4 *Bibliographie de la France*, vol. 9, no. 3, 15 jan.1820, p. 27 and e.g. vol. 9, no. 20, 13 mai 1820, p. 250.

Notes 179

5 *Bibliographie de l'Empire français*, vol. 4, no. 20, 20 mai 1815, p. 225; vol. 4, no. 32, 21 août 1815, p. 338.
6 *Bibliographie de la France*, vol. 15, no. 24, 25 mars 1826, p. 250 and following.
7 *Bibliographie de la France*, vol. 35, no. 14, 4 avril 1846, p. 62.
8 Mathurin-Joseph Brisset, *Le Cabinet de lecture*, Paris: Magen, 1843, vol. 1, p. 10: 'de séduisants aperçus de sentiments, de délicieux entortillages de phrases, de chastes dévergondages de pensée, suivis des tourbillons entraînants de la passion, de délires frénétiques et de tirades incendiaires!'
9 Brisset, *Cabinet de lecture*, pp. 13–14.
10 Brisset, *Cabinet de lecture*, pp. 16–18: 'Ennuyeusement vertueuses ou niaisement sentimentales'.
11 S—(ylvain) M—(aréchal), *Projet d'une loi portant défense d'apprendre à lire aux femmes*, Paris: Massé, 1801. Reprinted in Lille in 1841 and Belgium, 1847, then by Gustave Sandré in Paris, 1853, entitled: *Il ne faut pas que les femmes sachent lire, ou projet d'une loi...* This work, and its publishing history, are analysed in Geneviève Fraisse, *Reason's Muse: Sexual difference and the birth of democracy*, trans. Jane Marie Todd, Chicago (University of Chicago Press), 1994, pp. 1–26. I am grateful to Barrie Rose for bringing it to my attention.
12 Maréchal, *Projet*, article 5, translation from Fraisse, *Reason's Muse*, p. 10.
13 Maréchal, *Projet*, articles 39 and 79.
14 Maréchal, *Projet*, provision 61, translation from Fraisse, *Reason's Muse*, p. 25.
15 *Le Charivari*, 30 juin 1839, moeurs conjugales no. 6.
16 Lise Quéffelec, 'Le Lecteur du roman comme lectrice: Stratégies romanesques et stratégies critiques sous la Monarchie de Juillet', *Romantisme*, vol. 16, no. 53, 1986, pp. 9–21.
17 Eugène Labiche and Edouard Martin, *Le Voyage de Monsieur Perrichon, comédie en quatre actes*, Paris: Calmann-Lévy, 1949, Act 1, Scene 9. I am grateful to Jean-Yves Mollier for bringing this to my attention.
18 Kate Flint, *The Woman Reader, 1837–1914*, Oxford: Clarendon Press, 1993, chapter 4.
19 Gustave Flaubert, *Madame Bovary*, Paris: Classiques Garnier, 1961, 1ère partie, chapter VI. English edition by Penguin Classics, trans. G. Wall, Harmondsworth UK, 1992, p. 27.
20 Flaubert, *Madame Bovary*, English ed., p. 28.
21 Ibid., The italics are Flaubert's and usually denote a cliché.
22 Ibid., p. 30.
23 Ibid.
24 Flaubert, *Madame Bovary*, Garnier ed., ch. VII, p. 42; English ed., p. 35.
25 Ibid., Garnier ed., ch. IX, p. 54; English ed., p. 45
26 Ibid., English ed., p. 31.
27 Ibid., p. 47.
28 Ibid., p. 49.
29 Ibid., p. 66.
30 Ibid., p. 78.
31 Ibid., p. 215.
32 Ibid., p. 100.
33 Ibid., p. 131.
34 Ibid., p. 236.

180 Notes

35 Christiane Mounoud-Anglès, 'Le Courrier des lectrices de Balzac (1830–1840): Stratégies identitaires', in Mireille Bossis, ed., *La Lettre à la croisée de l'individuel et du social*, Paris: Kimé, 1994, pp. 98–104.
36 James Smith Allen, *In the Public Eye: a history of reading in modern France, 1800–1940*, Princeton NJ: Princeton University Press, 1991, pp. 77, 128, 236.
37 Allen, *In the Public Eye*, pp. 259–66.
38 Dupanloup, born in 1802, had been confessor to the Duke of Bordeaux and to Talleyrand. He became Bishop of Orléans in 1849. In 1871 he was deputy in the very conservative National Assembly, and in 1876 he became a senator.
39 Françoise Mayeur, 'Les Evêques français et Victor Duruy. Les cours secondaires de jeunes filles', *Revue d'histoire de l'église de France*, vol. 57, no. 159, juillet-déc.1971, pp. 267–304.
40 Cited in Jean-Louis Desbordes, 'Les Ecrits de Mgr.Dupanloup sur la haute éducation des femmes', in Françoise Mayeur and Jacques Gadille, eds, *Education et images de la femme chrétienne en France au début du XXe siècle, à l'occasion du centenaire de la mort de Mgr Dupanloup*, Lyon: Hermès, 1980, p. 28.
41 Mgr Félix Dupanloup, *Femmes savantes et femmes studieuses*, Paris: Douniol, 3rd edition, 1867, p. 24.
42 Desbordes, 'Ecrits de Dupanloup', cited p. 30.
43 Mgr. Félix Dupanloup, *La Femme studieuse: Quelques conseils aux femmes chrétiennes qui vivent dans le monde sur le travail intellectuel qui leur convient*, Paris: Douniol, 1870.
44 Dupanloup, *Femme studieuse*, pp. 49–51.
45 Lyons, *Triomphe du livre*, chapter 5, especially p. 98.
46 Desbordes, 'Ecrits de Dupanloup', p. 34.
47 Dupanloup, *Femme studieuse*, pp. 99–101.
48 Dupanloup, *Femmes savantes et femmes studieuses*, pp. 64–8.
49 Dupanloup, *Femmes savantes et femmes studieuses*, pp. 69–70.
50 Fish, *Is There a Text in this Class?*
51 *La Femme nouvelle*, vol. 2, no. 3, 1er fév.1905 and no. 11, 1er juin 1905. I am grateful to Glenda Sluga for alerting me to this source.
52 *La Femme nouvelle*, vol. 3, no. 2, 15 jan.1906, pp. 49–57 and no. 3, 1er fév.1906, pp. 102–4.
53 *La Femme nouvelle*, vol. 3, no. 2, 15 jan.1906, p. 50: 'Le mariage l'a douchée – à présent, c'est une matronne terre à terre, incapable de joies intérieures et de gaieté, compagne diligent et morose de son mari. Le contraste entre le rêve et la réalité a tué son âme. – Résultat déplorable, dû certainement à d'intempérantes lectures pendant sa première jeunesse.'
54 *La Femme nouvelle*, vol. 3, no. 2, 15 jan.1906, pp. 52–3.
55 *La Femme nouvelle*, no. 3, 1er fév.1906, p. 104: 'La lecture est un élargissement de la vie sociale: de même que dans la vie sociale, nous évitons le contact des maladies de peur de la contagion, préservons aussi des esprits jeunes, non encore assez fortifiés, de la contagion des héros de romans malsains'.
56 Lyons, *Triomphe du livre*, p. 245; Musée du Grand Palais, *Fantin-Latour: Catalogue d'une exposition (9 nov.1982–7 fév.1983)*, Paris, 1982, no. 20; Allen, *In the Public Eye*, p. 3. Allen lists many representations of reading in visual art in chapter 5 of his book.

5 Reading women: Defining a space of her own

1. Janice Radway, *Reading the Romance: Women, patriarchy and popular literature*, Chapel Hill: University of North Carolina Press, 1984.
2. Victorine B., *Souvenirs*, first edition published in Lausanne, 1909.
3. Michelle Perrot, ed., *History of Private Life, vol. 4: from the fires of revolution to the Great War*, Cambridge, MA: Belknap, 1990, pp. 500–2.
4. Eugénie de Guérin, *Journal*, Albi: Ateliers professionnels de l'Orphelinat St.-Jean, 60th ed., 1977, p. 195. 'Ce petit cahier ne doit jamais voir le jour. Ceci est sacré comme le secret de la confession'.
5. Beatrice Didier, *Le Journal intime*, Paris: Presses Universitaires de France, 1976, p. 115.
6. Louise Weiss, *Souvenirs d'une enfance républicaine*, Paris: Denoël, 10th ed., 1937. This forms the first part of her *Mémoires d'une Européenne*, 3 vols, Paris: Payot, 1970, which was followed by vols 4–6, published in Paris by Albin Michel (1971–76) and entitled 'nouvelle série'.
7. Bourdieu, *Distinction*.
8. Pierre-Jakez Hélias, *The Horse of Pride: Life in a breton village*, New Haven, CT: Yale University Press, 1978, p. 96, trans. J.Guicharnaud from *Le Cheval d'Orgeuil*, 'A la maison, outre le paroissien de ma mère et quelques receuils de cantiques, il y a deux livres importants. L'un, qui reste à demeurer sur l'appui de la fenêtre, est le dictionnaire français de Monsieur Larousse...l'autre est enfermé dans l'armoire de noces de ma mère, que nous appelons la presse. C'est la *Vie des Saints*, rédigée en breton.' I prefer my own translation here.
9. E.de Guérin, *Journal*, entries of 2 and 21 July 1839: '...une boîte funèbre, un reliquaire où se trouve un coeur mort, tout embaumé de sainteté et d'amour.'
10. Ibid., 27 July 1839.
11. Ibid., 17 August 1839.
12. Ibid., 19 October 1839.
13. Ibid., 27 November 1824 and 8 December 1834 for example.
14. Ibid., 5 January and 15 April 1835. 'Ces Vies de Saints sont merveilleuses, charmantes à lire, pleines d'instructions pour l'âme croyante.'
15. Ibid., 22 May 1835.
16. Ibid., 6 and 7 May 1837, 6 June 1838, 15 February 1840.
17. Ibid., 30 May and 13 June 1835.
18. Ibid., 9 January 1840.
19. Ibid., 10 March and 28 April 1835, 25 August 1839.
20. Ibid., 1 March 1838.
21. Ibid., 10 December 1834 and 28 April 1839.
22. Ibid., 11 April 1836.
23. Ibid., 11 April 1836 and 20 July 1838.
24. Ibid., 5 March 1839.
25. Ibid., 4 August 1838. 'Il est divin, il est infernal, il est sage, il est fou, il est peuple, il est roi, il est homme, il est femme, peintre, poète, sculpteur, il est tout.'
26. Ibid., 9 January, 2 April and 5 November 1840.

182 Notes

27 Ibid., 1 September 1835.

> Le diable m'a tentée tout à l'heure dans un petit cabinet où j'ai fait trouvaille de romans. 'Lis-en un mot, me disais-je. Pour voir celui-ci, pour voir celui- là,' mais le titre m'a fort déplu. Ca ne vaut rien, et ne peut rien apprendre que des désordres de coeur que j'ignore sans doute. Ce sont des lettres galantes d'une religieuse, la confession générale d'un chevalier galant et autres histoires de bonne odeur. Fi donc, que j'aille lire cela! Je n'en suis plus tentée maintenant et vais seulement changer ces livres de cabinet ou plutôt les jeter au feu pour qu'ils ne servent à rien. Dieu me garde de pareilles lectures'.

28 Ibid., 9 February 1838. 'Mais ces génies ont des laideurs qui choquent l'oeil d'une femme.'
29 Ibid., 4 August 1840.
30 Ibid., 3 September 1841.
31 Ibid., 7 January 1835. 'C'est toujours un livre ou plume que je touche en me levant, les livres pour prier, penser, réfléchir.'
32 Ibid., 20 November 1834. 'C'est moi qui suis lectrice, mais à bâtons rompus; c'est tantôt un clef qu'on me demande, mille choses, souvent ma personne, et le livre se ferme pour un moment.'
33 Ibid., 10 December 1834.
34 Hélène Legros, *Les Lettres d'Hélène*, ed. Dominique Halévy, Paris: Hermé, 1986. For an overview of the correspondence by an author who had access to all of it, see Anne Martin-Fugier, 'Les Lettres célibataires', in Roger Chartier, ed., *La Correspondance: les usages de la lettre au xixe siècle*, Paris: Fayard, 1991, pp. 407–26.
35 *Lettres d'Hélène*, pp. 266–7, 15 January 1897.

> Il faut tôt ou tard que nous cessions d'être immobiles et que nous ayons une idée, quelquechose d'uniquement à nous et que nous tâchons de réaliser... et quand l'accès est passé on a acquis plus d'expérience que les livres et la morale n'en peuvent donner, on est plus fort devant une foule de circonstances.

36 Ibid., p. 281, April 1897.
37 Ibid., pp. 305–6, 10 April 1898.
38 Ibid., pp. 290–1, 7 and 14 September 1897.
39 Ibid., pp. 22 and 78, 11 April 1894.
40 Ibid., pp. 52 and 58, 9 February and 8 March 1893.
41 Ibid., p. 108, 1 December 1894. The poems of 'Ossian', purporting to be the work of an ancient Celtic bard, were published by James Macpherson in 1763.
42 Ibid., p. 75, 30 March 1894.
43 Ibid., p. 47, 19 January 1893 and p. 91, 24 August 1894 (Loti); p. 51, January 1893 (*Manon Lescaut*); p. 151, 6 June 1895 (*Paul et Virginie*); p. 80, 18 April 1894 (Scott).
44 Ibid., p. 183, February 1896.
45 Ibid., pp. 30–4, October-November 1892.
46 Ibid., p. 145, 16 May 1895.

47 Ibid., p. 120, February 1895.
48 Ibid., pp. 40 and 45, December 1892 – January 1893; pp. 126–8, 13 February 1895. The full title in English is usually *Wilhelm Meister's Apprenticeship and Travels*, translated from *Wilhelm Meisters Lehrjahre* and *Wilhelm Meisters Wanderjahre*.
49 Ibid., p. 48, 19 January, 1893. 'D'abord, ceux où l'histoire n'est pas compliquée mais où il y a une masse de refléxions, dissertations, petites promenades à droite et à gauche – bien entendu, il faut que ce soit bien fait et que cela se rapporte au sujet... [*Wilhelm Meister*] Cela c'est mon bonheur suprême, c'est ce qu'on peut relire mille fois de suite.'
50 Martyn Lyons and Lucy Taksa, ' "If Mother caught us reading!" ': Impressions of the Australian woman reader, 1890–1933', *Australian Cultural History*, 11, 1992, p. 45.
51 *Lettres d'Hélène*, p. 125, end of February 1895.
52 Ibid., p. 56, 23 February 1893; p. 65, November 1893.
53 Ibid., pp. 197–8, end of March 1896.
54 Lynne Pearce, *Feminism and the Politics of Reading*, London: Arnold, 1997.
55 *Lettres d'Hélène*, p. 49, 19 January 1893. 'On ne pourrait pas les rêver plus parfaites, plus poètiques – et elles sont toutes aussi simples, aussi naives, aussi peu doctoresses que possible.'
56 Ibid., p. 89, 20 July 1894, 'ce n'est pas étonnant que la plupart des jeunes filles désirent se marier, quand ce ne serait que pour échapper à la vie bête et insignifiante qu'on leur fait presque partout.'
57 Ibid., p. 123, February 1895.
58 Ibid., p. 58, 8 March 1893.
59 Ibid., pp. 79–80, 18 April 1894 and following.
60 Ibid., p. 242, October 1896.
61 Ibid., p. 122, 15 February 1895.

J'avais fini le premier volume quand papa est survenu et m'a 'conseillé' de remettre ce livre de côté sur-le-champ. Furieuse que j'étais! D'autant plus qu'il n'y avait absolument rien de mal dans tout ce que j'en avais lu... C'est égal, il faut qu'il me considère comme une gosse de dix ans pour me défendre ce livre. Pourtant, je ne le lirai pas malgré la défense, il n'en vaut la peine – c'est un galimatias d'aventures biscornues... il n'y a rien qui me blesse comme de me voir défendre un livre – cela me met en rage contre tout – et je me console en pensant: 'J'en sais d'autres!'.

62 Ibid., p. 75, 30 March 1894.
63 Ibid., p. 110, December 1894 (*Wild Duck*); p. 115, January 1895 (*Brand*).
64 Ibid., p. 264, 7 January 1897.
65 Ibid., p. 51, January 1893.
66 Ibid., p. 115, January 1895. 'Quand on a commencé à faire la société de ce brave Ibsen, on ne peut plus s'en débarrasser, et les autres lectures paraissent fades.'
67 Ibid., p. 291, 14 September 1897.
68 Ibid., p. 137, April 1895. 'Je me suis sentie délivrée d'un fameux poids.'
69 Ibid., p. 273, 15 February 1897. 'Il me semble que tout le meilleur et le principal de ma vie, je l'aurai vécu par lettres, aussi je regarde ma main droite comme tout ce que j'ai de plus précieux.'

184 Notes

70 Ibid., p. 334, 16 August 1933. 'Je pense aussi souvent à elle qui a été si mêlée à notre vie – et il m'arrive, quand passe le facteur de l'après-midi, d'interroger le courrier comme s'il devait s'y trouver encore sa grande enveloppe bleue.'
71 Martyn Lyons and Lucy Taksa, *Australian Readers Remember: an oral history of reading*, Melbourne: Oxford University Press, 1992; Anne-Marie Thiesse, *Le Roman du quotidien: Lecteurs et lectures populaires à la Belle Epoque*, Paris: Chemin Vert, 1984.
72 Anne-Marie Thiesse, 'Mutations et permanences de la culture populaire: la lecture à la Belle Epoque', *Annales-économies, sociétés, civilisations*, vol. 39, jan–fév.1984, p. 75. 'On se les passait entre femmes. Le samedi soir, les hommes allaient au café, et les femmes venaient jouer aux cartes chez nous. Surtout, on échangeait alors nos feuilletons, des choses comme *Rocambole* ou *La Porteuse du Pain*.'
73 Anne-Marie Thiesse, 'Imprimés du pauvre, livres de fortune', *Romantisme*, vol. 43, 1984, p. 106. 'C'étaient des histoires d'amour; les feuilletons du *Moniteur* n'étaient pas particulièrement socialistes. Mon père ne lisait jamais le feuilleton, ah non!' See Appendix A.
74 Thiesse, 'Mutations et permanences', pp. 73–4 and 81.
75 Thiesse, 'Imprimés du pauvre', p. 91. 'Ma mère et moi on découpait le feuilleton du journal quand il était bien; on le cousait pour en faire un petit livre.'
76 Ibid., p. 106. (See Appendix A.)

> Il n'y avait pas de livres à la maison: c'était trop cher. J'ai eu des livres de prix chez les soeurs, mais pas à l'école laïque. Il y avait bien une bibliothèque municipale; je l'ai dévorée, mais il n'y avait pas grand-chose. Les institutrices me prêtaient des livres pour jeunes filles. Je lisais le dimanche après-midi, en allant garder les bêtes: je n'avais bien le temps de lire autrement, à cause de mon ouvrage de dentelle. Je lisais les feuilletons; les livres de l'institutrice, mes livres d'école, ou même le dictionnaire Larousse. J'ai toujours lu régulièrement le dictionnaire, je l'ai même apporté avec moi à la maison de retraite.

77 Thiesse, 'Mutations et permanences', p. 72.
78 Lyons and Taksa, *Australian Readers Remember*, pp. 158–63; Lyons and Taksa, ' "If Mother caught us reading!" ' pp. 39–50.
79 In a hitherto unpublished paper presented to the History of Reading Practices Workshop at the 6th Conference of the International Society for the Study of European Ideas, Haifa, August 1998.
80 *Lettres d'Hélène*, June 1892, p. 28 and 17 November 1894, p. 106. 'Quand je vois Robert et Maurice si occupés de leurs études auxquelles nous comprenons rien, je regrette de ne pas être comme eux et je suis furieuse contre ma condition de jeune fille.'
81 Martyn Lyons, 'New Readers in the Nineteenth Century' in G. Cavallo and R. Chartier, eds, *A History of Reading in the West*, Oxford: Polity, 1999, p. 323.
82 Thiesse, *Roman du quotidien*, title to section 1.
83 Thiesse, 'Imprimés du pauvre', p. 107. (See Appendix A.)
84 Voilquin, *Souvenirs d'une fille du peuple*; Victorine B., *Souvenirs*; Jeanne Bouvier, *Mes Mémoires ou 59 années d'activité industrielle sociale et intellectuelle*

d'une ouvrière, 1876–1935, Paris: La Découverte/ Maspéro, 1983 (1st ed. 1936).
85 Voilquin, Souvenirs d'une fille du peuple, p. 77.
'Ces divers ouvrages exaltant l'amour se rendaient complices de la nature, en agitant fortement mon imagination et en remplissant mon coeur de desirs inconnus.'
86 Ibid., p. 65. 'Je puisais dans ces romans des notions fausses sur la vie.'
87 For a discussion of this issue, see Grogan, *French Socialism and Sexual Difference*.
88 On this duality, see Marie-Claire Hoock-Demarle, 'Reading and Writing in Germany' in G. Fraisse and M. Perrot, eds, *A History of Women*, vol. 4, *Emerging Feminism from Revolution to World War*, Cambridge, MA: Belknap, 1993, pp. 145–65.
89 Philippe Lejeune, 'Les Instituteurs du XIXe siècle racontent leur vie', *Histoire de l'Education*, no. 25, janvier 1985, pp. 57–8.
90 Jacques Ozouf, *Nous les Maîtres d'Ecole. Autobiographies d'instituteurs de la Belle Epoque*, Paris: Julliard, 1967, p. 75. 'Mes pauvres parents durent voir le ciel s'entrouvrir. Ils mirent le pied dans l'entrebaillement afin que la porte ne se referme pas. Pour moi, c'était une sorte de conte de fées.'
91 See note 6 to this chapter.
92 Weiss, *Souvenirs*, p. 164. 'Nous vivions les 1001 Nuits'.
93 Ibid., p. 125.

En arrivant, tu vas cacher tes livres. Inutile que ton père les voie. Il est déjà assez mécontent que le lycée ait fait de toi une fille savante, alors que dans leurs classes tes frères ne sont pas en tout les premiers. Par ta facilité aux études, tu lui ressembles et c'est probablement ce qu'il ne parvient pas à te pardonner.

94 Ibid., p. 223. 'Un métier? Et pourquoi? Reste auprès de ta mère. Le journalisme auquel tu rêves te déclassera.'

6 Reading peasants: the pragmatic uses of the written word

1 E.de Guérin, *Journal*, entry of 7 mai 1837.
2 Gérard Coulon, *Une Vie paysanne en Berry de 1882 à nos jours*, Buzançais (self-published), 1979.
3 Ephraim Grenadou et Alain Prévost, *Grenadou, paysan francais*, Paris: Seuil, 1966.
4 Eugen Weber, *Peasants into Frenchmen : the modernization of rural France, 1870–1914*, London: Chatto & Windus, 1977. But see also Peter McPhee, *The Politics of Rural Life: Political mobilization in the French countryside, 1846–52*, Oxford: Clarendon Press, 1992.
5 Maurice Agulhon et al. *Histoire de la France rurale, vol. 3, De 1789 à 1914: Apogée et crise de la civilisation paysanne*, Paris: Seuil, 1992, pp. 171 & 172 (railways), p. 494 (social revolt), & p. 490 (the city).
6 Roger Chartier, *Culture populaire: Retour sur un concept historiographique*, Valencia: University of Valencia, Eutopìas, Documentos de trabajo vol. 52, 1994, p. 4. 'Le sort historiographique de la culture populaire est donc de toujours être étouffée, refoulée, abrasée et, en même temps, de toujours renaître de ses cendres.'

186 Notes

7   Radway, *Reading the Romance*, pp. 221–2.
8   Roger Thabault, *Education and Change in a Village Community: Mazières-en-Gâtine, 1848–1914*, trans. P.Tregear, London: Routledge Kegan Paul, 1971.
9   Furet et Ozouf, *Lire et ecrire*, p. 56.
10 Agulhon et al., *Histoire de la France rurale*, vol. 3.
11 Emile Guillaumin, *La Vie d'un simple*, Paris: Stock, 1943 & Livre de poche, 1972, pp. 190–1.
12 E.de Guérin, *Journal*, entries of 13 mai 1837 & 11 février 1840. 'Il vaut bien mieux un chapelet qu'un livre dans la poche d'un laboureur! Que ceux-ci cultivent les champs, que d'autres cultivent la science.'
13 Suzanne Tardieu, *La Vie domestique dans le Mâconnais rural pré-industriel*, Paris: Institut d'ethnologie, 1964, p. 358 & annexes.
14 Ibid., p. 232.
15 Roger Béteille, *La Vie quotidienne en Rouergue au 19e siècle*, Paris: Hachette, 1973, p. 78.
16 Ulysse Rouchon, *La Vie paysanne dans la Haute-Loire*, Le Puy en Velay: Imprimerie de la Haute-Loire, 1933, p. 24.
17 Guillaumin, *Vie d'un simple* (1943), p. 126.
18 Tardieu, *Vie domestique dans le Mâconnais*, pp.67–70, inventory of Claude D., *propriétaire* at Pouilly.
19 Daniel Fabre & Jacques Lacroix, *La Vie quotidienne des paysans du Languedoc au 19e siècle*, Paris: Hachette, 1973, p. 388.
20 Georges Rocal, *Le Vieux Périgord*, Toulouse: Guitard, 1927, p. 131.

> Ceci n'enleva pas la persuasion aux témoins des guérisons. Elle en fut accrue puisque la tradition affirme que les maléfices étaient communiqués sous forme d'écrits, enrobés de cire et avalés par le patient. Ce qui dans un cas avait nui pouvait, manié par une main bienfaisante, avantager!

21 Henry Massoul, *Au bon vieux temps. Souvenirs du Gâtinais et de la Brie*, Paris: Mercure de France, 1944–45, pp. 43–4.
22 Claude Seignolle, *Le Berry traditionnel*, Paris: Maisonneuve & Larose, 1969, pp. 269–71.
23 Daniel Fabre, 'Le Livre et sa Magie', in Chartier, *Pratiques de la lecture*, pp. 191–2. 'J'ai entendu dire par mes grands-parents qu'il y avait une institutrice qui le lisait et, quand elle le lisait, elle voyait des petites souris passer avec des bougies allumées.'
24 On the special association of shepherds with magic, see Daniel Fabre, *Ecritures ordinaires*, Paris: POL/Centre Georges Pompidou, 1993, pp. 269–313.
25 Fabre, 'Le Livre et sa Magie', pp. 200–3.
26 Martyn Lyons, 'Oral Culture and Rural Community in Nineteenth-Century France: the *veillée d'hiver*', *Australian Journal of French Studies*, vol. 23:1, 1986, pp.102–14.
27 Roger Devos & Charles Joisten *Moeurs et coûtumes de la Savoie du Nord au XIXe siècle: l'enquête de Mgr. Rendu*, Annecy: Académie Salésienne & Grenoble: Centre alpin et rhodanien d'ethnologie, 1978, p. 261 (response from St Nicholas-la-Chapelle).
28 Archives Départementales Seine-et-Oise 2V25/6, visites paroissiales, diocèse de Versailles, 1859.

Notes 187

29 Le Play, *Les Ouvriers européens*, p. 225 (agricultural day-labourer from the Sarthe, 1848); p. 237 (emigrant harvester and *petit propriétaire* from the Soissonnais, 1848–50); p. 243 (charcoal burner from Nièvre, 1842); p. 249 (rural forge-worker from Auvergne, 1850).
30 Fabre, 'Le Livre et sa magie', p. 185.
31 Pierre-Jakez Hélias, *Le Cheval d'Orgeuil: Mémoires d'un Breton au pays bigouden*, Geneva: Famot, 2 vols, 1979, vol. 1, p. 169.
32 Yann Brekilien, *La Vie quotidienne des paysans en Bretagne au 19e siècle*, Paris: Hachette, 1966, pp.90–1.
33 Eugène Le Roy, *Le Moulin du Frau*, Paris: Fasquelle, 1905, pp. 330–1.

C'est comme ça, que, chez nous, au fond d'une campagne du Périgord, on avait appris à connaître les Grecs et les Romains, dont les paysans, d'ordinaire, n'ont seulement point ouï parler, bien loin de se douter quels gens c'était.

34 Archives nationales, BB$_{30}$.370, report from *procureur-général du cour d'appel*, Aix, 14 March 1850; AN BB$_{30}$.388, report from *cour d'appel*, Toulouse, 4 January 1850.
35 Archives Nationales BB$_{30}$.370, report from *arrondissement* of Aix, 5 June 1851. 'Tous les mécontents s'enrôlent dans les chambrées. Les membres de ces chambrées s'abonnent à un journal d'opposition dont la lecture se fait à haute voix pour les paysans illettrés.'
36 Michel de Certeau, *L'Invention du quotidien – 1.Arts de Faire*, Paris: Gallimard, 1990, p. xxxvii.
37 Barnett Singer, *Village Notables in Nineteenth-century France: Priests, mayors, schoolmasters*, Albany: State University of New York Press, 1983, p. 39.
38 Ibid., pp. 114–15.
39 Le Play, *Les Ouvriers européens*, vol. 4, ch. 7, pp. 401–28.
40 Le Play, *Les Ouvriers européens*, vol. 5, ch.5, p. 207; vol. 4, ch. 9, p. 474.
41 Le Play, *Les Ouvriers européens*, vol. 5, ch.7, p. 337.
42 Jean-Jacques Darmon, *Le Colportage de librairie en France sous le Second Empire. Grands colporteurs et culture populaire*, Paris: Plon, 1972, p. 49.
43 Robert Mandrou, *De la Culture populaire au 17e et 18e siècles : la Bibliothèque Bleue de Troyes*, Paris: Stock, 1964. See also Geneviève Bollème, *Les Almanachs populaires aux xviie et xviiie siècles, essai d'histoire sociale*, Paris: Mouton, 1969, and G. Bollème, *La Bibliothèque Bleue, littérature populaire en France du 17e au 19e siècle*, Paris: Julliard, coll.Archives, 1971.
44 Mikhail Bakhtin, *L'Oeuvre de Rabelais et la culture populaire au moyen âge et sous la Renaissance*, Paris: Gallimard, 1970.
45 Roger Chartier, *Figures de la Gueuserie*, Paris: Montalba Bibliothèque Bleue, 1982, pp. 11–106.
46 Darmon, *Colportage*, pp. 126 & 301.
47 Archives Nationales, F18.567, dossier 124, procès-verbal du conseil-général du dépt. de la Mayenne, 13 Sept.1828.

Les livres impies et obscènes se multiplient d'une manière effrayante, on les imprime par milliers et on les colporte partout. Avant la Révolution, les oeuvres de Voltaire et autres impies étaient rares et d'un prix élevé : sous le règne de l'usurpateur, même, ces livres se répandaient peu... Sous le règne du fils aimé de l'Eglise, si admirable par ses vertus, il est affligeant que le poison de l'impiété se débite à vil prix dans toutes les parties de la France.

48 Charles Nisard, *Histoire des livres populaires ou de la littérature du colportage*, Paris: Dentu, 2 vols, 1864, reprinted New York (Franklin), 1971, vol. 2, pp. 232–8.
49 Ronald Gosselin *Les Almanachs républicains: Traditions révolutionnaires et culture politique des masses populaires de Paris (1840–1851)*, Paris: L'Harmattan, 1992, pp. 218–19.
50 Agulhon, 'Le problème de la culture populaire', p. 63.
51 Darmon, *Colportage*, pp. 102–5.
52 Ibid., p. 105.
53 Ibid., p. 104.
54 Michael B.Palmer, 'Some aspects of the French press during the rise of the popular daily, c.1860 to 1890', Oxford University D. Phil. thesis, 1972, p. 381. And see Palmer's *Des petits journaux aux grandes agences: Naissance du journalisme moderne, 1863–1914*, Paris: Aubier, 1983.
55 Palmer, 'Some aspects of the French press', p. 45.
56 Darmon, *Colportage*, p. 266.
57 Henri Norre, *Comment J'ai vaincu la misère: Souvenirs et refléxions d'un paysan*, présentés par Emile Guillaumin, Paris: Balzac, 1944, p. 44 (first published in 1914).
58 Coulon, *Vie paysanne*, pp. 119–20.
59 François-Florentin Bosquet, *De la moralité dans les campagnes depuis 1789*, Chalons-sur-Marne: Société Académique de la Marne, 1860.
60 Curmer, *De l'établissement des bibliothèques communales*, p. 5.
61 Robert, 'La Lecture populaire et les bibliothèques en 1861', pp. 101–2.
62 Ibid., pp. 103–4.

Si au fond d'un placard enfumé, vous rencontrez quelques vieux bouquins, vous gémissez de voir que ce sont les plus immoraux qui existent; le colportage éffréné du dernier règne a inondé nos campagnes de ces écrits impurs qu'on rougit de nommer et qui composent toute la bibliothèque du cultivateur. La lecture des romans à bon marché pénètre aujourd'hui partout et détruit les bons sentiments des populations rurales. Les feuilletons à bas prix, les livraisons périodiques inondent et empoisonnent nos campagnes.

63 Ibid., pp. 104–5.
64 Jean Hébrard, 'Les bibliothèques scolaires', in Dominique Varry, ed., *Histoire des bibliothèques françaises*, tome 3, Paris: Promodis/Cercle de la Librairie, 1991, pp. 546–77.
65 Archives Nationales, F17.9146.
66 Ibid., prefect of Indre-et-Loir, 31 juillet 1866.

On lit peu dans les campagnes, les paysans ne possèdent guère que des almanachs. Il n'en est pas ainsi dans la classe ouvrière, où le goût de la lecture est très répandu, et où on lit de mauvais romans et des livres souvent immoraux que les colporteurs trouvent moyen de faire échapper à l'estampille.

67 Ibid., prefect of Dordogne, 27 juillet 1866. 'L'ignorance et le mauvais goût président trop souvent au choix de ces livres, et l'administration doit plutôt s'attacher à réformer ce goût qu'à s'y conformer.'
68 Ibid., prefect of Loir-et-Cher, 23 juillet 1866. 'Les petits journaux illustrés à 5 à 10 centimes ont fait une concurrence désastreuse à la librairie ambulante.'
69 Ibid., *commissaire* de Montereau, 12 juillet 1866.
70 Ibid., prefect of Cher, 6 juillet 1866. 'Toute la série de romans plus ou moins futiles en renom d'Alexandre Dumas père et fils, de V.Hugo, G.Sand, Sue, Gauthier, etc., etc.'
71 Ibid., *commissaire* de Meaux, Seine-et-Marne, juillet, 1866. 'Afin de maintenir la génération actuelle dans les sentiments d'affection et de sympathie que les populations manifestent pour la dynastie de l'Empéreur.'
72 Ibid., report from Clermont-Ferrand, 13 juillet 1866.
73 Ibid., *commissaire* de Fontainebleau, Seine-et-Marne, 15 juillet 1866.
74 Lyons, *Triomphe du livre*, ch. 5.
75 Archives Nationales, F17.9146, *commissaire* de Beaume, Doubs, 23 juillet 1866.
76 Ibid., *commissaire* de Beaume, Doubs, 23 juillet 1866.
77 Jean-Jacques Darmon, 'Lecture rurale et lecture urbaine', *Europe*, no. 542, juin 1974 (issue on 'Le roman-feuilleton'), pp. 63–8.
78 Raymonde Anna Rey, *Augustine Rouvière, Cévenole*, Paris: Delarge, 1977, p. 79.
79 Thiesse, 'Imprimés du pauvre', and by the same author, 'Mutations et permanences'.
80 Anne-Marie Thiesse, *Le Roman du quotidien: Lecteurs et lectures populaires à la Belle Epoque*, Paris: Chemin Vert, 1984, pp. 18–19.
81 Sylvère, *Toinou*, p. 215.
82 Rey, *Augustine Rouvière*, p. 79.
83 Chartier, *La Correspondance*, p. 336.
84 Ibid., pp. 73–4.
85 Gérard Bacconnier, André Minet & Louis Soler, *La Plume au fusil: les poilus du Midi à travers leur correspondance*, Toulouse: Privat, 1985, p. 29.
86 Coulon, *Vie paysanne*, pp. 102–3.
87 Sylvère, *Toinou*, pp. 153–4. The risks of using professional scribes were well-illustrated in the recent film *O Central do Brasil* (Central Station).
88 Rey, *Augustine Rouvière*, p. 108.
89 Annick Cochet, 'L'Opinion et le Moral des Soldats en 1916, d'après les archives du contrôle postal', unpublished 3e cycle thesis, Paris-X-Nanterre, 1985, 2v., p. 455. 'Tu as bien compris. D'abord les boeufs, puis le carré de luzerne, puis le jardin. Tu en as pour tes six jours.'
90 Grenadou & Prévost, *Grenadou*, p. 93. 'Durant toute la guerre, j'ai rêvé la nuit que j'étais à Saint-Loup. Je me rêvais en moisson, je me rêvais à la charrue.'
91 Bacconnier et al., *Plume au fusil*, pp. 50–1.
92 Cochet, 'L'Opinion et le moral', pp. 479 & 493–4.
93 Daniel Halévy, *Visites aux paysans du Centre, 1907–34*, Paris: Librairie Générale, 1978, p. 76.
94 Halévy, *Visites aux paysans*, p. 394.
95 Ibid., pp. 119–24.

190 Notes

96 Ibid., pp. 60, 97 & 394.
97 Ibid., pp. 393–5 – reminiscences collected in 1900 by *La Quinzaine Bourbonnaise*. 'Tes lectures, je ne sais pas si, à la fin, ça te rendra fin ou bête'.
98 Sylvère, *Toinou*, p. 41.
99 Guillaumin, *Vie d'un simple* (1943), p. 291.
100 Thabault, *Education and Change*, pp. 137–40.
101 Ibid., pp. 224–5.
102 Fabre, 'Le Livre et sa magie', pp. 181–206.

7   Reading classes and dangerous classes

1 Roger Bromley, *Lost Narratives: Popular fictions, politics and recent history*, London: Routledge, 1988, pp. 24–60.
2 Briquet, *Agricol Perdiguier*, pp. 359–65.
3 Jeanne Bouvier, *Mes Mémoires ou 59 années d'activité industrielle, sociale et intellectuelle d'une ouvrière, 1876–1935*, Paris: Maspéro, 1983; & Bonnie G.Smith, *On Writing Women's Work*, Florence: European University Institute Working Paper 91/7, 1991, p. 6.
4 Arnauld, *Mémoires*, p. 226. 'Brisons nos idoles pour ne plus nous occuper que de notre bonheur commun; lisons Jean-Jacques Rousseau, lisons Lamennais, Lamartine, Victor Hugo et Châteaubriand; ces grands hommes nous retremperont l'âme et assainiront notre jugement.'

Appendix B

1 Archives Nationales F.17.9146, ministerial circular to Prefects, 27 June 1866.

Le choix des livres destinés à composer les bibliothèques scolaires est en ce moment de ma part l'object d'études approfondies et minutieuses. Il m'importe beaucoup, au moment où je fais dresser la liste des ouvrages qui semblent le mieux répondre aux besoins des populations urbaines et rurales, de savoir quels sont les livres qui jouissent aujourd'hui dans nos campagnes surtout d'une vogue et d'un succès assurés. Je vous prie donc de vouloir bien me faire connaître le plus tôt possible les principaux ouvrages qui, offerts par les colporteurs ou étalés dans les foires sont achetés en grand nombres.

Bibliography

Archival sources

Archives Nationales
BB18 and BB30 = general correspondence of Ministry of Justice, especially BB18.1374, no. 6342.
BB18.1449, dossier 3160, circular from Ministry of the Interior, 6 September 1849.
BB30.370, Reports from Aix-en-Provence, 1850–51.
BB30.388, Reports from Toulouse, 1850–51.
F1a 632, Bibliothèques communales et populaires, 1850–65.
F 17* 3236–8, Procès-verbaux de la commission des bibliothèques populaires, communaux et libres, 1882–1914.
F17.9146, Replies to the 1866 questionnaire on reading habits in the countryside.
F18.567, dossier 124.

Archives Départementales Seine-et-Oise
2V25/26, visites paroissiales, diocèse de Versailles, 1859.

Periodicals

L'Atelier: Organe des intérêts moraux et matériels des ouvriers, Paris: EDHIS facsimile reprint, 1978, 3 vols, with introduction by Maurice Agulhon.
Bibliographie de l'Empire français
Bibliographie de la France, Paris, 1810–
Bulletin de la Société Franklin (BSF), vols 1–8, 1868–76.
Le Charivari
La Femme nouvelle
La Ruche populaire: Journal des ouvriers rédigé par eux-mêmes (sous le direction de Vinçard), Paris, 1839–49.

Autobiographical texts

Arnaud, Jean-Baptiste, *Mémoires d'un compagnon du Tour de France*. Rochefort: Giraud, 1859.
Audoux, Marguerite, *Marie-Claire*. Paris: Grasset, 1987.
B. (Brocher), Victorine, *Souvenirs d'une morte vivante*. preface by Lucien Descaves, Paris: Maspéro, 1976 (first edition published in Lausanne, 1909).
Benoît, Joseph, *Confessions d'un prolétaire*. Paris: Editions Sociales, 1968 (first published Lyon, 1871).
Bouvier, Jeanne, *Mes Mémoires ou 59 années d'activité industrielle sociale et intellectuelle d'une ouvrière*. 1876–1935, Paris: La Découverte/Maspéro, 1983 (1st ed. 1936).

Commissaire, Sebastien, *Mémoires et souvenirs*, 2 vols. Lyon: Méton, 1888.
Dumay, Jean-Baptiste, *Mémoires d'un militant ouvrier du Creusot (1841–1905)*, ed. Pierre Ponsot. Grenoble: Maspéro, 1976.
Egapel, X (pseudonym of Constant Lepage), *Soixante Ans de la vie d'un prolétaire*. Paris: Vanier, 1900.
Gauny, Gabriel, *Le Philosophe plébéien*, ed. Jacques Rancière. Paris: La Découverte/Maspéro, 1983.
Genoux, Claude, *Mémoires d'un enfant de la Savoie suivis de ses chansons*, preface by Béranger. Paris: Le Chevalier, 1870.
Gossez, Rémi, ed., *Un Ouvrier en 1820: Manuscrit inédit de Jacques-Etienne Bédé*. Paris: Presses Universitaires de France, 1984.
Grenadou, Ephraim and Prévost, Alain, *Grenadou, paysan francais*. Paris: Seuil, 1966.
Guérin, Eugénie de, *Journal*, Albi (Ateliers professionnels de l'Orphelinat St.-Jean), 60th ed., 1977.
Guillaumin, Emile, *La Vie d'un simple*. Paris: Stock, 1943 and Livre de poche, 1972.
Hélias, Pierre-Jakez, *The Horse of Pride: Life in a Breton village*. New Haven, CT & London: Yale University Press, 1978 (trans J.Guicharnaud from *Le Cheval d'Orgeuil: Mémoires d'un Breton au pays bigouden*, Geneva, Famot, 2 vols, 1979).
Laffitte, Jacques, *Mémoires de Laffitte, 1767–1844*, ed. Jacques Duchon. Paris: Firmin-Didot, 1932.
Legros, Hélène, *Les Lettres d'Hélène*, ed. Dominique Halévy. Paris: Hermé, 1986.
Lejeune, Philippe, 'Les Instituteurs du XIXe siècle racontent leur vie', *Histoire de l'Education*, no. 25, janvier 1985, pp. 53–104.
Lejeune, Xavier-Edouard, *Calicot, enquête de Michel et Philippe Lejeune*. Paris: Montalba, 1984.
Malon, Benoît, 'Fragments de Mémoires', *Revue socialiste*, vol. XLV, janvier-juillet 1907 (several parts).
Meunier, Louis-Arsène, 'Mémoires d'un ancêtre ou tribulations d'un instituteur percheron', *Cahiers percherons*, 65–6, 1981, pp. 38–44. Meunier's memoirs were first published as supplements to the teachers' journal *L'Ecole nouvelle* in 1904.
Ménétra, Jacques-Louis, compagnon vitrier au XVIIIe siècle, *Journal de ma vie*, ed. Daniel Roche, preface by Robert Darnton. Paris: Albin Michel, 1998 (first published Paris, Montalba, 1982).
Nadaud, Martin, *Mémoires de Léonard, ancien garçon maçon*, intro. by Maurice Agulhon. Paris: Hachette, 1976 (first published at Bourganeuf by Duboueix in 1895).
Norre, Henri, *Comment J'ai vaincu la misère: Souvenirs et refléxions d'un paysan*, présentés par Emile Guillaumin. Paris: Balzac, 1944 (first published in 1914).
Ozouf, Jacques, *Nous les Maîtres d'Ecole. Autobiographies d'instituteurs de la Belle Epoque*. Paris: Julliard, coll. archives, 1967.
Peneff, Jean, ed., *Autobiographies de militants CGTU-CGT*. Nantes: Université de Nantes, cahiers du LERSCO no. 1, 1979.
Perdiguier, Agricol, *Mémoires d'un compagnon*. Moulins: Cahiers du Centre, 1914.
Rey, Raymonde Anna, *Augustine Rouvière, Cévenole*. Paris: Delarge, 1977.
Sylvère, Antoine, *Toinou, le cri d'un enfant auvergnat, pays d'Ambert*, preface by P.-J.Hélias. Paris: Plon, 1980.
Traugott, Mark, ed. and trans., *The French Worker: Autobiographies from the early industrial era* (Bédé, Voilquin, Perdiguier, Nadaud, Truquin, Dumay, Bouvier). Berkeley, CA: University of California Press, 1993.

Truquin, Norbert, *Mémoires et aventures d'un prolétaire à travers la Révolution, l'Algérie, la République argentine et le Paraguay*. Paris: Librairie des Deux Mondes, 1888.

Voilquin, Suzanne, *Souvenirs d'une fille du peuple ou la Saint-Simonienne en Egypte*, introduction by Lydia Elhadad. Paris: Maspéro, 1878 (first published 1866).

Voisin, Joseph, dit Angoumois, *Histoire de ma vie et 55 ans de compagnonnage*. Tours: Imprimerie du Progrès, 1931.

Weiss, Louise, *Souvenirs d'une enfance républicaine*. Paris: Denoël, 10th ed., 1937. (This forms the first part of her *Mémoires d'une Européenne*, 3 vols, Paris, Payot, 1970, which was followed by vols 4–6, published in Paris by Albin Michel in 1971–76 and entitled 'nouvelle série'.)

General secondary works

Agulhon, Maurice, 'Le Problème de la culture populaire en France autour de 1848', *Romantisme*, no. 9, 1975, pp. 50–64.

Agulhon Maurice, 'Les Chambrées en Basse-Provence: histoire et ethnologie', *Revue historique*, no. 498, 1971, pp. 337–68.

Agulhon, Maurice, Gabriel Désert and Robert Specklin, *Histoire de la France rurale*, vol. 3, *De 1789 à 1914: Apogée et crise de la civilisation paysanne*. Paris: Seuil, 1992.

Allen, James Smith, *In the Public Eye: a history of reading in modern France, 1800–1940*, Princeton NJ: Princeton University Press, 1991.

——, *Popular French Romanticism: Authors, readers and books in the 19th century*. Syracuse, NY: Syracuse University Press, 1981.

Auspitz, Katherine, *The Radical Bourgeoisie: the Ligue de l'Enseignement and the origins of the Third Republic, 1866–1885*. Cambridge: Cambridge University Press, 1982.

Bacconnier, Gérard, André Minet and Louis Soler, *La Plume au fusil: les poilus du Midi à travers leur correspondance*. Toulouse: Privat, 1985.

Barbier, Frédéric, 'Livres, lecteurs, lectures' in Dominique Varry, ed., *Histoire des bibliothèques françaises*, vol. 3, *Les Bibliothèques de la Révolution et du XIXe siècle, 1789–1914*. Paris: Promodis/Cercle de la Librairie, 1991, pp. 579–623.

Bertocci, Philip A, *Jules Simon: Republican anticlericalism and cultural politics in France, 1848–1886*, Columbia MI: University of Missouri Press, 1978.

Boivin, Marcel, 'Les Origines de la Ligue de l'Enseignement en Seine-Inférieure, 1866–71', *Revue d'histoire économique et sociale*, vol. 46, no. 2, 1968, pp. 203–31.

Bollème, Geneviève, *Les Almanachs populaires aux XVIIe et XVIIIe siècles, essai d'histoire sociale*. Paris: Mouton, 1969.

Bollème, Geneviève, *La Bibliothèque Bleue, littérature populaire en France du 17e au 19e siècle*. Paris: Julliard, coll.Archives, 1971.

Boulogne, Arlette, 'L'Influence de Pierre-Jules Hetzel, éditeur, sur les institutions de lecture populaire', in Christian Robin, ed., *Un Éditeur et son siècle: Pierre-Jules Hetzel, 1814–1886*. Paris: ACL, 1988, pp. 255–67.

Bourdieu, Pierre, *La Distinction: Critique sociale du jugement*. Paris: Eds de Minuit, 1979.

Briquet, Jean, *Agricol Perdiguier, compagnon du Tour de la France et représentant du peuple, 1805–1875*. Paris: Rivière, 1955.

Certeau, Michel de, *The Practice of Everyday Life*. Berkeley, CA: University of California Press, 1984 (translated from Michel de Certeau, *L'Invention du Quotidien – 1.Arts de Faire*, Paris, Gallimard, 1990).
Chartier, Roger, *Figures de la Gueuserie*. Paris: Montalba Bibliothèque Bleue, 1982.
Chartier, Roger, *The Order of Books: Readers, authors and libraries in Europe, between the fourteenth and eighteenth centuries*. Stanford: Stanford University Press, 1994.
Chartier, Roger, *Culture populaire: retour sur un concept historiographique*. Valencia: University of Valencia, Eutopìas, Documentos de trabajo vol. 52, 1994.
Chartier, Roger, ed., *Pratiques de la Lecture*. Marseilles: Rivages, 1985.
Chartier, Roger, ed., *La Correspondance: les usages de la lettre au XIXe siècle*. Paris: Fayard, 1991.
Chatelain, Abel, 'Ligue de l'Enseignement et éducation populaire en Bourgogne au début de la Troisième République', *Annales de Bourgogne*, vol. 27, 1955, pp. 104–14.
Chevalier, Louis, *Classes laborieuses et classes dangereuses à Paris pendant la première moitié du XIXe siècle*, Paris: Plon, 1958 (English version published in London, Routledge & Kegan Paul, 1973).
Cochet, Annick, 'L'Opinion et le Moral des Soldats en 1916, d'après les archives du contrôle postal', unpublished 3e cycle thesis, Paris-X-Nanterre, 2 vols, 1985.
Cuvillier, A, *Un Journal d'ouvriers:* L'Atelier, *1840–1850*. Paris: (Felix Alcan), 1914.
Darmon, Jean-Jacques, *Le Colportage de librairie en France sous le Second Empire. Grands colporteurs et culture populaire*. Paris: Plon, 1972.
Darmon, Jean-Jacques, 'Lecture Rurale et lecture urbaine', *Europe*, no. 542, June 1974 (issue on 'Le Roman- feuilleton'), pp. 63–8.
Didier, Beatrice, *Le Journal intime*. Paris: Presses Universitaires de France, 1976.
Dubuc, André, 'Les Colporteurs d'Imprimés au XIXe siècle en Seine-Inférieure', *Actes du 105e Congrès National des Sociétés Savantes, Caen 1980, section d'histoire moderne et contemporaine, tome 2 – Histoire de la Normandie et questions diverses*. Paris, 1984, pp. 147–61.
Dufour, Cécile, ouvrière en modes, 'A M.de Lamartine', *La Ruche populaire*, sept.1839, pp. 15–18, and see Lamartine's response in the November issue.
Duveau, Georges, *La Vie ouvrière en France sous le Second Empire*. Paris: Gallimard, 1946.
Duveau, Georges, *La Pensée ouvrière sur l'éducation pendant le Seconde République et le Second Empire*. Paris: Domat Montchrestien, 1948.
Fabre, Daniel, *Ecritures ordinaires*. Paris: POL/Centre Georges Pompidou, 1993.
Faure, Alain and Jacques Rancière, eds, *La Parole ouvrière, 1830–1851*. Paris: Union Générale d'Editions, série 10/18, 1976.
Fish, Stanley, *Is There a Text in this Class? The Authority of interpretive communities*. Cambridge, MA: Harvard University Press, 1980.
Flint, Kate, *The Woman Reader, 1837–1914*. Oxford: Clarendon Press, 1993.
Fraisse, Geneviève, *Reason's Muse: Sexual difference and the birth of democracy*, trans. Jane Marie Todd. Chicago: University of Chicago Press, 1994.
Fraisse, Geneviève and Perrot, Michelle, eds, *A History of Women*, vol. 4, *Emerging feminism from revolution to World War*. Cambridge, MA: Belknap, 1993.
Gimet, François, *Les Muses Prolétaires*. Paris: Fareu, 1856.
Gosselin, Ronald, *Les Almanachs Républicains: Traditions révolutionnaires et culture politique des masses populaires de Paris: 1840–1851*. Paris: L'Harmattan, 1992.

Graham, Hamish, 'How did 19th-century Workers get into Frédéric Le Play's "Bad Books"?', *Australian Journal of French Studies*, vol. XXIII, no. 1 (4th George Rudé Seminar issue), 1986, pp. 130–44.

Grogan, Susan, *French Socialism and Sexual Difference: Women and the new society, 1803–44*. London: Macmillan (now Palgrave), 1992.

Hébrard, Jean, 'Comment Valentin Jamerey-Duval apprit-il à lire: un autodidaxie exemplaire', in R. Chartier, ed., *Pratiques de la lecture*. Marseilles: Rivages, 1985, pp. 23–60.

Hébrard, Jean, 'Les Nouveaux Lecteurs', in *Histoire de l'Edition française, vol. 3, Le temps des éditeurs, du romantisme à la Belle Epoque*, edn. H.-J. Martin and R. Chartier. Paris: Promodis, 1985, pp. 471–509 and Fayard/Cercle de la librairie, 1990, pp. 526–65.

Hoggart, Richard, *The Uses of Literacy : Aspects of working-class life*. Harmondsworth UK: Penguin, 1958.

Hoock-Demarle, Marie-Claire, 'Reading and Writing in Germany' in G.Fraisse and M.Perrot, eds, *A History of Women, vol. 4, Emerging Feminism from Revolution to World War*, Cambridge, MA: Belknap, 1993, pp. 145–65.

Julliard, Jacques, *Pelloutier et les origines du syndicalisme d'action directe*. Paris: Seuil, 1971.

Lejeune, Philippe, *L'Autobiographie en France*. Paris: A. Colin, 1971.

Lejeune, Philippe, *Le Pacte autobiographique*. Paris: Seuil, 1975.

Lejeune, Philippe, *Moi aussi*. Paris: Seuil, 1986.

Lejeune, Philippe, *On Autobiography*, ed. P. J. Eakin. Minneapolis: University of Minnesota Press, 1989.

Lyons, Martyn, 'The Audience for Romanticism: Walter Scott in France, 1815–51', *European History Quarterly*, 14:1, 1984, pp. 21–46.

Lyons, Martyn, 'Oral Culture and Rural Community in Nineteenth-Century France: the *veillée d'hiver*', *Australian Journal of French Studies*, vol. 23:1, 1986, pp. 102–14.

Lyons, Martyn, *Le Triomphe du livre: une histoire sociologique de la lecture dans la France du 19e siècle*. Paris: Promodis, 1987.

Lyons, Martyn, 'The Autodidacts and their Literary Culture: Working-class autobiographers in nineteenth-century France', *Australian Journal of French Studies*, vol. XXVIII, no. 3, 1991, pp. 264–73.

Lyons, Martyn, 'Towards a National Literary Culture in France', *History of European Ideas*, vol. 16, nos.1–3, 1993, pp. 247–52.

Lyons, Martyn, 'Fires of Expiation: Bookburnings and Catholic missions in Restoration France', *French History*, vol. 10, no. 2, June 1996, pp. 240–66.

Lyons, Martyn, 'New Readers in the Nineteenth Century: Women, children, workers' in G. Cavallo and R. Chartier, eds, *A History of Reading in the West*. Oxford: Polity, 1999, pp. 313–44.

Lyons, Martyn, and Lucy Taksa, ' "If Mother caught us reading!": Impressions of the Australian woman reader, 1890–1933', *Australian Cultural History*, 11, 1992, pp. 39–50.

Lyons, Martyn, and Lucy Taksa, *Australian Readers Remember : an oral history of reading*. Melbourne: Oxford University Press, 1992.

Macé, Jean, *Morale en action: Mouvement de propagande intellectuelle en Alsace*. Paris: Hetzel, 1865.

McPhee, Peter, *The Politics of Rural Life: Political mobilization in the French countryside, 1846–52*. Oxford: Clarendon Press, 1992.

Mandrou, Robert, *De la Culture populaire au 17e et 18e siècles: la Bibliothèque Bleue de Troyes*. Paris: Stock, 1964.

Martin, Henri-Jean and Roger Chartier, eds, *Histoire de l'edition française, tome 3*. Paris: Promodis, 1985.

Mollier, Jean-Yves, 'Le roman populaire dans la bibliothèque du peuple', in Jacques Migozzi, ed., *Le Roman populaire en question(s)*. Paris: PULIM, 1996, pp. 585–98.

Mollier, Jean-Yves, *Michel et Calmann Lévy, ou la naissance de l'édition moderne, 1836–91*. Paris: Calmann-Lévy, 1984.

Mollier, Jean-Yves, *L'Argent et les Lettres: Histoire du capitalisme d'édition, 1880–1920*. Paris: Fayard, 1988.

Mollier, Jean-Yves, 'Histoire de la lecture, histoire de l'édition', in Roger Chartier, ed., *Histoires de la lecture: un bilan de recherches*. Paris: IMEC/Maison des Sciences de l'Homme, 1995, pp. 207–13.

Mounoud-Anglès, Christiane, 'Le Courrier des lectrices de Balzac (1830–1840): stratégies identitaires', in Mireille Bossis, ed., *La Lettre à la croisée de l'individuel et du social*. Paris: Kimé, 1994, pp. 98–104.

Musée du Grand Palais, *Fantin-Latour: Catalogue d'une exposition (9 nov.1982– 7 fév.1983)*. Paris, 1982.

Newman, Edgar Léon, 'Sounds in the Desert: the socialist worker poets of the Bourgeois Monarchy, 1830–1848', *Proceedings of the Third Annual Meeting of the Western Society for French History. December 1975*, no place (USA), 1976, pp. 269–99.

Newman, Edgar Léon, 'The Historian as Apostle [Perdiguier]: Romanticism, religion and the first socialist history of the world', *Journal of the History of Ideas*, vol. 56, no. 2, April 1995, pp. 239–61.

Palmer, Michael B., 'Some aspects of the French Press during the Rise of the Popular Daily, c.1860 to 1890', unpublished Oxford University D.Phil. thesis, 1972.

Palmer, Michael B., *Des Petits Journaux aux grandes agences: Naissance du journalisme moderne, 1863–1914*. Paris: Aubier, 1983.

Pellisson, Maurice, 'Les Lectures Publiques du Soir, 1848–50', *La Nouvelle revue*, vol. 30, 1er octobre 1904, pp. 317–26.

Perrot, Michelle, 'A Nineteenth-Century Work Experience as Related in a Worker's Autobiography: Norbert Truquin', in Steven J. Kaplan and Cynthia J. Koepp, eds, *Work in France: Representations, meaning, organization and practice*. Ithaca NY & London: Cornell University Press, 1986, chapter 10.

Pierrard, Pierre, *La Vie ouvrière à Lille sous le Second Empire*. Paris: Bloud et Gay, 1965.

Quéffelec, Lise, 'Le Lecteur du roman comme lectrice : stratégies romanesques et stratégies critiques sous la Monarchie de Juillet', *Romantisme*, vol. 16, no. 53, 1986, pp. 9–21.

Radway, Janice, *Reading the Romance: Women, patriarchy and popular literature*. Chapel Hill, NC, 1984.

Ragon, Michel, *Histoire de la Littérature prolétarienne en France*. Paris: Albin Michel, 1974.

Rancière, Jacques, 'The Myth of the Artisan: Critical reflections on a category of social analysis', in Steven L. Kaplan and Cynthia J. Koepp, eds, *Work in France:*

Representations, meaning, organisation and practice. Ithaca NY & London: Cornell University Press, 1986.

Rémusat, Charles de, *Mémoires de ma vie*, ed. C. Pouthas. Paris: Plon, 1958–67.

Richter, Nöé, *La Lecture et ses Institutions: la lecture populaire, 1700–1918*. Le Mans: Editions Plein Chant & l'Université du Maine, 1987.

Richter, Nöé, *La Conversion du mauvais lecteur et la naissance de la lecture publique*. Marigné: Edition de la Queue du Chat, 1992.

Richter, Nöé, *L'Oeuvre des Bons Livres de Bordeaux: les années de formation, 1812–1840*. Bernay (Société d'histoire de la lecture), 1997.

Richter, Nöé, *Lecture populaire et ouvrière: Lecture et travail*. Bernay: Société d'histoire de la lecture, 1998.

Roche, Daniel, *The People of Paris: an essay in popular culture in the 18th century*. Leamington Spa, UK: Berg, 1987.

Rose, Jonathan, 'Rereading the English Common Reader: a preface to the history of audiences', *Journal of the History of Ideas*, vol. 53, no. 1, 1992, pp. 47–70.

Sainte-Beuve, Charles-Augustin, 'De la littérature industrielle' (1839), in *Portraits contemporains*. Paris: Calmann-Lévy, 5 vols., 1888–9, vol. 2, pp. 444–71.

Savart, Claude, *Les Catholiques en France au XIXe siècle: le témoignage du livre religieux*. Paris: Beauchesne, 1985.

Singer, Barnett, *Village Notables in Nineteenth-century France: Priests, mayors, schoolmasters*. Albany: State University of New York Press, 1983.

Sonenscher, Michael, review of Rémi Gossez, ed., *Un Ouvrier en 1820: manuscrit inédit de Jacques-Etienne Bédé*, *History Workshop Journal*, 21, summer 1986, pp. 173–9.

Thiesse, Anne-Marie, 'Imprimés du pauvre, livres de fortune', *Romantisme*, vol. 43, 1984, pp. 91–109.

Thiesse, Anne-Marie, 'Mutations et permanences de la culture populaire: la lecture à la Belle Epoque', *Annales-économies, sociétés, civilisations*, vol. 39, jan–fév.1984, pp. 70–91.

Thiesse Anne-Marie, *Le Roman du Quotidien: Lecteurs et lectures populaires à la Belle Epoque*. Paris: Chemin Vert, 1984.

Vincent, David, *Bread, Knowledge and Freedom: a study of 19th century working-class autobiography*. London: Europa, 1981.

Viollet, Alphonse, *Les Poètes du Peuple au 19e siècle*, intro. by M.Ragon. Paris & Geneva: Slatkine reprint, 1980, an anthology first published in 1846.

Weber, Eugen, *Peasants into Frenchmen: the modernization of rural France, 1870–1914*. London: Chatto & Windus, 1977.

Yalom, Marilyn, 'Women's Autobiography in French, 1793–1939: a selected bibliography', in *French Literature Series* (University of South Carolina), vol. 12, 1985, pp. 197–205.

Education and literacy

Clark, Linda, *Schooling the Daughters of Marianne: Textbooks for the socialization of girls in modern French primary schools*. Albany NY: State University of New York Press, 1984.

198 Bibliography

Fleury, M and A.Valmary, 'Les Progrès de l'instruction élémentaire de Louis XIV à Napoléon III d'après l'enquête de Louis Maggiolo (1877–79)', *Population*, 12, jan–mars 1957, pp. 71–92.

Furet, François and Jacques Ozouf, 'Literacy and Industrialisation: the case of the Département du Nord in France', *Journal of European Economic History*, vol. 5:1, spring 1976, pp. 5–44.

Furet, François and Jacques Ozouf, *Reading and Writing: Literacy in France from Calvin to Jules Ferry*. Cambridge: Cambridge University Press and Maison des Sciences de l'Homme, 1982. (This is an abbreviated translation of *Lire et ecrire : l'alphabétisation des français de Calvin à Jules Ferry*, Paris, Editions de Minuit, 1977.)

Furet, François and W.Sachs, 'La Croissance de l'alphabétisation en France, 18e-19e siècle', *Annales-économies, sociétés, civilisations*, vol. 29, 1974, pp. 714–37.

Gildea, Robert, *Education in Provincial France, 1800–1914: a study of three departments (Nord, Gard, Ille-et-Vilaine)*. Oxford: Clarendon Press, 1983.

Gontard, Maurice, *L'Enseignement primaire en France de la Révolution à la loi Guizot, 1789–1833*. Paris: Les Belles Lettres, 1959.

Gontard, Maurice, *Les Ecoles primaires de la France bourgeoise, 1833–1875*. Toulouse: Centre régional de documentation pédagogique, 1976.

Grew, Raymond and Patrick J.Harrigan, *School, State and Society: the growth of elementary schooling in 19th century France – a quantitative analysis*. Ann Arbor MI: University of Michigan Press, 1991. See also the critical debate in *Annales-économies, sociétés, civilisations*, vol. 41:4, 1986, pp. 885–945.

Grew, Raymond, Patrick J.Harrigan and James Whitney, 'The Availability of Schooling in 19th Century France', *Journal of Interdisciplinary History*, XIV, summer 1983, pp. 25–63.

Hébrard, Jean, 'Ecole et alphabétisation au XIXe siècle', *Annales-économies, sociétés, civilisations*, vol. 35:1, jan- fév 1980, pp. 66–80.

Lorain, Paul, *Tableau de l'instruction primaire en France*. Paris: Hachette, 1837.

Mayeur, Françoise, 'Les Evêques français et Victor Duruy. Les cours secondaires de jeunes filles', *Revue d'histoire de l'église de France*, vol. 57, no. 159, juillet–déc.1971, pp. 267–304.

Ozouf, Mona, *L'Ecole, l'Eglise et la République, 1871–1914*. Paris: Cana/Jean Offredo, 1982.

Prost, Antoine, *Histoire de l'enseignement en France, 1800–67*. Paris: Armand Colin, 1968.

Strumingher, Laura S, *What Were Little Girls and Boys Made Of? Primary education in rural France, 1830–1880*. Albany NY: State University of New York Press, 1983.

The nineteenth-century discourse on reading

Audiganne, A., *Les Populations ouvrières et les industries de la France: Études comparatives*, 2 vols. New York (Franklin facsimile reprint), 1970 (first published in Paris, 1860).

Bethléem, abbé Louis, *Romans à lire et romans à proscrire*. Cambrai: Masson, 4th ed., 1908.

Bosquet, François-Florentin, *De la moralité dans les campagnes depuis 1789*. Chalons-sur-Marne: Société Académique de la Marne, 1860.
Brisset, Mathurin-Joseph, *Le Cabinet de lecture*. 2 vols. Paris: Magen, 1843.
Chartier, Anne-Marie and Jean Hébrard, *Discours sur la lecture, 1880–1980*. Paris: Bibliothèque publique d'information, Centre Georges Pompidou, 1989.
Cormenin, Baron Louis-Marie de la Haye, *Entretiens de village*. Paris: Pagnerre, 1846.
Curmer, Léon, *De l'Etablissement des bibliothèques communales en France*. Paris: Guillaumin, 1846.
Delessert, François François, *Opinion dans la discussion sur le budget de l'Instruction publique, 13 mai 1836*. Paris: Chambre des Députés, 1836.
Desbordes, Jean-Louis, 'Les Ecrits de Mgr.Dupanloup sur la haute éducation des femmes', in Françoise Mayeur and Jacques Gadille, eds, *Education et images de la femme chrétienne en France au début du XXe siècle, à l'occasion du centenaire de la mort de Mgr. Dupanloup*. Lyon: Hermès, 1980.
Dupanloup, Mgr. Félix, *Femmes savantes et femmes studieuses*. Paris: Douniol, 3rd edition, 1867.
Dupanloup, Mgr. Félix, *La Femme studieuse: Quelques conseils aux femmes chrétiennes qui vivent dans le monde sur le travail intellectuel qui leur convient*. Paris: Douniol, 1870.
Flaubert, Gustave, *Madame Bovary*. Paris: Classiques Garnier, 1961 (English edition by Penguin Classics, trans. G. Wall, Harmondsworth UK, 1992).
Frémy, Arnould, *Comment lisent les Français d'aujourd'hui?*. Paris: Calmann-Lévy, 1878.
Hulot, abbé M., *Instruction sur les romans*. Paris, 1825.
L'Etang, Espérance-Augustin de, *Le Colportage, l'instituteur primaire et les livres utiles dans les campagnes*. Paris: Dupray, 1865.
L'Etang, Espérance-Augustin de, *Des Livres utiles et du colportage comme moyen d'avancement moral et intellectuel des classes rurales et ouvrières*. Paris: Maillet, 1866.
Le Play, Frédéric, *Les Ouvriers européens: Études sur les travaux, le vie domestique et la condition morale des populations ouvrières de l'Europe*. Paris: Imprimerie Impériale, 1855. (A second edition was published with the same title in six volumes by Mame et fils in Tours, 1877–79. Then appeared F.Le Play, *Les Ouvriers des deux mondes: études sur les travaux, le vie domestique et la condition morale des populations ouvrières, 2e série, vol. 1*. Paris, Firmin-Didot, 1887.)
Lerminier, Jean-Louis, 'De la Littérature des ouvriers', *Revue des Deux Mondes*, vol. 4, 1841, pp. 574–89.
M—(aréchal), S—(ylvain), *Projet d'une loi portant défense d'apprendre à lire aux femmes*. Paris: Massé, 1801 (reprinted in Lille in 1841 and Belgium, 1847, then by Gustave Sandré in Paris, 1853, entitled: *Il ne faut pas que les femmes sachent lire, ou projet d'une loi*).
Nettement, Alfred, *Etudes critiques sur le feuilleton roman*, 2 vols. Paris: Perrodil, 1845–6.
Nisard, Charles, *Histoire des livres populaires ou de la littérature du colportage*, 2 vols. Paris: Dentu, 1864 (reprinted New York, Franklin, 1971).
Poulot, Denis, *Question sociale: le sublime, ou le travailleur comme il est en 1870 et ce qu'il peut être*, ed. Alain Cottereau. Paris: Maspéro, 1980 (first published 1870).

Robert, Charles, 'Notes sur l'état de la lecture populaire en France', *Bulletin de la Société Franklin*, no. 50, 15 juin 1872, pp. 180–9 and no. 52, 15 juillet 1872, pp. 214–24 (2 articles).
Stendhal, *Correspondance de Stendhal (1800–1842)*, ed. A. Paupe and P.-A. Chéramy, 3 vols. Paris: Bosse, 1908.
Stendhal, *Le Rouge et le Noir*. First published Paris: Levasseur, 1831.
Tolain, Henri, 'Le Roman Populaire', *La Tribune ouvrière*, vol. 1, no. 3, 18 juin 1865, pp. 9–10.
Turinaz, Mgr, évêque de Tarentaise, *Les Mauvaises Lectures: la presse et la littérature corruptrices (Lettre pastorale)*. Paris: Librairie de la Société Bibliographique, 1881.

Libraries

Bellet, Roger, 'Une Bataille culturelle, provinciale et nationale, à propos des bons auteurs pour bibliothèques populaires', *Revue des sciences humaines*, vol. 34, 1969, pp. 453–73.
Carbonnier, Marianne, 'Une Bibliothèque populaire au XIXe siècle: la bibliothèque populaire protestante de Lyon', *Revue française d'histoire du livre*, 47e année, no. 20, juillet-août-septembre, 1978, pp. 613–45.
Hassenforder, Jean, *Dévéloppement comparée des bibliothèques publiques en France, en Grande-Bretagne, et aux Etats-Unis, dans la seconde moitié du 19e siècle, 1850–1914*. Paris: Cercle de la Librairie, 1967.
Hébrard, Jean, 'Les bibliothèques scolaires', in Dominique Varry, ed., *Histoire des bibliothèques françaises*, 4 vols., tome 3. Paris: Promodis/Cercle de la Librairie, 1991, pp. 546–77.
Louandre, Charles, 'La Bibliothèque Royale et les bibliothèques publiques', *Revue des deux mondes*, vol. 13, 15 mars 146, p. 1055.
Lyons, Martyn, 'La Transformation de l'espace culturel français: le réseau des librairies et des bibliothèques, 1870–1914' in Jacques Girault, ed., *Ouvriers en banlieue, xixe et xxe siècles*. Paris: Editions de l'Atelier, 1998, pp. 390–407.
Marie, Pascale, 'La Bibliothèque des Amis de l'instruction du 3e arrondissement', in Pierre Nora, ed., *Les Lieux de mémoire – 1, La République*. Paris: Gallimard, 1984, pp. 323–51.
Parent-Lardeur, Françoise, *Les Cabinets de lecture: la lecture publique à Paris sous la Restauration*. Paris: Payot, 1982.
Pellisson, Maurice, *Les Bibliothèques populaires à l'étranger et en France*. Paris: Imprimerie Nationale, 1906.
Pelloutier, Fernand, *Histoire des Bourses du Travail*. Paris: Publications Gramma/Gordon and Breach, 1971, pp. 141–3 (first published 1902).
Rappe, Daniel, 'La Bourse du Travail de Lyon des origines à 1914', unpublished mémoire de maîtrise d'histoire contemporaine, Université Lumière, Lyon- 2, 1997.
Richter, Noë, *Les Bibliothèques populaires*. Le Mans: Université du Maine, 1977.
Richter, Noë, 'Les Bibliothèques populaires et la lecture ouvrière', in Dominique Varry, ed., *Histoire des Bibliothèques françaises: Vol. 3, Les Bibliothèques de la Révolution et du 19e siècle, 1789–1914*. Paris: Promodis/Cercle de la Librairie, 1991, pp. 513–35.

Robert, Charles, 'La Lecture populaire et les bibliothèques en 1861', *Bulletin de la Société Franklin*, vol. 4, no. 45, 1er avril 1872, pp. 100–110.
Saint-Albin, Emmanuel de, *Les Bibliothèques municipales de la ville de Paris*. Paris: Berger-Levrault, 1896.
Sainte-Beuve, Charles-Augustin, *A Propos des bibliothèques populaires* (speech in Senate, 25 juin 1867). Paris, 1867.
Simon, Jules, 'L'Instruction populaire et les bibliothèques populaires', *Revue des deux mondes*, vol. 47, 15 September 1863, pp. 349–75.
Spire, Juliette, 'La Bibliothèque de la Bourse du Travail à Paris: étude des acquisitions de 1898 à 1914', unpublished mémoire de maîtrise, Université de Paris-1, 1985.
Varry, Dominique, ed, *Histoire des bibliothèques françaises:* vol. 3, *Les Bibliothèques de la Révolution et du 19e siècle, 1789–1914*. Paris: Promodis/Cercle de la Librairie, 1991.
Watteville, Baron de, *Rapport à M.Bardoux, ministre de l'Instruction Publique, sur le service des Bibliothèques scolaires, 1866–1877*. Paris: Imprimerie nationale, 1879.

Regional studies which mention peasant reading

Béteille, Roger, *La Vie quotidienne en Rouergue au 19e siècle*. Paris: Hachette, 1973.
Brekilien, Yann, *La Vie quotidienne des paysans en Bretagne au 19e siècle*. Paris: Hachette, 1966.
Coulon, Gérard, *Une Vie paysanne en Berry de 1882 à nos jours*. Buzançais (self-published), 1979.
Devos Roger and Joisten, Charles, *Moeurs et coûtumes de la Savoie du Nord au XIXe siècle: l'enquête de Mgr. Rendu*. Annecy: Académie Salésienne and Grenoble: Centre alpin et rhodanien d'ethnologie, 1978.
Fabre, Daniel and Lacroix, Jacques, *La Vie quotidienne des paysans du Languedoc au 19e siècle*. Paris: Hachette, 1973.
Halévy, Daniel, *Visites aux paysans du Centre, 1907–34*. Paris: Librairie Générale, 1978.
Le Roy, Eugène, *Le Moulin du Frau*. Paris: Fasquelle, 1905.
Massoul, Henry, *Au Bon Vieux Temps. Souvenirs du Gâtinais et de la Brie*. Paris: Mercure de France, 1944–45.
Rocal, Georges, *Le Vieux Périgord*. Toulouse: Guitard, 1927.
Rouchon, Ulysse, *La Vie paysanne dans la Haute-Loire*. Le Puy en Velay: Imprimerie de la Haute-Loire, 1933.
Seignolle, Claude, *Le Berry traditionnel*. Paris: Maisonneuve & Larose, 1969.
Tardieu, Suzanne, *La Vie domestique dans le Mâconnais rural pré-industriel*. Paris: Institut d'ethnologie, 1964.
Thabault, Roger, *Education and Change in a Village Community: Mazières-en-Gâtine, 1848–1914*, trans. P. Tregear. London: Routledge & Kegan Paul, 1971.

Index

advice literature ix, 19, 25–8, 29, 30, 31, 41, 43, 48, 59–60, 92–7, 100, 153, 157, 158
Aesop, *Fables* 49, 60
Agulhon, Maurice 132, 139, 141
Albigeois 9, *see also* Tarn
Allier, dept of 143, 152
almanacs 30, 46, 133, 134, 135, 139, 140, 141, 143, 146, 162
Alsace 4, 35, 36, 37, 39–40, 47, 124, 125
anarcho-syndicalism 68, 70
Annales school of history vii
anticlericalism 45, 50, 51, 52, 53, 61, 62, 73, 77, 84, 113, 127, 144, 160, *see also* Volney, Voltaire
Arabian Nights, Tales of the (1001 nuits) 125, 147, 164
Ardèche, dept of 117, 150, 158
Ardennes, dept of 147
Ariège, dept of 9
Arnauld, Jean-Baptiste 75, 77, 160
Atelier 25–8, 41, 58, 59, 61, 62, 72
Audiganne, A. 37
Audoux, Marguerite 159
Auspitz, Katherine 36
autobiographies ix, x, 2, 19, 21, 30–1, 43–4, 49–57, 60, 63, 64, 70–6, 86, 101, 102, 116–9, 122–8, 130, 143, 150, 152, 158–60
autodidacts 2, 27–8, 30–2, 41–2, 43–4, 48–57, 61, 63, 64, 70–1, 75–80, 122–3, 160
Auvergne 117, 118, 119, 162
Avignon 13, 23, 60, *see also* Vaucluse

B., Victorine *see* Brocher, Victorine
Balzac, Honoré de 14, 33, 58, 69, 76, 89, 91, 130
Barbier, Frédéric 45–6
Baudelaire, *Fleurs du Mal* vii
Baylac, Jean-Pierre 135

Bédé, Jacques-Etienne 75–6
Benoît, Joseph 62, 78, 79
Béranger 19, 60, 141
Berry 143
bestsellers viii, 4, 148
Bethléem, abbé 13–15
Bibliothèque bleue see colportage literature
Bibliothèque des dames chrétiennes 82, 105
Blanc, Louis 33, 38, 66, 67
Blois 56, 105, 146
bonapartism 11, 15, 19, 22, 29, 41, 144, 157
bonapartist literature 129, 141, 147, 149, 164
Bonvin, painter 120
book-burnings 12–13, 22–3, 134
bookshops, secondhand 31, 55
Bordeaux 4, 23–4, *see also* Gironde
Bossuet 29, 72, 93, 94, 95, 104
Bourdieu, Pierre 41, 54, 70–1, 102, 160
Bourses du Travail x, 67–70
Bouvier, Jeanne 74, 122, 159
bovarysme 86–91, 92, 96–7
Brest 23
Brisset, M-J, *Le Cabinet de Lecture* 83–4, 89
Brittany 4, 5, 103, 137, 140, 149
Brive 47
Brocher, Victorine 62, 63–4, 71, 73, 102, 122
Brunetière 33, 72
Buonarroti 62, 68
Byron 97, 110

Cabet, Etienne 21, 26, 33, 38, 50, 61, 62, 67
cabinets de lecture 10, 18, 55, 63, 64, 81, 83–4, 89, 122, 156
Calmann-Lévy 3, 156

Carnot, Hippolyte 24
Casanova, *Memoirs* 14
catechisms 3, 5, 8, 136, 139, 140
Catholic missions 12–13, 22–3
Catholic reading model 92–5, 103, 104, 128, 157
Certeau, Michel de 16, 138
chambrée 21, 137–8
Champagne 139
Charente, dept of 145
Charpentier format 10, 23
Chartier, Roger ix, 61, 131, 140
Châteaubriand, René 55, 61, 63, 64, 76, 88, 89, 97, 125, 148, 160, 164
Cher, dept of 124, 147
Chevalier, Louis 12, 156
children as readers ix, 7–9, 35, 46–7, 48, 125, 158, 163
Christian Brothers (Frères de l'Ecole Chrétienne) 6, 8, 20, 26, 27, 51–2
Christian socialism 26, 62
Cochet, Annick 152
Cognac 9
Collection des meilleurs romans français dédiés aux dames 82
colportage literature viii, 18, 20, 21, 29, 93, 134, 135, 136, 139–43, 144–9, 150, 153, 164
Commissaire, Sébastien 55
Commission des bibliothèques populaires 33–4
commonplace books 94
compagnonnage 67, 72, 73–5, 77
Cooper, Fenimore 33
Corneille, Pierre (and seventeenth-century classics) 29, 33, 36, 41, 55, 59, 60, 61, 64, 72, 93, 97, 148, 165
Cottin, Sophie 82, 122
Craik, El 48
Creuse, dept of 21, 78, 146, *see also* Limousin
Curmer, Léon 20, 144

Dante 29, 64
Darwin, Charles 67, 68, 93, 95, 113
Daumier, Honoré 85, 98
Delessert, Orléanist deputy 20, 21
Déroulède 33, 70

diaries *see journal intime*
Dickens, Charles 33, 111, 153, 154
Diderot 144
Didier, Béatrice 102
Didot *aîné* 82, 105
Don Quixote 64, 148, 164
Dordogne 7, 134
Doyle, Conan 33
drinking habits 20, 21, 28, 31, 38, 54, 77, 136
Ducray-Duminil 76, 83
Dumas, Alexandre *père* 3, 10, 33, 48, 55, 111, 113, 136, 143, 147, 148, 149, 150, 164
Dumay, Jean-Baptiste 53, 57, 74, 75, 77
Dupanloup, Mgr 92–5, 96, 97, 103, 104
Duruy, Victor 92, 147, 164
Duveau, Georges 9, 59

education 49–50, 51–2, 57, 158, 162
employers' resistance to 9, 50, 51, 133
girls' 7, 92, 124
mutual system 8
parental resistance to 7, 8–9
see also Christian Brothers, Falloux Law, Ferry education laws, Guizot Law, schools
Emerson 126
Erckmann-Chatrian 33, 125, 154
Eure, dept of 147

Fabre, Daniel 135, 154
Falloux Law 7, 92
Fantin-Latour, Henri 98–9
Fayard, publisher 10
fear of reading ix, 1–2, 11–16, 17–19, 22–3, 41, 45, 53, 66, 85, 86, 87, 97–8, 106–7, 129, 136, 140–1, 144, 156–7
feminist press 2, 95
feminist reading models 95–8, 128, 157
Femme nouvelle 95–7
Fénélon 24, 29, 59, 72, 93, 105, 148, 164

Ferry education laws 6, 9, 13, 40, 132, 145, 152, 158
Feydeau 14
fiction *see* novels
Flammarion, publisher 10, 156
Flaubert, Gustave *see Madame Bovary*
Fleury, *Catéchisme historique* 93
Flint, Kate 87
Fontainebleau 147
foreign language reading 47, 56, 62, 64, 90, 110, 111, 114, 124–6
Fourierism 26, 66, 67, 141
France, Anatole 14, 33, 68, 69, 121, 163
Franco-Prussian War, 1870 2, 21, 151
Franklin Society 28–35, 37, 41, 47, 58, 59
Frémy, Arnauld 2, 21
Frères de l'Ecole Chrétienne *see* Christian Brothers
Furet, François vii, 9

Garonne-Haute, dept of 137, *see also* Toulouse
Gauny, Gabriel 52, 54, 57
Genoux, Claude 25, 56–7, 62, 64
Gide, André vii
Gilfedder, Jeanette x, 119–20
Gilland, Jérôme-Pierre 25, 59, 72, 79
Girard 30, 66
Gironde, dept of 75, 138, *see also* Bordeaux
Goethe 55, 58, 111–2, 114
Gorky, Maxim 33
Gosselin, publisher 81
Grenadou 130, 152
Grew, Raymond 6–7
Guérin, Eugénie de 100, 101, 102, 103–8, 114, 116, 119, 127–8, 129, 133, 158
Guillaumin, Emile, *Vie d'un Simple* 14, 130, 133, 153–4
Guizot Law, 1833 6, 8, 20, 132

Hachette 15, 39, 142, 148, 156
Hardy, Thomas 15, 33, 34
Hassenforder, Jean 29

Hébrard, Jean x, 145
Hélias, Pierre-Jakez 103, 130, 137
history reading 27, 29, 38, 39, 40, 47–8, 51, 59, 62, 67, 68–9, 94, 105–6, 147, 148
Hoggart, Richard 44
Homer 59, 82
Hugo, Victor 14, 25, 38, 39, 60, 63, 69, 76, 106, 107, 121, 136, 141, 147, 148, 160, 163
 Les Misérables 3, 14, 64
 Notre-Dame de Paris 14, 33, 58, 59, 89, 107, 153

Ibsen, Heinrik 33, 114
Indre, dept of 147
inventories post-mortem 133

Jamerey-Duval, Valentin 49
Jasmin, *coiffeur* 71
Jaurès, Jean 67, 68
journal intime 94, 101–8, 115, 135, 158

Kock, Paul de 14, 143, 145, 148, 165

Labiche, *Voyage de M. Perrichon* 86
Laffitte, Jacques 72–3, 76, 77
Lafontaine (and seventeenth-century classics) 29, 33, 36, 41, 55, 59, 60, 61, 64, 72, 97, 137, 148, 164
Lamartine, Alphonse de 25, 33, 38, 60, 64, 72, 89, 97, 106, 110, 135, 148
Lamennais 25, 66, 82, 105, 160
La Rochelle 40
Larousse dictionary 72, 103, 118, 163
Lavisse, Ernest 33
Le Creusot 53, 75
Legros, Hélène 100, 101, 108–16, 117, 119, 120, 127, 128, 158
Lejeune, Philippe 71, 75, 123
Lejeune, Xavier-Edouard 55, 63, 64, 71, 76
Le Havre 39–40, 62
Lepage, Constant 62, 63
Le Play, Frédéric 18, 45–7, 136, 138–9
legitimism 11, 63, 92, 129
LeRoy, Eugène 33, 137, 153

letter-writing 138, 150, 151–2, 154
Lévy, Michel, publisher 10
Lhomond 24, 148
libraries viii, 2, 10, 15, 17, 18, 19, 20, 22, 28–35, 37, 41, 46, 47–8, 58, 59, 120, 144, 145, 157
  Catholic 23–4
  in Britain 17, 20, 28–9, 41, see also Mechanics' Institutes
  in the workplace 35, 36, 37, 39–40, 46
  municipal 28, 34–5, 47–8, 118, 162
  private 5, 45–6, 59
  school 135, 136, 145–9, 150, 154, 163, 164
  workers' 43, 45, 53, 59–60
lighting for reading 52–3, 118
Ligue de l'Enseignement 30, 35–6, 37, 40, 41
Lille 28, 37
Limousin 78, 143, 151, see also Creuse
L'Isle, Leconte de 110
literacy rates 1–2, 3–5, 9, 131–2, 137, 138
  male/female 1, 5–6
  reading only 5–6, 138
  schooling and 7–8, 9, 135
  urban 4–5
Lives of the saints 23, 93, 103, 104, 137, 140, see also religious reading
Loire, dept of 147
Loire-Atlantique, dept of 138
Lons-le-Saulnier 8
Lorraine 4, 49, see also Metz, Nancy
Loti, Pierre, *Pêcheur d'Islande* 3, 14, 33, 111, 112, 121, 153, 163
Louandre, Charles 20
Lyon 5, 12, 29, 37, 50, 51, 61, 62, 65, 121, 133, 163

Macé, Jean 30, 35–6, 40
Mâconnais 133–4
Madame Bovary 69, 87–91, 97, 98, 113, 122, see also bovarysme
Magasin pittoresque 26, 36, 59
magazines, illustrated 21, 32, 99, 150, 154, 156
Maggiolo, Louis 3–4

magic power of books 49, 134–5
Malon, Benoît 71
Mandrou, Robert 136, 140
Manet 98, 99
Maréchal, Sylvain 84–5, 111
Marie, Pascale 66
Marne, dept of 144
Marx, Karl 10, 68, 125
Massif Central 5, 140, 146, 149, 151
Massillon 93, 104
Massoul, Henri 134
Maupassant, Guy de 14, 136
mauvais livres, campaigns against 12–13, 17, 22–3, 134, 136, 144, 156
Mayenne, dept of 141
Meaux 147
Mechanics' Institutes 17, 27, 37, 39, 41
Ménétra, Jacques-Louis 49
Mérimée, Prosper 111, 121, 163
Merlaud, Alexandre 130, 143, 151
Metz 55, see also Lorraine
Meunier, Louis-Arsène 62
Meuse, dept of 8
Michelet 19, 22, 26, 27, 38, 40, 66, 68, 91, 97, 106, 135, 148
Milton, John 29, 93
Mirbeau, Octave 69, 159
Molière (and seventeenth-century classics) 29, 33, 36, 41, 55, 59, 60, 61, 64, 72, 93, 97, 106, 148, 164
Mollier, Jean-Yves x
Montesquieu 59
Montpellier 8, 96
Mulhouse 30, 36, 37

Nadaud, Martin 9, 21, 27, 52, 53, 61, 74, 78, 79, 153
Nancy 96, see also Lorraine
newspapers 1, 2, 10, 19, 21, 28, 38, 46, 52, 55, 58, 63, 71, 76, 85, 117, 132, 133, 137, 138, 139, 142, 147, 150, 154, 156, 162, 163
  workers' press 25–8
Nièvre, dept of 46
Nisard, Charles 141, 142

206 *Index*

non-fiction reading   31, 32, 39, 47–8, 57–65, 66, 68, 69, 94–5, 143, 148
Nord, dept of   13, 21
Nord, Philip   36
Normandy   140
Norre, Henri   130, 143, 152
novels   1, 3, 10, 13, 16, 23, 26, 32–4, 45, 47–8, 55, 57–65, 69, 81, 82–6, 86–91, 94–5, 97, 100, 101, 105–7, 108–16, 117, 121, 122, 127, 128, 135, 136, 139, 143, 144–5, 146, 147–9, 150, 156, 157, 163
  English   14–15, 83, 93, 153, see also Scott, Walter

Ohnet *see Porteuse du Pain*
Oise, dept of   46
oral history   ix, 101, 116–9, 120–1, 130, 135, 150, 158, 159–60, 162–3
oral reading   18, 24, 38, 46, 49, 50, 51, 55, 60, 61, 79, 85, 86, 99, 105, 122, 126, 137, 154
Ossian   110
Owenism   26
Ozouf, Mona   15

Paris   12, 21, 24, 27, 30, 37, 45, 49, 50, 52, 54, 55, 56, 58, 61, 63, 72, 75, 78, 81, 83, 86, 89–90, 91, 115, 116, 124, 126, 148, 153–4, 156, 159, 163
  June Days, 1848   18–19, 22
  libraries in   29, 34, 47–8, 66, 68
  literacy rates in   4–5
Paris Commune, 1871   4, 12, 21, 53, 56, 62, 67, 68, 73, 113, 122
Pascal   29, 93, 97, 105
patois and regional languages   52, 60, 71, 78, 118, 129, 150, 152, 154, 162
  Breton   4, 103, 137
  Occitan   71, 158
  Provençal   60, 78
Paul et Virginie   33, 88, 89, 111, 148, 164
Pearce, Lynne   112
peasant integration   130–1, 149–50, 154–5

peasants as readers   ix–x, 2, 7, 8, 9, 11, 12, 14, 16, 20, 21, 23, 117, 123–4, 129–55, 156, 158, 161, 164–5
Pelloutier, Fernand   67–70
Perdiguier, Agricol   58, 59–61, 63, 72, 74, 77–8, 79, 159
Périgord   33, 134, 137, 146
Petit Albert   49, 134–5
Petit Journal   46, 139, 142–3, 147, 150, 156
Petrarch   64
Plutarch's *Lives*   29
poetry   27, 47, 76, 90, 105, 106, 110, 126, 135, 142, 150
  worker-poets   27, 59, 70–2
Ponson du Terrail   135, 142, 150
La Porteuse du Pain   3, 117, 150
Poulot, Denis   33, 37–9
Protestant influences   21, 35, 36, 46, 148
Proudhon   58, 66, 67, 135
Provence   4, 11, 21, 137, 139
public readings   24–5, 40
publishers   1–2, 10, 11, 15, 65, 82–3, 156, 159
publishing by instalments   10, 55, 59, 82, 117, 120, 144, 147, 149, 156
Puy-de-Dôme, dept of   52, 147, 150
Pyrenees   135, 139, 149

Les Quatre Fils Aymon   140, 147, 164
questionnaire of 1866   130, 144–9, 164–5
Quinet, Edgar, *Histoire de mes idées*   97

Racine (and seventeenth-century classics)   29, 33, 36, 41, 55, 59, 60, 61, 64, 72, 93, 97, 148, 165
Radway, Janice   101, 131
railway bookstalls   13, 86, 139, 142, 149
Rancière, Jacques   74
Raspail   148
reading:
  autonomy of the reader   16, 19, 41, 44, 55, 61, 65, 66, 100, 101, 114, 120, 128, 131, 160
  communities   61, 62, 77, 79, 95, 101, 160, 161

crises 55
employers' opposition to 53
fragmented 21, 32
identificatory 91, 112
illicit 118–20, 135
intensive 32, 94
interstitial 119–20
parental opposition to 53
programmes 54, 93–4
religious 3, 23, 30, 32, 45–6, 59, 62, 82, 88, 93, 97, 103–8, 127, 133–4, 139, 140
re-reading 32, 64, 94, 111, 114
silent 98–9
utilitarian 61, 90, 143, 161
see also oral reading, fear of reading, lighting for reading
Rémusat, Charles de 18
Renan, Ernest 52, 66, 93
Rendu, Mgr 136
Republic (Third) 13, 15–16, 21, 36, 123, 132, 136, 149, 157
Restoration period 12, 17, 22–3, 24, 82, 93, 141, 156
Revolutions:
 1789 1, 3, 4, 5, 18, 22, 23, 38, 41, 59, 64, 65, 67, 68, 141, 148
 1830 21, 22, 78
 1848 2, 12, 18, 19, 21, 22, 24, 25, 28, 37, 38, 41, 45, 50, 55, 73, 129, 137, 139, 141, 157
Richter, Nöé 54
Robert, Charles 20, 30, 144, 145
Robinson Crusoe 33, 148, 164
Rollin, *Ancient History* 62
romans-feuilletons 10, 26, 27, 58, 69, 85, 95, 96, 117, 118, 119, 140, 142, 144, 149, 150, 154, 162
Rose, Jonathan x, 43, 60
Roubaix 5
Rouen 23, 37, 40, 89
Rouergue 133
Rousseau, Jean-Jacques 12, 22–3, 49, 59, 61, 62, 64, 66, 72, 113, 123, 125, 144, 148, 160
Roussillon 135, 154
Rouvière, Augustine 150, 151
Ruche populaire 25–7, 64, 72

rural exodus 2, 4, 131, 158

Saint Augustine 82, 104, 105
Saint-Etienne 65
Saint-Pierre, Bernardin de 82, 88, 89, 106, 164, *see also Paul et Virginie*
Saint-Simonians 26, 52, 63, 68, 122, 123
Sainte-Beuve 10, 65–6, 106
Sand, Georges 14, 26, 33, 59, 60, 63, 66, 69, 72, 74, 85, 89, 90, 96, 129, 147, 148, 153
Saône-et-Loire, dept of 20
Savoy 56, 136
Schiller 29
schools:
 attendance 7, 9, 44, 132
 Catholic 6, 15, 162, *see also* Christian Brothers
 primary 1, 6–9, 13, 15, 60, 93, 131, 132, 145, 152, 154, 158
 see also education
schoolteachers 3, 6, 8, 15, 20, 30, 36, 55, 62, 95–6, 102, 110, 118, 122, 123–4, 126, 127, 130, 135, 136, 138, 144, 145, 150, 151, 155, 158, 162, 163
Scott, Walter 14, 33, 36, 64, 81, 83, 88, 89, 90, 106, 107, 111
Second Empire 6, 9, 17, 19, 25, 28, 60, 132, 138, 139, 140, 146, 154
Ségur, comtesse de 125
Seine-et-Marne, dept of 147
Seine-et-Oise, dept of 144
Seneca 30
separate spheres 84–6, 92–5, 95–7, 119, 122, 123, 126
serialization of fiction *see romans-feuilletons*
Sévigné, Mme de 93
Shakespeare 29, 36, 55, 60, 93, 124, 125
Simon, Jules 7, 15, 28, 29, 30, 37, 144
Smiles, *Self-Help* 31
socialism 11, 15, 18, 22, 26, 29, 33, 37, 39, 50–1, 56, 58, 61–2, 66, 67, 68, 117, 125, 129, 137, 141, 144, 162,

socialism (*continued*)
   see also Blanc, Cabet, Fourierism,
      Saint-Simonians
Société catholique de bons livres   24,
   46
Société des Amis de l'Instruction   66–7
Société Franklin see Franklin Society
Somme, dept of   47, 50, 120, 163
Staël, Germaine de   64, 97, 107, 122
Stendhal   vii, 3, 14, 81, 83
   Le Rouge et le Noir   3, 14, 53
Sue, Eugène   10, 14, 26, 30, 34, 39, 58,
   59, 66, 69, 89, 95, 141, 143, 144,
   148, 149, 164
Sylvère, Antoine ('Toinou')   52, 130,
   150, 151, 154

tailors   18
Taine, Hippolyte   14, 93, 112
Taksa, Lucy   ix
Tardieu, Suzanne   133
Tarn, dept of   103, 129, 133
Thabault, Roger   131, 154
theatre   47, 49, 60–1, 90, 94, 105, 110,
   114, 163, see also Feydeau, Ibsen,
   Labiche
Thiers as historian   40, 48, 148, 164
Thiesse, Anne-Marie   116–18, 120,
   150, 158, 162
Tinayre, Marcelle, *La Rebelle*   121, 163
Tolain, Henri   58–9, 60, 63, 69
Tolstoy, Leo   33, 110, 111, 112, 126,
   150, 151
Toulon   23
Toulouse   4, 24, 154, see also Garonne-
   Haute
Tours   146
trade unionism   26, 53, 67–70, 122
Troyes   142
Truquin, Norbert   50–1, 57, 62, 79–80,
   158
Turinaz, bishop   13

Uncle Tom's Cabin   153, 154

Vallès, Jules   14
Vaucluse, dept of   117, see also
   Avignon
veillée   135–6

Verne, Jules   3, 32, 33, 48, 69, 136,
   150, 153
Versailles   136
Vienne, dept of   7
Vienne-Haute, dept of   20
Vigny, Alfred de   25, 97, 110
Virgil   59
Voilquin, Suzanne   63, 122–3,
   127
Voisin, Joseph   75
Volney   61, 62, 64, 123, 144
Voltaire   12, 22–3, 26, 40, 52, 59, 60,
   61, 62, 63, 66, 72, 106, 108, 123,
   141, 144, 148

war of 1914–18   121, 125, 127, 135,
   149, 151–2, 163
Weber, Eugen   149, 155
Weiss, Louise   100, 101, 102, 124–8
Werdet, publisher   57, 82
Whistler   98–9
Wilde, Oscar   34
women as readers   ix, 1, 2, 5, 6, 11, 14,
   16, 35, 43, 58, 63, 66, 81–99,
   100–28, 135, 156, 157, 161,
   162–3
   networks see women readers'
      networks
   represented in art   98–9
   surveillance of   86, 109–110, 111,
      113, 115, 121
   see also separate spheres
women readers' networks   110, 114,
   115, 117, 120–1, 150, 162, 163
workers as readers   ix, 1, 2, 9, 11, 12,
   15, 16, 17–42, 43–80, 102, 117,
   121, 156, 157, 160–1, see also
   autodidacts, workers' networks
workers' networks   53, 55–6,
   118
working day, length of   9–10

Yonne, dept of   40

Zeldin, Theodore   vii–viii
Zola, Emile   11–12, 14, 34, 52, 68, 69,
   130, 142, 153
   L'Assommoir   38
   Germinal   12, 153